Bill Friday's
QUICK
PRINTING
ENCYCLOPEDIA

PRUDENTIAL PUBLISHING COMPANY
P.O. Box 10751- P
So. Lake Tahoe, CA 95731

© Copyright 1982 Wm. Friday

"Instant Printing"
1976
"Instant Printing 2"
1979
"Instant Printing - Third Edition"
1980
Name changed to
"Quick Printing Encyclopedia"
1982

ISBN - 0 - 934432 - 10 - 4

About the Author

In the mid 1940s, Bill Friday helped pioneer the first direct-image plate and camera/platemaker for the Lithomat Company. He purchased a Multilith press to experiment with these new products. From then to the present, there have been few periods when he hasn't been personally trying out new types of quick printing materials and equipment.

Since the 1960s, he has been involved full time as an owner/operator of quick printing shops, including an experimental shop opened in 1980 where he regularly assists in the operation of every piece of equipment.

He is the author of five books, including the industry's best seller, "Instant Printing." He is the holder of an Honorary Lifetime Membership in the National Association of Quick Printers, awarded "for outstanding contributions made toward the betterment of the industry." Over fifty of his articles have appeared in leading trade publications. Many of his articles have reported shop vists and interviews with leading quick printers throughout the U.S. and Canada.

He is a former oil field roughneck, motorcycle and car racer, yacht and Coast Guard skipper, airplane pilot, and top level executive for three of the world's largest conglomerates. His most rewarding accomplishment, in terms of personal satisfaction and the one he is most proud of, is becoming a successful quick printer.

PREFACE

Quick printing has swept around the world in a very few years. Bill Friday was one of the pioneer owner-operators of a quick printing shop, becoming involved in the mid 1940s with the first crude direct-image plates and platemakers. Later, when quick printing entered the successful stage, he opened shops in the Los Angeles market where he prospered. His operation became a model for others to copy.

In the first edition of *Instant Printing,* published in 1976, Bill Friday laid bare his entire operation — plans, methods, tactics, formulas, forms, price lists, failures, and successes. Truth recorded truly! The book was an instant success. Friday has since received many honors from the printing industry, including an Honorary Lifetime Membership in the National Association of Quick Printers and invitations to speak at national and regional printing conventions.

This fourth edition contains all of the original material, updated and revised to reflect Friday's continuing quick printing experience. New chapters and enlargement of previous chapters record the experiences of many other quick printers. Results obtained in the experimental shop Friday opened in 1980 are also reported.

There is no doubt that quick printing is changing. Success depends on knowing how others have succeeded and applying individual ingenuity to changing conditions. Improvement of opportunities offered by the quick printing industry is the stated aim of this book.

ACKNOWLEDGMENTS

Writing articles for printing magazines, especially interview-type articles, has allowed me to explore many quick printing shops. Owners have been generous in sharing their experiences and knowledge.

To the many who have contributed to this book, I am extremely grateful — for information and particularly for your friendship.

In researching this edition, I updated my library with every new book I could find on printing subjects. Of particular value were the Armed Services training manuals. I found the Navy manuals to be the most helpful, partly because my introduction to offset printing was in the Navy Reserve. But the main reason is that the Navy operates many small print shops on ships. They use quick printing type equipment and have to solve many of the same problems as quick printers.

To the many quick printers who have attended my seminars, thank you for providing me with more information than I'm sure I dispensed.

Finally, thanks to my wife and the other tolerant people in our experimental shop. It isn't easy to work in a shop where the boss changes equipment, materials, and systems as soon as they start working right.

This book is dedicated to the thousands of individuals with enough confidence in themselves to have ventured into the risky business of quick printing.

May you succeed!

CONTENTS

CONTENTS

CONTENTS

CONTENTS

CONTENTS

10

CONTENTS

CONTENTS

CONTENTS

CONTENTS

CONTENTS

CHAPTER 1

QUICK PRINTING
YESTERDAY & TODAY

QUICK PRINTING
YESTERDAY AND TODAY

The phrase "quick" or "instant" printing is not new, but the industry, as we know it today, had its birth with the introduction of the Itek camera-platemaker and Eastman photo-direct plates. There were many other types of photo-direct plates and platemakers on the market before the Itek-Eastman combination,but all had shortcomings that prevented them from gaining acceptance in commercial printing.

EARLY SHOPS

The early shops were called "Instant Printing Shops." Some even tried to trademark the name "Instant Printing" without success. Many small print shops used "instant" in their names while continuing to operate with process cameras and metal plates. Hence the birth of the ridicule, "Printing while you wait, and wait, and wait."

THE BIRTH OF INSTANT PRINTING

In the 1940s, long before I opened an instant printing shop, I helped introduce the first photo-direct plate and platemaker. We sold hundreds of inplant installations, but sold the system to only two commercial print shops. The quality of work produced by the plates was barely acceptable to inplant printers. Paying customers of commercial printers would not buy the level of quality produced. Twenty-five years passed before instant printing was widely accepted by commercial printing customers.

One of the shops that experimented with that first instant printing system was owned by Walter Graham, currently an author and lecturer known throughout the printing world. He had just opened his first printing shop in Omaha, Nebraska. His experiments with my quick printing equipment were of tremendous help in selling inplant printers, even though he concluded the process wasn't suitable for his commercial shop.

The photo-direct paper plate, later to be known as the Lithomat plate, was developed in the early 1940s by an obscure chemist, working in his basement. The system was purchased by the Army for use in the jungles of the Pacific. Producing maps and other printing with process cameras and plate burners in sniper-filled jungles presented problems that were partially solved by this new plate and platemaker.

The new direct-image plate required only a small lighted box with a glass on top. It could be carried under one arm and operated from a small electric generator. The Army placed an order for $5,000,000 worth of plates, chemicals, and equipment. The chemist sold out and the Lithomat Corporation was created to manufacture the Army's requirements.

After the war in the mid 1940s, the system was redesigned for the commercial market. The plateburner was housed in a wooden box with a spring-loaded top that pressed copy and plate together on a pane of glass.

To get an even exposure from fluorescent lights in the bottom of the box, a large plywood shutter had to be jerked violently from a slot between lights and sensitized plate. It took six seconds of exposure time and three minutes to process the plate in trays of chemicals — truly this was instant printing. The platemaker sold for $85.00. The cost of plate and chemicals was estimated at 58 cents. This compared to $3.50 for zinc plates used by most offset printers at the time.

It was a saleable idea, but the quality problems proved insurmountable. Twice in 1948, we had to replace all plate material because the entire surface, not just the image area, was inking. Lithomat sold out to A. B. Dick. This was the beginning of A. B. Dick's involvement with offset printing.

CURRENT QUALITY

Current systems and materials are capable of producing a level of quality acceptable to all but the most discriminating buyers. There are still many problems with inks, chemicals, plate materials, and machinery and a high degree of ingenuity is needed to operate successfully. One of the secrets is knowing what type of work not to accept.

RAPID GROWTH

In the past, only the inplant market was big enough to warrant the development cost of specialized equipment for small printing shops. All of the equipment used by early quick printers was manufactured with inplant customers in mind. Rapid growth of the industry to the present 13,000 quick print shops in the U.S. is attracting attention. More and more manufacturers are developing equipment especially for quick printers.

WORLD GROWTH

The popularity of quick printing is not limited to the United States. Quick printing shops are operating in all parts of the world. My book *Instant Printing* was recently translated into Japanese. It is selling for 2000 yen with fifty pages of supplier advertisements. Quick Printing has also reached boom proportions in much of Europe.

CURRENT AVERAGE SALES

Surveys conducted by independent consultants, associations, and trade magazines have concluded that today's average shop has sales of approximately $200,000 per year. This figures out to about two and a half billion dollars for all U.S. shops. It is obvious from these figures that quick printing has "arrived."

PREDICTED U.S. GROWTH

Frost & Sullivan, Inc., worldwide industry consultants, recently produced a 278 page report entitled "Quick Print and Associated Equipment and Supplies Markets: 1980-1985." The report sells for $1,075 and is intended primarily for manufacturers of quick printing equipment and supplies. The existence of such a report is evidence of the attention manufacturers are finally directing toward quick printers.

Frost and Sullivan estimate a 158% increase in numbers of quick printing companies from 1980 through 1985. Some quick printers might groan at this predicted increase in competition. I can, however, look back to the 1960s when we had one of only three shops on Ventura Boulevard in Los Angeles and were barely breaking even. A few years later there were twenty-five shops on Ventura Boulevard, and we were making an excellent profit.

The number of shops will increase as consumer demand increases. Increased demand means more opportunity for experienced and progressive quick printers.

SPECIALIZATION

Specialization has arrived in the quick printing business. Decisions regarding equipment and markets are more difficult. Experimentation can be costly. Some of the new automated presses sell for $60,000 or more.

Your best bet is to start with proven methods and equipment and feel your way from there. It's a tough business even with proven equipment. You need to stay current, but you cannot afford to experiment with every new machine. A heavy percentage of new equipment does not prove out in actual usage.

Two methods that started slowly, but are finally proving profitable in specialized operations, are the electrostatic platemaker and the completely automated platemaker press. In some urban areas, the so-called "system" presses have captured a large portion of short-run, multiple-page jobs.

The photo-direct (silver-coated) plate, however, is far from dead. To the contrary, improved quality of plate material is opening doors to business formally reserved for metal plates.

Many quick printers are still operating with only one type of plate and camera/platemaker. In urban areas, it is possible to build a large and profitable business by specializing in one type of quick printing. A handful of "one system" operators are using only electrostatic plates and relying on metal plates for fine line and fine halftone work. Most "one system" operators are using photo-direct plates.

Many quick print shops are concentrating on high quality, long run, or two-color work. Instant is a thing of the past for them. A quick printer in Los Angeles did traditional quick printing for ten years. Now he does nothing but short run process color work for advertising agencies — on the same A. B. Dick presses he was using for quick printing — metal plates, of course.

QUICK ISN'T "INSTANT" ANYMORE

Quick printing today does not necessarily mean "instant." Some shops still have signs like, "500 copies in 10 minutes or it's free," but most jobs are ready in a matter of hours or days. Do-it-yourself photocopiers placed in the lobbys of some shops provide instant copies, but full service copying is often backed up to next day delivery.

COMPETITION WITH COMMERCIAL PRINTERS

Contrary to the belief of many commercial printers, the quick printer does not and will not pose a threat to his future. The quick printer did deal a blow to the small job printer, or at least forced him to convert to quick printing or move into full scale commercial printing.

The commercial printer is moving rapidly into more expensive and complicated methods. Even though the quick printer is also becoming more sophisticated in equipment and methods, it is not likely that he will ever pose any kind of a threat to the progressive commercial printer.

QUICK PRINT DEPARTMENTS FOR COMMERCIAL PRINTERS

Some conventional printers have installed quick printing departments. The principal problem has been the difficulty in separating quick printing from their regular operation. Customers want quick printing prices and service, but if they are dealing with a conventional printer, they also want the full range of services.

Quick printing pricing and the size of the average job does not allow for these extras. A quick printer depends on location, sign, and advertising to bring customers to him. Even though the average size of a quick printing job has gone from eleven dollars ten years ago to better than fifty dollars today, this is far short of an average needed to justify the services offered by most commercial printers.

In order to operate without salesmen, a shop needs to be located on a main thoroughfare. A quick printing shop on a back street is doomed from the start. Of course, a commercial printer can open a quick printing shop as a completely separate operation with a different name and succeed. The point is the same — quick printing and full scale commercial printing are as difficult to blend as oil and water.

XEROX COMPETITION

There is considerable concern among quick printers about Xerox copy centers. There is also some concern about Xerox type copiers replacing offset printing presses. Conglomerate owned businesses can afford, if they desire, to engage in unfair competition by selling at a loss.

In the past, government agencies have issued cease and desist orders for such unfair practices. Without government intervention, such practices could be a real threat to small businesses in general. There is no chance, however, of Xerox or any other large company coming up with greater shop operating efficiency than can be obtained by individual quick printers.

Printing, particularly quick printing, does not fit into "bigness" very well. Printing has always been the most fragmented of all major segments of U.S. industry. Quick printing will probably always remain a haven for independent entrepreneurs.

The chance that Xerox type copiers will replace

offset printing presses is "no chance at all." Electrostatic copying will grow — so will offset printing. There will, however, be a big increase in quick printing equipment that is controlled to some degree by microelectronics. This will up the cost of starting or staying in a quick printing business and perhaps squeeze a few underfinanced companies.

COMPUTERS

The computer has arrived in quick printing. Several thousand shops are using computers for accounting and payroll. The computerized phototypesetter is rapidly replacing strike-on machines. A few quick printers are using computers for estimating the selling price of jobs.

Prudential Publishing is in the process of developing computer software that will estimate jobs and print out quotations. Their computer is also being used to assemble and calculate average prices charged for popular items in various regions of the U.S. By combining this information with pricing formulas, their computer will print out complete price lists of obtainable prices for two hundred or so items.

TRADE ASSOCIATIONS

The formation and rapid growth of quick printing

trade associations has added considerable prestige to the quick printing industry. Today, there are two such organizations — the National Association of Quick Printers and the American Quick Printing Association.

N.A.Q.P.

The National Association of Quick Printers is the brainchild of George Pataky, owner of "Quick Copies of Asheville" in North Carolina. In 1976, Pataky, with the help of his family, copied names of quick printers from the library of telephone directories at the local phone company. The response to his initial mailing encouraged him to charter the N.A.Q.P.

Today, this association has over three thousand members. Two annual meetings held in major cities of the U.S. bring quick printers together for an exchange of information. A major exhibit by manufacturers of quick printing equipment and products is held in conjunction with the midsummer meeting. The N.A.Q.P. Co-op arranges discounts resulting in thousands of dollars of savings for individual printers. Discounted educational material is distributed to members through an affiliate organization, the N.A.Q.P. Foundation. A monthly bulletin keeps members informed of current trends and happenings in the industry.

Surveys of various types are conducted and published as an aid to management.

AMERICAN QUICK PRINTING ASSOCIATION

The A.Q.P.A., organized in 1980 as an affiliate of P.I.A., has yet to really get off the ground. However, with P.I.A. backing, the prospect of this association developing into a viable organization is good.

TRADE PUBLICATIONS

Until the mid 1970s, little mention of quick or instant printing was seen in printing trade publications. Today, publications such as the prestigious American Printer and Lithographer have quick printing departments. Most national and regional publications publish frequent articles about quick printing. Quick Printing Magazine has developed into a major publication with over fifteen thousand subscribers.

Other magazines are being put together to serve the growing population of quick printers. Graphic Arts Monthly has announced publication of a monthly newsletter for quick printers. Prudential Publishing has launched a monthly Pricing/Purchasing Advisory Bulletin in conjunction with a counter price book and computer pricing service.

MANAGEMENT KNOW-HOW

Like any other business, there are many failures, and the survivors in quick printing will be good businessmen with a working knowledge of every aspect of the business — from president to janitor. The quick printing business is here to stay as it offers a service the public needs and wants. I hope this book will help the business to grow in a profitable direction.

Finally, before you get hooked or stay hooked on quick printing, I offer a word of caution.

Your chance of success is no better or worse than it would be in any other business. You need capital and some usable talent, and a little luck won't hurt!

CHAPTER 2

MANAGEMENT

MANAGEMENT

Management is said to be both an art and a science. An art because it deals with human reactions which are not always logical. A science because it deals with precise methods, authority, and responsibility.

Actually, every chapter in this book could be titled, "Management." Everything that happens or does not happen is the responsibility of the manager.

This book will not make you a successful manager of a quick printing shop, however, the fact that you are reading this book or any other book on the subject indicates that you have the right idea on how to be a successful manager. Venturing into business without all of the information and tools you can gather is like entering a wilderness without a map or compass. Yet every year thousands charge blindly into quick printing without planning, knowledge, or adequate capital.

The trick is to gather the information that time and common sense allow. This brings the odds more in your favor. You must then be prepared to guess and gamble. There are no "sure things" in any business - just good odds and bad odds.

TIME TO MANAGE

A quick printer who is running a press, answering the telephone, waiting on the counter, fixing equipment, selling and delivering jobs, keeping records, etc., etc. has no time left to manage. Necessity may force him to start out doing everything, but unless he eventually hires others and delegates responsibility, he will never be in a position to grow through the benefits of management. The size of his shop will be limited by the amount of personal energy he expends.

WHO ARE THE MANAGERS?

In a big business, management responsibility is shared by many executives. Most quick printers can afford only one executive - the owner! Everything that happens - every department is his responsibility. Shop owners with top corporate executive experience are often overwhelmed by the great variety of responsibilities of even a small quick printing shop.

MANAGER'S RESPONSIBILITY

An owner's responsibility extends beyond the direct operation of his shop - it extends to customers, suppliers, and creditors. These vital supporters of business will desert at the first sign of irresponsibility.

As a youngster I worked one summer on an oil drilling rig. Heavy equipment swung from the derrick as tons of drilling pipe were lowered or pulled from the hole. Serious injury was all too common. I can close my eyes and still hear the cry of the driller, "That's steel, boy, you handle it or it will handle you." No better philosophy can guide you in handling business problems. You handle them or they will handle you.

The ability to make decisions, to be wrong, to accept responsibility for the consequences, and keep on making decisions is the key. This is what management responsibility is all about. If you have mastered this ability, it will lead you into the other areas necessary for success.

ORGANIZING ABILITY

Some people can't seem to get it all together. It's not likely you'll see this type in quick printing management - at least not for long. A successful quick printing manager must be able to organize people, production, finances, and a multitude of other small and large elements - delegating authority but exerting control.

History provides many examples where a handful of organized, coordinated men have overturned empires. Organization can weld a group of people into a unified whole without the demoralizing aspect of conflicting functions.

Like the parts of an engine, you can have a jumble or a smooth-working machine. No one ever fully understands the importance or the difficulty of organization until the full load of doing it in a small business falls on his shoulders. You must put all of the parts together, assemble them, tune them, and run the thing with very little help.

To do this, you must plan all of the details and put these details on paper. You don't need a great memory to succeed, but you do need a great reference system. A handy tool is a pocket-size loose-leaf notebook. Write everything down that you think you might need to refer to in the future - names, telephone numbers, suppliers, prices, formulas, prospective employees, costs, production times, insurance agents, etc., etc. (See Record Keeping section for complete filing system.)

DRIVE AND LEADERSHIP

These two characteristics go hand-in-hand - they depend on each other for effectiveness. If a quick print shop is to grow, a following must be developed among employees, investors, and customers. Few will follow a leader who doesn't have drive.

PHYSICAL ABILITY

It takes a lot of physical energy to manage a quick printing shop. Getting a shop off the ground requires long hours. Troubleshooting is an important function of quick printing management. This can involve physical strength and stamina. Even a shop operating forty hours a week draws heavily upon the physical energies of a manager. It is not a business for someone in poor health.

PERSEVERANCE

Every quick printing shop owner faces periods of low income or loss. It takes time to turn some things around. Without perseverance, there will be overwhelming temptations to throw in the towel.

MECHANICAL APTITUDE

Machinery will inevitably quit operating - often at the most inconvenient times. Down time has killed many quick printing shops. Service men are hours, often days away. Parts may take weeks to arrive. The ability to somehow, someway get a machine going is not only an asset, it is a necessity in quick printing. You may be lucky enough to hire someone who can provide this vital function for you - not likely!

This mechanical troubleshooting function, not considered a management essential in all types of business, is high on the list of assets in quick printing management.

PLANNING

When I got my first car, driving was one of life's greatest delights. Not knowing where to go, we sometimes played a game - if the first car coming toward us had a license plate ending in an odd number, we turned left at the next intersection or road - an even number, we turned right. Unless we met a car, we continued straight ahead, sometimes coming to a dead end. These uncharted, haphazard trips were fun, but not productive to getting anywhere in particular.

Many quick printing shops, I have observed, seem to be operating with comparable changes in direction for no better reasons. Planned changes in direction will produce a much greater forward movement.

RESEARCH AND DEVELOPMENT

Research and development are two of the most important functions of quick printing management.

Quick printing has come of age. Manufacturers are now aware of the potential. This recognition will speed the development of new equipment and materials. I am not recommending the purchase of every new, highly touted piece of equipment that comes on the market. This can lead to bankruptcy as much of the new equipment does not prove out in actual use. But it pays to keep an eye on the experiments your peers are conducting. One of the benefits I derive from writing magazine articles is the opportunity it gives me to interview quick printers using new types of equipment.

Research and development can be carried on in ways other than buying new equipment. New methods of advertising, recruiting employees, training, bookkeeping, pricing, compensation, etc. can be tested. Of course, methods that are working should not be thrown out before developing better alternatives.

A successful quick printing manager operates with all the tried and tested methods he can find - and then he makes small, but often significant, improvements, fitting the methods to his particular requirements.

JOB DESCRIPTIONS

What am I supposed to do? How much is expected of me? Who do I take orders from? What are advancement possibilities? How am I doing? These are major questions in the minds of employees. Only through custom-designed job descriptions can morale-building answers be properly given.

Following is a basic formula for developing job descriptions for quick printing employees:

1. Find out exactly what each employee is doing at present. (This often provides surprises.)

2. Write a description of present functions.

3. Determine if there is a more logical, efficient, equitable way of doing each job.

4. Prepare a new job description, delegating authority, responsibility, income and advancement guidelines.

5. Set up a regular - every six months - review period where you can privately discuss goals and accomplishments with each employee, using the job description as a guide.

COMPANY POLICIES

Perhaps the greatest benefit a franchised business has over an independent is a set of firm operating policies. Few independent quick printers have a well-defined written policy to cover major operating circumstances. Pressures from inside and outside the business are constant and often overwhelming unless bulwarked with a written policy. Of course, policies can and should be reviewed and changed, but not under the pressure of everyday business. Policy changing flexibility can, however, be a valuable asset to an independent operator if it is used wisely.

COMPANY OBJECTIVES

Take aim - not only at money - but at goals. Money follows. Even though a lot of effort is exerted, a touchdown is never scored until the ball crosses the goal line. That's the time to negotiate - or raise prices. If your goals reward customers with better service or other worthwhile benefits, they will reward you by paying higher prices - probably reluctantly. They may try to find the same benefits elsewhere at a cheaper price, but most will eventually return.

In a seven-mile stretch of a main boulevard in Los Angeles, there are twenty-seven quick print shops. Prices displayed on many of the windows are ridiculously low. Yet with all of this cut-price competition, several shops with high selling prices are making it big. The shops trying to make it on price either can't afford to or don't know how to provide the service or quality that customers are willing to buy.

DECISION BALANCE SHEET

Before making a major decision, you should design a simple balance sheet of your plan. On the left side of the paper, put down every requirement: time, cost, personnel, facilities, equipment, etc. On the right side opposite each requirement, fill in what you have available to fulfill the requirement. Don't roll the plan until you have all of the parts.

FORM FOR PLANNING

Set up a record of the plan. Every plan will need to be changed or canceled as time goes by. It is vital for you to know how it is doing. Memory is often a terrible record. You can keep a record of most operations on a single sheet of paper. Draw columns with a pencil. Design the form so that you can enter results by week, month, or whatever period you need and so you can compare one period against another. As you accumulate figures of past performance, project ahead, using these figures as a basis for your projection.

WHEN TO CHANGE OR BAIL OUT

If your projections do not indicate success, make changes or bail out. This is when you need to make up a new plan balance sheet. You are wiser now -

you have experience, and all experience is valuable even if it is not successful experience. Don't send good money after bad! Examine your plan balance sheet in the light of what exists now.

Consider yourself as starting from scratch - would you put the plan into effect? Don't plan for miracles to happen, but don't bail out if you see "daylight." A little "daylight" is about all most quick printers see in the early days. If you weren't a "tightrope walker," you wouldn't even be here. You would be drudging away, drawing a safe paycheck. The important thing is to avoid as many surprises as possible by planning and looking ahead. Unless you closely examine all obstacles and opportunities, you have about as much chance of making it as a squirrel has of crossing a busy freeway.

HOW TO GET BETTER

Ninety percent of your time needs to be spent working with the day-to-day problems of running your business. You will have little exposure to peers, so most of your knowledge will come from reading. Book knowledge, however, is next to worthless unless you can apply and test it. Experience is the catalyst. A new business owner who tries to learn without reading is cheating himself out of the benefit of thousands of years of recorded experience. No matter how new a type of business may be, most of the methods used will have been tried and proven over many years - and the results recorded.

You should allot 10% of your time to reading. This gives you a solid base to start from. You can strengthen that base by experimenting and developing improvements of past successful systems.

Quick Printing Associations

This can be one of the best investments a new owner can make. Conventions offer an opportunity to talk with peers from throughout the country - peers who are not competitors and who will freely share information. A large percentage of the nation's most successful quick printers attend at least one convention every two or three years. Associations publish magazines, bulletins, surveys, and books - all aimed at quick printers. (See "Resources" for names and addresses.)

Printing Trade Magazines

There are over twenty national and regional printing trade publications - free to qualified quick printers. Most are aimed primarily at commercial printers, but include periodic articles about quick printing. Don't pass up the inplant publications. They are particularly valuable as they cover the type of small equipment used by most quick printers. In fact, nearly all quick printing equipment was first used and proven by inplant printers. If you just scan through several trade publications every month, you will be assured that nothing of importance in the way of equipment is getting past you. If it's working, it will be written about or advertised. (See "Resources" for names and addresses of trade publications.)

Computers With almost avalanche momentum, computers are engulfing the quick printing business. Routine problems such as billing, accounting, and payroll have been successfully handled for some time. Now problems peculiar to quick printing are being tackled with computer programs. Prudential Publishing Company, the publisher of this book, has entered the computer programming field with pricing software and a computer generated counter price book.

WHERE NEW OWNERS COME FROM

Most present owners of quick print shops had no previous experience in the printing business. One of today's largest and most successful operators, Bill James, owner of Glendale Instant Printing, had no prior printing or business experience - and very little capital. His wife operated the first tiny shop while he continued working full time at his engineering job. Ten years later he had the world's largest quick printing shop under one roof.

Unfortunately, very few employees of quick printing shops end up starting their own shops. Even if they could raise the capital, they would probably go into some other business as they have seen how tough it is to make it in quick printing. This is true in all fields - the grass always looks greener!

Most new owners are men who have been in management positions with large or medium sized businesses. They want to get out of the "rat race" and build the security that can come with business ownership. A few expect to make a fortune, but most are not that naive. They are looking for a better life style - not a fortune.

WHY MOST NEW OWNERS FAIL

Most shops crash before they get off the ground. The owners haven't taken the time to learn enough to have a good shot at success - many can't even "talk" the language. It is important to have enough knowledge about quick printing to convince others that you are going to make it. Convincing others is often difficult. You are following in the footsteps of dreamers, con men, wild gamblers, and the worst. combination of all - the dumb and devious. These forerunners have made skeptics out of your potential investors, creditors, partners, and employees. You need to convince these people that you are offering a reward, not a sting. You need to be good at verbal communication to get people to gamble on you.

Also needed is the ability to stay in business. Lack of staying ability wipes out about ninety percent of the people who get over the first hurdle. Verbal communication takes on less importance. After two or three years in business, your investors, creditors, partners, and employees will be influenced more by what you have done than by what you say you can do.

CHAPTER 3

QUICK RATE
YOUR CHANCES
OF SUCCESS

QUICK RATE YOUR CHANCES OF SUCCESS

Many new owners are dismayed at the complexities of operating a quick printing shop. They find that few things go as they are "supposed" to go.

New owners often expect to make a "killing" right off the bat. They reason, and correctly so, that many of the existing shops offer poor service and poor quality. They conclude, incorrectly, that customers will flock to their well-managed establishment. All too often they learn too late that new customers can stay away in droves.

A good location, proper equipment, capable employees, sales, and advertising help to build business. Good service, good quality, dependability, and knowledgeable pricing help to retain business. Sounds simple enough, but unless you have done it before, these necessary elements

47

can be difficult to develop and maintain. You can go broke before you learn enough, unless, of course, you have enough money to finance your school of hard knocks.

This little test is just that — a "little" test! Perhaps it will help you in making your decisions.

If you score 9 points on this rating system, you have a good chance of success in the quick printing business. If your score is low but your determination is high enough, you might beat the odds — many have!

TECHNICAL EXPERIENCE

Few quick print shop owners have been blessed with previous printing experience. The ones who have made it have had to learn fast. It is impractical to depend entirely on employees or servicemen to keep quick printing equipment operating. Many shops have gone under because of excessive down time while waiting for service men.

It is difficult to find good pressmen. If "press mechanic" is added to the qualification requirement, it is darn near impossible!

If you have a high mechanical aptitude or a natural feel for machinery, you can learn much faster. For this reason, mechanical aptitude has been taken into consideration in the following ratings.

Technical experience ratings:

Less than 1 year experience or
low mechanical aptitude - 0 points

1 year experience or
  so-so mechanical aptitude - 1 point
2 years experience or
  high mechanical aptitude - 2 points
3 years experience or
  a natural feel for machinery - 3 points
4 or more years experience - 4 points

MANAGEMENT EXPERIENCE

This is an asset many quick print shop owners have before going into business. Most have gained management experience at someone else's expense. Their previous bosses have paid their salaries and hapless employees have been sacrificed to their inexperience. This, unfortunately, is a price that must be paid to develop managers.

The average quick print shop owner cannot afford to hire capable top management talent. The price is too high. The average owner must have it or acquire it. The manager's job is the most difficult to fill, the highest paid, and the least appreciated.

Management experience ratings:

Less than 2 years - 0 points
  (The zero rating is given for less than two years experience because most companies will give a manager at least two years to hang himself. If you haven't made it past the two year mark with a company,you can't be sure you really have it.)
2 years experience - 1 point
3 years experience - 2 points
4 years experience - 3 points
5 or more years experience- 4 points

MONEY

A minimum amount of money may well be an asset in starting out. You are then forced to make a profit or go under. The threat of failure may prod you into successful habits. Once developed, these habits can carry you through good times and bad.

Exactly how much money is essential? The amount depends on the size of your shop, but you need at least enough cash for the following:

Initial lease payments on your shop. This can range from one month's rent in advance to first and last months' rent plus a substantial deposit.

Remodeling. A commercial lease, unlike a house lease, rarely includes interior remodeling expense. All counters, carpet, wiring, lighting, partitions, signs, etc., etc. will probably be at your expense. (Improvements that are fastened down usually stay when you leave so the length of the lease is important.) You may be able to get short term credit on a sign and some of the remodeling, but short term credit will not substantially affect the amount of initial cash you need.

Initial inventory and supplies. This includes such items as paper, ink, chemicals, film, rags, stationery, bookkeeping supplies, etc. Beware of salesmen's recommendations regarding initial requirements. You may be joining the club many of us have been in. The dues are five years or a lifetime supply of slow-moving items.

Down payments on equipment. If you purchase equipment, the down payment will run about 20%.

Lease plans require, at the very least, first and last months' payments. Most want first and last two payments. Some demand first and last four or five payments. You should be able to get a five-year lease on new equipment — at least three years on used equipment purchased from a dealer with lease connections. Group all small equipment into a single lease. Leasing companies do not like small monthly payments.

Initial advertising expense. If ever you will need advertising, you will need it when you start out. About the only place you can get long term credit on advertising is from the yellow pages. This comes with your monthly telephone bill. Five thousand dollars is not an exorbitant initial advertising budget for a new shop.

Accounts Receivable. 50% of the average quick printer's business is charged. Payment will average forty-five days if you're careful in granting credit - can easily run one hundred and twenty days. Big, well-financed customers may ride you, especially when interest rates are high. $10,000 in accounts receivables is not unusual for a six-months-old quick print shop.

Operating expense. You should have enough to pay your fixed expenses for at least six months. Unfortunately, this is insurance that is waived by many new owners. It can give you a chance to make a few mistakes and still recover. Insufficient operating expense is listed by most statisticians as the number one cause of failure in a small business.

Money ratings:

The amounts listed are minimums for a small shop if you have good credit. If you plan to pay cash for everything, you should triple or quadruple these amounts.

Less than $20,000 — 0 points
$20,000 — 1 point
$30,000 — 2 points
$40,000 — 3 points
$50,000 or more — 4 points

YOUR SCORE

If you come up with less than nine points, the odds are against you. This doesn't mean you can't make it. Some of the most successful quick printers started with a few hundred dollars and very little useable experience. The shoestring survivors have one thing in common. They all went through several years of killing hours and starvation income. Even with the highest rating of twelve, you can expect three to five years of difficulties before the big dough starts rolling in.

CHAPTER 4

FINANCING

FINANCING

FOUR BASIC NEEDS

The four basic financing needs for the new quick printing shop are:

1. Money to buy equipment.
2. Money to lease and remodel a shop.
3. Money for inventory.
4. Money for operating expense.

A new business has little chance of borrowing money for items 2 and 4, so it is necessary for you to have enough cash to pay the initial lease payment on a building, remodel to suit your requirements and have enough left over for operating expense. The item that is most often underestimated is operating expense. The amount needed depends upon the size of your initial operation, but unless you have $20,000 to $25,000 to carry you through the initial year or so, you are probably going to have serious, if not crippling, financial problems in even a small quick printing operation.

FINANCING EQUIPMENT

If you are starting in business for the first time, your best bet is to purchase equipment from a dealer who has a good working relationship with a leasing company. (Most do.) If your personal credit rating is A-1, it will help a little, but until you have a track record in business, you will find all financing hard to come by. Most leases are close cousins to purchase agreements. The principal difference is the amount of interest charged (on a lease it isn't called interest, but it's the same difference) and the fact that the title remains with the seller until the end of the lease. Most leases have purchase options that average about 10% of the purchase price. Spread your lease payments out as long as the "lender" will allow as you will need all of the cash you can get your hands on for the first few years. After a piece of equipment is paid off and the option to purchase is exercised, it is of little value in raising additional cash even though it may be in perfect working condition.

GET THE BEST RATES AND $$ THOUSANDS IN CASH FROM THE GOVERNMENT

Be independent — shop for rates. You've heard the old saying, "I don't care how much it costs; I'm not going to pay it anyway." Lenders are influenced by your concern over how much you will have to pay, much the same as you are when you are selling someone on credit. It is no time to be modest about your financial standing or the value of real estate or other assets you list on the application for credit. Do not fail to ask for the right to claim the Investment Tax Credit (if it is still allowed by the Federal Government) on any equipment you lease. (You can always take it if you purchase.) Many leasing companies will give you this right if you ask in advance, and even if they refuse, they may be impressed that you expect to have enough of a tax liability to make use of the Investment Tax Credit. On a $20,000 piece of equipment, this can mean a $2,400 saving in Federal Income taxes, and you can carry it back to previous years when you may have paid heavy taxes which can come back to you and provide badly needed cash. When past tax payments are used up, you can carry the credit ahead and deduct it from future tax liabilities.

MONEY FOR INVENTORY

This is a form of loan that is a lot easier to come by than other loan requirements because it is short term, and the profit potential of a regular customer is often many times the amount of the risk. Keep asking for credit and you will find many dealers who will go along with you for one order. Pay your bills promptly, and you will have obtained many thousands of dollars in financing. Most credit managers expect you to earn any discounts offered by paying within the discount period. It is a black mark on your credit standing if you do not earn discounts.

BANK LOANS

There is not much chance for a new business to borrow on business assets, but after you have established a record of success, banks will be anxious to loan you money. A small business should select a large bank. Many small businesses make the mistake of starting out with a small bank only to find after several years of establishing a good relationship that the small bank is hard pressed for cash because of a few big loans or adverse business conditions. There is a much better chance for a small business to obtain a loan from a bank so big and wealthy that they are hard pressed to find a place for their cash to earn the kind of interest you will be paying.

INVESTORS

If you don't have enough money, or you can't borrow enough, you may have to consider selling a piece of your business to investors. At best, you will be taking on backseat drivers, and at worst, you will get pushed to the back seat with an investor doing the driving. Never forget the 51% rule. Unless you own more than half of your business, you are, in reality, working for someone else instead of being an independent businessman.

The type of investor you go after depends on the form of business organization you have set up. The two most common forms are Sole Proprietorship and Corporation.

INVESTMENTS IN THE
SOLE PROPRIETORSHIP

Investment opportunities in a sole proprietorship are limited because an investor has very little protection and no ready market if he decides to bail out. Legal papers can be drawn up outlining agreements, but for all practical purposes, an investment in a Sole Proprietorship is much like a loan with no repayment provision. In effect, you are saying, "If I make it and if I want to, I will give you, the investor, a piece of the profits" — that's it! If the investor becomes a legal partner, he may be liable for your debts or actions. For these reasons, most investors in sole proprietorships are limited to trusting relatives or friends. Term loans usually lead to better relationships in the long run. The principal difference between a term loan and an investment is that the amount and time of repayment is spelled out in a term loan contract while an investment depends upon profit left after the sole proprietor takes out all of the profit that he desires. Also, there is no question of partnership liability in a term loan. The terms can be anything that is mutually agreeable, but watch out for over-optimism in agreeing to repayment. A big chunk coming due at one time can shock or kill a going business. Unlike an investment, you may have to repay a term loan even if your business goes broke.

INVESTMENTS IN SMALL CORPORATIONS

Investors are easier to obtain if you are set up as a corporation. The security for the investor in a closely controlled corporation is not much better than it would be in a sole proprietorship, but the fact that the corporate form of business is designed primarily for the purpose of attracting investors lends a degree of stature to corporate shares. On the other hand, loans are not as easy for a corporation to obtain as all normal loans are canceled in the event of bankruptcy. Many lenders will require your personal guarantee in addition to taking corporate assets as security. This, of course, means that if the corporation goes broke, you are personally liable for the loan.

ORGANIZING AS A SOLE PROPRIETORSHIP

Most quick printers start as sole proprietorships, which is the simplest form of business organization. Because the full responsibility for debts and actions is on the proprietor, the legal requirements for reporting are much lighter than for a corporation.

The determination of which form of business has the best tax advantage requires a qualified expert to review each individual situation, but generally, most quick printers do better as proprietors in the early years. Losses can easily be charged off against other income. Investment tax credits can result in refunds of income taxes paid on personal income in past years. Tax rates are usually lower, as compared with a corporation, until taxable income climbs well above $10,000, a level which few quick printers reach in the first year or two. It is simple to change to a corporation later.

The principal disadvantage of a proprietorship is the risk of some unexpected liability against the business wiping out your personal fortune. Some types of business incur greater hazards in this regard than others. For most quick printers, the risks not covered by insurance are small.

ORGANIZING AS A PARTNERSHIP

"Partner" is a friendly sounding word — odd that it describes a relationship that often results in so much dissension. Most business relationships develop dissension at some time or another, but where leadership is clearly defined, the dissension is settled faster. The principal problem with a partnership is that legal leadership is often divided evenly, creating a tug-of-war situation, with problems remaining in the center that could be solved by going in either direction.

Most successful partnerships have legal agreements outlining exact details of responsibility and profit sharing. Agreements should also cover tax reporting methods, salaries, division of special income, limitations of liability, and buy-sell arrangements. Partnerships are legally dissolved upon the death of a partner. Unless advance arrangements are made for the remaining partners to buy out the deceased partner's share, complications involving heirs can cause the business to fail.

Before starting business as a partnership, the advantages of the corporate form of business should be explored as an alternative.

ORGANIZING AS A CORPORATION

The principal reason for the corporate form of business is to limit the legal liability of the people investing in the business. In a sole proprietorship or partnership, business failure can result in the loss of most of your personal assets. In a corporation, you only lose the money you have put into the business. This is in theory — in practice, most creditors of new corporations require a personal guarantee, so your personal assets are not protected from all debts. Outside investors, however, are fully protected against loss of personal assets except assets that are specifically committed to the corporation. This makes it easier to attract investors.

Organizing a corporation is a fairly simple task. Most lawyers overcharge for their services in this regard. You can even do it yourself by writing to the Department of Corporations in the state you decide upon and following their instructions. You do not have to incorporate in the state you intend to operate in. You can incorporate in any state, even if you do not live or operate there. Over one third of all U.S. corporations are incorporated in Delaware which has liberal laws and minimal fees. All you need is a street mailing address in the state you choose. A "Registered Agent" will provide everything you need, including the mailing address and forwarding service.

ORGANIZING AS A
SUBCHAPTER S CORPORATION

The principal advantage of this type of corporation is that dividends are taxed only once, whereas in a regular corporation, they are taxed twice. All Subchapter S earnings (or losses) are distributed proportionately among the owners and taxed as personal income only. Other corporate advantages, such as limited liability, are the same as for regular corporations. There are, however, limitations and disadvantages. The regular corporation provides better tax advantages for investors who want to leave corporate earnings in and let them grow. Also, state taxes of Subchapter S income may be higher in some cases than earnings from regular corporations.

Eligibility requirements for Subchapter S status:

1. No more than ten stockholders (husband and wife can be counted as one).
2. Individuals only as shareholders — no corporations.
3. Must be a United States organized corporation.
4. Must not have non-resident alien stockholders.
5. Only one class of stock can be issued.
6. Must not be a member of an affiliated group of corporations.
7. 20% or more of income must be earned from operations in U.S.
8. Not more than 20% of income from "investments."

Losses can be used to offset personal income, an advantage not available in regular corporate organization.

You can change your form of organization by filing the proper forms with the I.R.S., but all shareholders in a Subchapter S corporation must consent and sign the form.

CHAPTER 5

PROFESSIONAL
SERVICES

PROFESSIONAL SERVICES

A quick printer, especially one starting out, certainly needs guidance, but in seeking it, he often ends up a tidbit for one of the many vultures preying upon small business.

LEGAL

Lawyers are trained to "practice" in an arena where the winner is often the most deceitful contestant. This training makes it difficult for lawyers to understand normal business dealings, which are usually based on an assumption of forthrightness and trust. If you take all of your problems involving legal risk to a lawyer, you will often find yourself out of the frying pan and into the fire. Your best bet is to buy a book on business law published for your state and use it to avoid problems. Try to settle most problems with common sense and compromise. A compromise may be costly, but the cost is often much less than legal "service."

There are times, of course, when a lawyer is an absolute necessity. An attorney may help you organize your company. He may even be able to help negotiate leases or contracts. The big question is, how do you select a good one? All advice on selecting a good lawyer boils down to common sense and an awful lot of luck.

C.P.A.

C.P.A.'s are licensed, have an accounting degree, at least two years accounting experience, and have passed a state examination. They do the same work as an accountant, but usually charge more because of their professional status. By nature, they are cautious — by training, they are equipped to deal with big business accounting problems. Few C.P.A.'s are properly equipped to serve a quick printer, where risk taking is an everyday affair and accounting problems involve relatively small, potential savings. A plain garden variety accountant who is familiar with small business problems is often a better bet.

The more accounting you personally do, the more you will understand the financial workings of your business. The most you can expect from an accountant is correct mathematics and the proper completion of forms. A financial statement, no matter how well prepared, will not give you the decision making information you need to properly manage your business. You need to be involved in the financial and accounting process all along the way.

Accountants or C.P.A.'s can be hired to do all or part of your bookkeeping. A set price is best. Hourly rates have a way of getting out of hand.

CONSULTANTS

The old adage, "advice is cheap," doesn't apply to the rates charged by most so-called small business consulting companies. The "advice" is often less than worthless — more often than not it is damaging because it is dispensed as "expert" advice. To be an expert, a person must be currently involved in a particular business. Few, if any, consultants are actively involved in the day to day operation of a quick printing shop. And even then, to be helpful, their shop would need to be of the same type as yours. There is great variety in quick printing today.

Consultants are used primarily by big businesses. They are experts in one narrow field. Their advice and guidance on a specific problem can be very valuable to a large business. The market for the services of a qualified expert in quick printing would not provide a living wage for a consultant.

DO IT YOURSELF

Your best bet is to read everything you can find on quick printing. Visit quick printers outside of the area where you will be competing and talk with the owners. Join printing associations—both national and local. (See "Resources" for names and addresses.) Subscribe to trade magazines. A word of caution on reading and listening to others — you will find a great difference of opinion among successful quick printers. There are many paths that lead to success. If you investigate several successful operations, you may be confused at the differences of opinions and methods. You can't follow them all, but you can take the best from each.

CHAPTER 6

LOCATION SELECTION

LOCATION SELECTION

MOST SHOPS FAIL BEFORE THEY START

The selection of a location is the most important single decision an owner will make. It is many times as important as the location of a business that uses outside salesmen. Unless location is given proper consideration, all subsequent efforts to succeed will fail. Every city has its own peculiarities, so the following should be blended with the knowledge you have of local conditions.

HOW FAR WILL CUSTOMERS TRAVEL

This depends, of course, on the density of the area. In a densely populated area, most of your customers will come from an area within two miles of your shop with about 75% of your business coming from within a mile of your shop. In small towns, you may even draw from surrounding towns.

HOW MANY POTENTIAL CUSTOMERS

The average quick printing shop needs 2,000 to 3,000 potential customers within this four mile radius. You will never sell more than ten to fifteen percent of the printing buyers in your area, so unless you locate in an area where you have these buyers in adequate number, you will not make it operating as a quick printing shop. Of course, you can convert to outside salesmen, but why pay the high cost of a quick printing location if you are not going to benefit from it? You will be better off, in this case, in a low cost location on a back street.

TYPE OF CUSTOMERS NEEDED

One of the most common mistakes of the new owner is to locate in a retail shopping area, either in a shopping center or on a street in the center of retail shops. The rent is usually nearly double in an area of concentrated retail shops as compared to what it is a few blocks away from the shops but still on a main street. The principal problem with this type of location is that you will be surrounded by retail shoppers, not printing buyers. The customer who frequents retail shops during the week day is not the type of printing buyer you can make a profit on. Your profitable customers will be small and medium sized businesses or small branches of large businesses. Most of these people have offices in multistoried office buildings. You should be near many office buildings (but not inside of one). The small retailer is, of course, a potential customer, but he is far down on the list of potential profitable types of customers.

PARKING

Adequate parking is an absolute must. Most of your customers will be coming to you, not you to them. Even if you offer a delivery service, most of your delivery customers will make frequent trips to your shop to discuss printing problems or to pick up rush orders. If they cannot park at or near your door, they will not do business with you.

MAIN OR SIDE STREET

A location on a street with a "key" name is worth ten

times the rent of an unknown street. Your customers will come from the yellow pages, from mailers, and from word-of-mouth. A ten-inch map won't cure the problem of a location on an unknown street, even if the street happens to be a few steps off of the "key" street. Most customers don't have the exact address in their minds. They come to the general area and start looking for a sign. As an example of this, for several years we were located across the street from another quick printing shop. We had the largest and best placed sign, and we did the most advertising, however, every six months or so our competitor across the street would send out several thousand flyers. He later told me that he got very little return from these flyers. But we always got a big return from his flyers. New customers would come into our shop with his flyer, his address, and his name which was entirely different sounding than ours. They were simply coming to the general location and looking for a sign that said "printing," and our sign was larger and better placed than his. Even when they found out that they were in the wrong place, most stayed and bought from us. They had responded to the advertisement because it hit them at a time they had a printing requirement, and the location mentioned was close by and easy to get to. In effect, they were responding to a "known" location, not to a particular company.

Buyers of quick printing are a long way from becoming "brand" conscious. They will try almost any place that is convenient, and if they are treated right, most will return.

LEASE, RENT, OR BUY

Most quick print shop owners do not have the capital to buy a location in a prime spot. Also the selection is narrowed as compared to the lease or rent locations. If you have the capital and can find the right location, there is nothing wrong with buying. The biggest problem facing most new owners is the length of the lease. It is going to take three or four years to build your business to a good profit, and if you have a short term lease, most of your efforts can go out the window. Even if you have to move just a mile or two away, you will lose a very heavy percentage of your customers. A long lease will obligate you also, but this is one of the smaller risks you will be taking. A building is a lot easier to sub lease (in case you fail) than it is to sub lease or sell the other obligations you will be taking on.

I wouldn't go into any location without at least a five year lease, and a five year with a five year option is even better. If your landlord balks at a long lease, suggest options that will give him protection. For instance, if he balks at a long lease for the reason that most landlords balk, which is the restraint a long lease might have on a sale of the building, suggest a clause with six months notice and six months free rent if he wants you to vacate. This leaves it open for him to take any profitable deal that might come his way, and it gives you more protection than you would have from a short term lease. You then know that you have the location for ten years unless the landlord sells or gets mad enough to forfeit six months rent. Options covering tax increases or inflation are routine and will cover many objections by landlords to long leases.

CHAPTER 7

SHOP DESIGN

SHOP DESIGN

THREE REASONS DESIGN IS IMPORTANT

Shop design is important for three basic reasons:

1. Appearance
2. Convenient flow of work
3. Space saving

MAKE YOUR SHOP SELL

Unlike the conventional printer who sends out salesmen, the quick printer does most of his selling across the counter. Many large customers of conventional printers never see the printer's place of business. They form their impression of him by his advertising and by the appearance and actions of his salesman.

Nothing can substitute for quality work and all of the other things a customer normally expects, but a quick printer cannot afford to underestimate the impact the appearance of his shop has on potential customers. I said, **potential customers.** Unless you can turn potential customers into customers, you will never have a chance to show them what great

work you do. If they already know how good you are, they might continue giving you their business even if they are not impressed by the appearance of your shop, but you can't depend on **building** your business in this manner.

DON'T SHOW IT ALL

Proper shop design should allow your customer TO SEE ONLY WHAT YOU WANT HIM TO SEE. This may not sound too important, but a lot of problems are caused by a customer seeing too much. For instance, a customer should be able to see the press running, but he should not be able to see the delivery end of the press. Why? Because a lot of crud comes out the delivery end of your press before you get the job lined up to run. Few customers can understand why so many sheets of their job are being thrown away. Many will try to salvage the runup from the wastebasket. It is not to your advantage for your customer to see or obtain work that you see fit to throw away. There are times when you may be having trouble with a job, or the job may be confidential.

PRESS LOCATION

Your presses should be located behind a partition approximately 4 to 4½ feet high. The exact height depends on the distance the partition is behind your front counter where your customer stands. If the customer is waiting, he can see the top area of the press and see that work is being done on his job, so he is satisfied.

TOTAL SHOP SPACE NEEDED

The space in the average quick print shop will cost four or five times as much per square foot as space in a print shop or manufacturing plant located off of a main thoroughfare. The design and arrangement of any plant or shop is important, but because of the cost of space, this aspect takes on added importance to the management of a quick printing shop. There are always exceptions to any rule, but as a general guide, a range of from 800 square feet to 1200 square feet will best fit the requirements of most shops. If the location is priced so cheap that more space can be afforded, it is probably a poor location for a successful shop. If it is too small, it leaves no room for growth. A lot can be done with a small amount of space if every effort is made to utilize every square foot. The best way to do this will be covered in detail later in this chapter.

FRONT LOBBY

The front lobby should be small—not only to conserve space, but to create the illusion of being crowded when only a few people are at your counter. People like to do business with busy people. They figure, perhaps rightly, that if you are busy, you must be offering something worthwhile, and vice versa.

COUNTER

Your counter should be large enough to accommodate not more than three people at a time. Unless you are the super quick printer, you will not have more than two trained people on your counter, so there is no need for more room at your counter. If they have to stand back and wait, they are more impressed than they are if they are at your counter and not being waited on. There is the impression carried over from lunch counters that when they are at the counter, they should be served promptly. Also,if you have a lot of extra counter space, customers will start using it for collating, stuffing mailers, etc.

GET THEM IN AND OUT — FAST!

Don't serve coffee. Don't furnish counter stools. Don't encourage them to use your lobby or counter as a hangout or loafing place. Your biggest bottleneck is your counter. There is no way of

predicting when three, four, or even five or six customers will walk in and expect prompt service. You may sit for hours with no activity and then, wham, they all come at once. The last thing you need is for your counter to be tied up by a couple of bums who have nothing to do back at the office. Most of your good customers, the ones who pay their bills, are busy people. They could care less about a cup of coffee. They want their job fast, and they want to get back to work. Provide two or three seats in your lobby, but not at your counter. The loafers want to be up at the counter where the action is. They won't stay long if placed away from the counter without a cup of coffee.

77

KEEP IT CLEAN AND UNCLUTTERED

It goes without saying that your counter and lobby should be neat and clean, but less obvious is the need to keep it uncluttered. There are a few items you will want to call to the attention of your customers. Remember that a good advertisement has plenty of white space. The advertising you place in your lobby should be placed with the same principle in mind. You won't have a big volume of traffic, and they won't have a lot of time to browse, so give them only a few items to look at. For instance, if you are pushing "From the desk of" pads, make up an attractive display of pads and remove all else from your lobby during the pad promotion. You'll be surprised how much attention your pad display will get.

DON'T SELL STATIONERY

It is poor judgment to display a variety of small items ranging from greeting cards to pencils. One of the greatest mistakes made in quick print shops is the assumption that the sale of small items to a customer is extra profit. Your two greatest shortages are time and space, and small dollar volume items take up large amounts of both and give little profit in return. In order to make money selling small retail items, it is necessary to have enough of a variety to attract a heavy flow of customers, such as a stationery store. Very few shops have been successful in combining these two operations for reasons mentioned in other chapters. You can use low cost retail clerks to sell stationery, but these clerks will not attract profitable printing customers.

ONE ENTRANCE ONLY

The cost of space is too great to devote space for a walkway through the shop for customers. Besides the safety and security risks of having customers walk through the shop, there is the disadvantage of giving up needed privacy.

USE SUBTLE APPROACH

This may sound like a contradiction of my "uncluttered" advice, but if used with discretion, this idea will sell a lot of merchandise for you. USE YOUR LOBBY TO STORE LARGE JOBS. If you are working on a large job that won't be picked up for a few days, you can impress your customers by selecting part of the job and stacking it in your lobby. It is a subtle way of saying, "We're so busy we're running out of space." It also lets your customers know that you do large jobs as well as small ones. You can do the same thing with cartons from your regular stock of paper. Stack eight or ten cases in your lobby for a few days, and it looks like you are so busy you are running out of space.

KEEP SOME AREAS PRIVATE

All you need to show to your counter customers is the area where their "while you wait" job is being produced. Even if they aren't waiting for a job, they hear the press running, and this creates the desired impression. It also keeps your pressman on his toes. There is nothing more effective toward improving quality than for him to hear complaints, compliments, or to face a complaining customer.

Most of your shop should be kept private. You will be using part-time workers for large jobs involving collating, stapling, etc., and they should be in an area which is not in plain view of your counter. You can't always select part-time help with "image" in mind, and some of them are pretty scroungy. Some college students are good workers, but their looks would scare customers into your competitor's shop.

You can't keep everything neatly stored, and some of your storage area should be out of sight. A small, private office is nice to have if you can spare the space, but you should have a desk at the front counter where most of your billing, etc. can be done during slack periods. If you have an office, it should not be used as a hideaway. Your customers want to see YOU and be greeted by YOU when they come in. If they have a large job to talk about, they want to talk to the head man. If you spend too much time hiding in your office, you could be passing up some large and profitable business.

PUT IT ON WHEELS

If possible, put your work area counters on wheels. Work area space is at a premium and can easily become clogged with a few big jobs. You need lots of counter top space around your presses and in the binding area, but if you build in enough counter area to handle rush periods, you are wasting a lot of valuable space for counters used a small percentage of the time. The answer is to put the counters on wheels and move them around to the areas where they are needed. Keep the counters small, about 12 inches deep and not more than 3½ to 4 feet long. Height should be normal work area height and shelves should be spaced to take jr. size cartons as well as loose jobs. These rolling counters can't be bought at any place I know of, but they are easy to have made or to make yourself. Use steel, swivel, heavy duty wheels, not rubber-tired wheels. Rubber wheels roll easy when not loaded down, but they are hard to push and steer with a heavy load of paper. KEEP THEM NARROW. I repeat this advice as we made the mistake of starting with large rolling counters and ran into a lot of problems moving them around. Passage areas are often cluttered, leaving just enough space to walk through. A 12" wide rolling counter may be a bit more tipsy than a wider shelf, but it will fit into a lot more places. If a large work area is needed for a particular job, place several small rolling counters together. When not in use, they are rolled out of the way.

LIGHTING

Provide plenty of light. Many quick printing shops

are poorly lighted, creating eye strain and causing quality and safety problems. Inexpensive drafting type lights can be mounted on a wall close to each press to supplement the light on the press which is not powerful enough for good quality control. In addition, there should be bright overhead lighting to prevent eye strain. The Itek camera may need shielding from some of the lighting to obtain even copy. This can be accomplished by placing a ½" sheet of plywood on top of the Itek camera and hanging sheets of rubylith down the sides. This provides a nice appearance and the lights from the camera still show which lets the customer know that things are "happening" to his job.

FINISHED JOB STORAGE

Nothing turns a customer on or off as fast as a display of organization or confusion. Provide alphabetical shelves for finished jobs. Most completed jobs are small enough to be placed on shelves. A copy of the job order should be placed on the shelf in alphabetical sequence. If a customer asks about a job before it is complete, the job ticket is easily located and from there the job can be traced to determine how near it is to completion. When a job is complete, it should be placed on the shelf with the job order and any other papers or originals that need to be signed or returned to the customer. When a customer calls for his work, it is quickly located. Of course, you should have filed a master control copy of every job order and invoice in case the shelf copies are misplaced and to assure that every job is paid for or entered into the records. (More on record keeping in another chapter.)

JOB ORDERS

Work orders should be seen at a glance. A slanted shelf at eye level is a convenient way to sort out job orders in the press and binding areas. If orders are attached to large envelopes (we use 11" x 16" job envelopes), they can be placed, along with originals, in the order to be produced. A glance will indicate what the load is and jobs can be moved around to accommodate rush jobs that need to be sandwiched in. The shelf area should be long enough to take care of rush periods. (Ours is 8' long.) To prevent the appearance of emptiness (many customers will glance at the work order shelves when they enter the shop), keep the shelf near full at all times by using dummy job orders and envelopes to fill in the empty space not being used for real orders. ALWAYS LOOK BUSY.

Shop design for specialized areas will be covered under chapters dealing with the individual specialties.

CHAPTER 8

HIRING AND FIRING

HiRING AND FIRING

Hire good people and pay them well. The difficult word in this phrase is "good." No matter how expert you become at hiring, there will be many times when you will hire an employee who doesn't fit your job. It is unfair to hold on to such an employee—unfair to him, to your other workers, and to you. This chapter covers the methods of hiring and firing I have found practical for a quick printing business.

DO YOU REALLY NEED A "STAR" PRESSMAN

In any business the skill of any craftsmen used is important. In a quick printing shop, it is VITAL that you have at least one "Star" pressman. Finding a

star isn't as easy as it may sound, considering the fact that approximately 90% of the small press operators available are not capable of doing acceptable direct image work, and only about one out of ten "acceptable" pressmen turns out to be a "star."

ACTUAL PROFIT COMPARISONS

First you have to convince yourself that a "star" will be worth what you are going to have to pay him, so let's examine value based upon our experience. The figures given are relative and will differ with each shop, depending on the type of work being done, prices charged, etc., however, the principal point is the comparison of one set of figures against the other sets.

Category 3 Pressman: (Barely acceptable) Turns out approximately $300 of business per day on an average based on a month's production. He uses a higher percentage of material and his quality is marginal.

Category 2 Pressman: (Average but not a "Star") Turns out approximately $400 average per day of acceptable quality business, but has problems with difficult jobs and must be supervised closely.

Category 1 Pressman: Turns out approximately $550 average per day of high quality business and handles most difficult jobs and press problems without help. This is star performance.

RATE OF PAY: (For illustration purposes only - varies greatly from city to city)
    Category 3: $5.00 per hour.
    Category 2: $6.00 per hour.
    Category 1: $7.50 per hour.

There's a big spread between the barely acceptable pressman's pay and the pay needed to land a star, but let's examine the comparative worth. Category 3 will run business off faster than you can land it and is worth less than nothing, so let's consider the comparative worth between Category 2 and 1 as this is the area where most well-run shops find themselves. Let's assume you could hire an acceptable pressman for $6.00 per hour and a star would cost you $7.50 per hour.

Let's assume that material cost is about average or 25% of the total job, leaving 75% gross profit before other expenses.

The "acceptable" pressman will produce an average of	$400.00 per day
Cost of material used	100.00
Gross Profit	**300.00**

The "star" pressman will produce an average of	550.00
Cost of material used	137.50
Gross Profit	**412.00**

Assuming 25% more pay for a star pressman, the extra pay amounts to $12.00 per day. The extra gross profit amounts to $112.00 per day, making the star worth $100.00 per day more than an acceptable pressman.

Actually, our experience showed an even greater difference because stars could turn out difficult jobs. This attracted many customers willing to pay a higher price, especially when the other shops they had tried could not even do the job.

HOW TO FIND A STAR PRESSMAN

First, determine what the level of pay for acceptable pressmen is in your area. You will have to go 25% above this level to even get initial interest from a star. Don't hedge! The pressman you want is no dummy. He will know what the level of pay is, and he will probably be getting a rate which is near the top of the "acceptable pressmen" level. You are not looking for someone who is out of work. You are looking for a pressman who is either being underpaid, overworked, or who has some reason for looking at the ads occasionally.

HOW TO WORD A NEWSPAPER AD

Most ads say something like: "Experience required," "top pay," "pay open," "pay depending upon experience," "pay $5.00 to $7.00," etc. When you are fishing for a star, you can't expect him to bite at ambiguous bait. You need to spell it out. Example: You will want to list the usual things such as type of equipment, location, telephone, etc., but when it comes to the bait, we use the following: Experience: "Must have 5 yrs. quick print shop experience." Salary: "$1,275 per month based on 5 day, 40 hrs., overtime paid." Why $1,275 per month instead of an hourly rate? Because nearly everyone is guilty of figuring on a basis of 4 weeks per month, and if the rate of pay was stated as $7.50 per hour, which is the same as $1,275 per month, most people would multiply $7.50 x 40 hours and come up with $300.00 per week which they would multiply by 4 weeks and come up with $1,200.00 per month. By stating a monthly figure, you give the applicant a truer picture of the income he can expect.

WEED OUT THE CHAFF

You will receive many calls from completely unqualified people even though you have stated an experience requirement. If you grant interviews to these unqualified people, you will be wasting a lot of their time and yours. You can eliminate most of the unqualified with the following procedure:When you first answer the telephone, do not let the applicant take the initiative. Immediately start off with questions such as: "How much quick print shop experience do you have?", "What type of presses have you operated?", (get details, time, place, etc.), "Are you now working?", "When did you leave your last job?" (Look out for the person who has been out of work just long enough to use up his unemployment eligibility.) "What is your name, telephone number?" By this time you have enough information on paper to make an evaluation as to whether the applicant is worth an interview, but do not make an appointment at this point or indicate any preference for the applicant. Explain as follows: "We are screening all applicants by phone while the ad is running, and we will arrange an interview with the two applicants we feel are most qualified for the job. Thank you for calling. If we decide it would be worth your time and ours for an interview, we will be in touch with you within the next few days. When are you available at this number?" At this point, hang up and make notes regarding your impressions and date your notes. This is important as your impressions will soon be dulled with the rush of everyday business and other applicants' calls. After all of your calls are in, take out your notes and decide if you have an applicant worth an interview. You don't find a star every time, so unless you have a good sounding applicant, chuck the whole batch and start over with a new ad.

DON'T BOTTLENECK YOUR FUTURE

The greatest hazard to recruiting a star is the

tendency to give up and accept someone barely qualified and hope for the best. The odds are too great! Keep looking for good basic qualifications. Once you hire someone less than a star, you have shut off the recruiting and closed out any chance you have to make the kind of money you expected to make when you went into business. The big money is there, but you need a "star" to guide you to it.

EMPLOYMENT AGENCIES

Commercial agencies can be useful, but the principal problem is the method in which they are compensated. They are paid nothing for their efforts unless you hire one of their applicants. This obviously puts them in the position of "sellers," and you should judge their evaluations of applicants with this in mind. If you use a commercial agency, look for an established agency, specializing in printing jobs as they are more likely to be trying to build a reputation and repeat business.

State employment agencies do not charge a fee, but you may be flooded with applicants who are responding simply to meet the requirements for continuing their unemployment checks. In among the weeds, there are usually some good crops if you have the time to do some thinning out.

KNOCKOUT FACTORS

In addition to the obvious list of requirements and desirable traits, you should compile a list of knockout factors. Be realistic and keep the list short—some lists I have seen would take out 98% of the entire population. This list can cut down the number of applicants actually interviewed as these factors can usually be uncovered in a telephone interview.

FIRING

There is no more undesirable task than firing people. The better you become at hiring and managing, the less firing you will need to do. People are complicated, and for reasons sometimes beyond anyone's control, employees develop into a liability that the business cannot afford. In a quick printing shop, this task should not be delegated. It should be done by the boss.

All too often the "boss" feels he must justify his action by downgrading the employee. No employee will accept this, and he will forever hate any boss who fires him in this manner. He has his ego to preserve, and it is valuable to him that he keep his self-respect.

Figure out a reason that is true, but one that lets the employee go on to the next job with his head high and without scars. A reason might be, "We are going to have to fill your position with someone with a type of experience that more closely fits our particular requirements."

Time the firing interview so that it is over quickly with little opportunity for discussion. Any discussion at this point will develop into a defense of position on both sides, and no worthwhile progress will be made.

After an employee is fired, the best course to take

with other employees is to button up. If you try to justify your actions, you will lose respect. The fired employee is the underdog. You can afford to be "big" about it or small!

REFERENCE CHECK

After an application is received, you may want to go directly into a preliminary interview. However, it is best to delay a hiring decision until references have been checked.

A reference check is a must if you are to get a true picture of the applicant. It is only normal that applicants present their stories in as favorable a light as possible. Since they want to be hired, it would be unnatural for them to do anything else. In their eagerness to impress a prospective employer, they may substitute fiction for fact by:

**Slanting Their Work
Histories in Their Own Favor**

This is done by almost everyone. Some, however, carry this to an extreme. Some accomplished "job shoppers" have learned by experience to tell smooth, plausible stories in a most convincing manner.

Covering Up

Unfavorable facts in an applicant's work history are sometimes concealed by:

   1. Stretching dates of employment to cover poor references
   2. Inflating salary figures
   3. Claiming a higher level of responsibility than

HIRING AND FIRING

(This form reduced approximately 40%)

APPLICATION FOR EMPLOYMENT

Answer all questions as completely as possible. Use reverse side to give additional information when necessary.

Date_____

NAME_____
     Last   First   Middle   Social Security No.

ADDRESS _____
      Street & No.   City   State   Zip

How long at above address?_____Telephone No. _____

Previous address_____How long there? ___

Position being applied for _____ Full Time___ Part time___

If part time specify days and hours available _____

IS THERE ANY REASON AN APPLICATION FOR SURETY BOND MIGHT BE REFUSED?_____

EDUCATION

High school name & address _____

Major studies in high school_____Did you graduate?___

College or Trade school - List studies completed & give name and address.

_____

WORK EXPERIENCE

GIVE YOUR BUSINESS RECORD FOR PAST THREE EMPLOYERS IN DETAIL, GIVING NAMES AND ADDRESSES OF EMPLOYERS, LOCATION OF WORK, POSITION HELD AND RESPONSIBILITIES	DATE MO.	DATE YR.	POSITION HELD	SALARY REC'D	REASON FOR LEAVING
1. PRESENT OR LAST EMPLOYER	FROM				
	TO				
2. PREVIOUS					
3. PREVIOUS					

SIGNATURE

Do not write below this line - For office use only.

INTERVIEW AND REFERENCE NOTES:

_____

Date Employed_____Position_____ Date of birth _____

Marital status_____Spouses name _____

93

was actually reached

    4. Giving a glossed-over reason for leaving

Falsifying

Occasionally an applicant will deliberately lie about his qualifications. Because people will slant their stories in their own favor and because some will cover up and falsify, it is essential that their histories be checked with other sources so that complete accurate facts will be available.

WHAT TO CHECK

You will want to check particularly on:

Dates of previous employment
Of particular significance are unexplained, unaccounted for gaps. Sometimes an applicant will stretch the employment dates in order to account for time spent on a job he does not want you to know about.

Previous salary figures
The salary figures given on an application blank are frequently inflated.

Positions previously held
These are frequently misrepresented.

Real reasons for leaving previous positions

Personal habits such as gambling and drinking

METHODS OF CHECKING

Checks with Previous Employers

There is no one better qualified to give you additional information about the applicant's ability, his drive to succeed, his cooperativeness, etc., and to verify the facts he has furnished than the supervisor for whom he has worked in each organization. He knows firsthand how the person worked out on the actual job.

Getting the kind of information you need takes tact; it takes probing; it takes careful interpretation. Checks with previous employers can be done in three ways:

1. By mail. This is the poorest way. Experience has shown that employers are reluctant to put in writing any information of a negative character.

2. Personal inquiry. From a quality standpoint, the personal call on a former employer is without doubt the very best method. It is certainly recommended if the previous employer is in town and can be easily reached. The time consumed in making the call will be well worthwhile.

3. Telephone check. Distance and the lack of time frequently make a personal call impossible. The telephone check is an efficient, practical method which has had excellent results. With the proper approach, you should be able to induce previous employers to tell you things which they would not put in writing.

WHY THE TELEPHONE CHECK IS EFFECTIVE

**It is the fastest way to get
information about the applicant**
Ordinarily each telephone check requires only five to ten minutes.

More and better information is obtained
If you use the proper approach in a telephone conversation, you can easily induce previous employers to "open up" and say things they never would put in writing. When the facts you uncover do not seem to correlate with those on the application form, you can probe for further information—a technique which is impossible if you use a written inquiry.

It is an inexpensive means of investigation
Even in those cases when it is necessary to make long distance calls, the cost is usually well justified by the value of the information obtained.

**The information is in your hands
before the second interview**
Making this check before the interview has important advantages. It is easier for you to plan your questions if you have advance information. You will know what areas to stress, what items require careful probing, and what aspects of the applicant's background need clarification.

Who to contact
There are two sources you can contact: (1) The applicant's immediate supervisor, the person he reports to. (2) The Personnel Department. You will get better results by contacting the supervisor. He will be able to give you many details about the individual's capacities and personality characteristics which do not appear on the personnel records. In cases where exact dates of employment are of particular interest, it may be necessary to contact both.

NOTE: Be sure you have indicated your intention of checking former employers so that if there are any he does not want contacted, he will tell you.

HOW TO MAKE THE TELEPHONE CHECK

Preparation
Before telephoning, make a note regarding the dates of employment, nature of his work, salary at leaving, and reason for leaving.

Approach for Personnel Department
Because no employer or personnel department will give out information unless they know who is calling and why the information is needed, you should identify yourself and indicate the purpose of your call:

"This is Bill Friday. (Give your title and company.) I would like to verify some information given to me by Mr. Alfred Smith, a former employee of yours, who is applying for a position with us."

The word "verify" will ease the way for you as it implies that you already have the necessary information and that all you want from him is verification. Actually, it will serve as a wedge to obtain additional information beyond mere verification.

Resistance
Occasionally you will come across a contact unwilling or very reluctant to reveal any information. If you do, you may overcome this resistance in one of the following two ways:

1. Refer to the information the applicant has given you regarding dates of employment, job duties,

salary, reason for leaving, etc. Ask for verification. This often breaks the ice and lets the former employer know that you have a bona fide application for employment. He may then be willing to answer questions.

2. If the person contacted cannot give out information because of company policy, ask to speak to his supervisor. If the supervisor gives you the same story (after explaining to him that you understand perfectly that company policy does not permit him to give information over the phone, but you would like to make a decision about the person that day), then ask to speak to his supervisor. It may be necessary to make two or three such contacts before the right person has been reached. In most cases, however, this straightforward approach will get you the information you want.

Techniques
A special advantage of the telephone check lies in the fact that you can tell a lot from the inflection and tone of the voice of the speaker. For example, the question, "Would you re-employ him if you had an opening?" must be interpreted not only by what he says, but how he says it. A change in tone, evasiveness, hesitation can tell you a great deal. An enthusiastic "Darn right I would!" is one thing. A wavering "Yeah ... I guess I would" is still another. Naturally, if the company has a policy of not rehiring former employees, you will have to allow for a "no" answer. This is such an important question that it is worth following up with another to determine what the answer would be if there were not such a policy.

The questions near the end, "What are his strong points?", "What are his weak points?" serve not only as a double check to catch any information you may have missed, but in answering the question on weak points, your contact may give you more detailed information of an important and possibly disqualifying nature.

When you spot an inconsistency, follow it up. You may discover some very significant facts. If the information furnished by the employer conflicts with the applicant's story, try to reconcile the facts to determine whether the applicant made honest errors or was attempting to mislead you. Probe with questions such as, "How do you mean?", "Why do you say it that way?", "Would you care to explain a little more?" Etc., etc.

Closing
When you have the information you require, close on a note of thanks and assure the contact that his confidence will be respected.

Check more than one
Getting the viewpoints of more than one previous employer is always advisable. It is recommended that you check at least three to guard against the possibility of weighing too heavily information which is biased either for or against the applicant. Occasionally an employer may be resentful toward employees whose departure may have caused him to be inconvenienced.

TELEPHONE REFERENCE CHECK FORM

A form is helpful and should be custom designed for your partricular requirements. The following outline should serve as a starter:

Date
Name of applicant

Name of company
City and state
Telephone
Person to contact
Position

Before making the call, fill in the foregoing and the following: Nature of job, Dates of employment, Earnings on leaving, Reason for leaving. If information conflicts with applicant's story, try to reconcile the facts to determine whether applicant made honest errors or was attempting to mislead.

Suggested Approach for
Immediate Supervisor
"Mr. ..., this is ... (title and company). We are considering Mr. ... for a position as a (   ). He has listed you as a former employer, and I'd like to verify some of the information he has given us. Of course, everything you tell me will be held in the strictest confidence."

Suggested Questions
   1. Mr. ... lists his dates of employment with your company as: Starting____ Ending____ Does this check with your records or memory? (Checks? Yes — No)

2. What was the nature of his work? (Application states ____. Checks? Yes — No)

3. How were his results compared with others? Excellent____ Average____ Poor____

4. Did he work hard? Industrious____ Enough to get by____ Below average____

5. How was his attendance on the job? Excellent____ Some days lost____ Poor____

6. How did he get along with others? Very well____ Fair____ Poor____

7. Any bad drinking or gambling habits? No____ Yes____ (comments)

8. He says his earnings were ____ when he left. (Checks? Yes — No)

9. Why did he leave your company? (Application states____. Checks? Yes — No) If does not check, explore for true reason.

10. What would you say were his strong points?

11. What would you say were his weak points?

12. Would you re-employ him if you had an opening? (Yes — No) If not, why not?

13. Is there anything else you would like to tell me that might help in forming an accurate estimate of Mr. ...'s qualifications?

Thank you for the information. Again I would like to assure you that this information will be held in confidence and used solely for the purpose of judging our applicant's qualifications for our job.

Rating

Rating and comments should be completed immediately after hanging up while inflections in tone and other impressions are fresh.

Good reference
Some reservation
Definitely questionable
Comments
Check made by

JOB INTERVIEW

The interview is the core of your entire selection procedure. No device has as yet been found which can take the place of a face-to-face chat. It is a means not only of obtaining factual information, but of obtaining a firsthand impression of the applicant's personality and the impact he makes on people. The interview has three principal objectives:

1. To obtain the facts about the applicant.
2. To check the first impressions gained from the application and any reference checks that may have been made.
3. To make sure the applicant clearly understands the requirements of the job.

Interviewing is both an art and a skill. In each case, a high degree of effectiveness can be obtained by following sound principles and basic techniques. Here are some key points to remember—points that will help you to get the true picture.

Prepare in Advance
Select a spot that provides complete privacy and

freedom from interruptions. Have at hand all the forms and tools you will need.

Put the Applicant at Ease

Extend a friendly greeting and begin informally. Make him feel welcome. The applicant will give you more information about himself with less effort on your part if he is at ease. For this reason, it is generally a good idea to start the interview with some pleasant remark about a topic in which the applicant may be presumed to be interested. Spend a few minutes in casual conversation, small talk about something current—a ball game, or even the weather—anything to get on common ground and relax the tenseness which may be present.

Don't Jump to Conclusions

We are generally busy and shortcuts are welcome; but unfortunately, jumping to conclusions results in expensive decisions, excessive turnover, and leads only to the necessity for further searching.

Phrase Your Questions Carefully

Avoid leading questions. A question which requires some kind of reply is better than one which can be answered with a "yes" or "no." For example, "Why did you leave your last position?" is a better question than, "Did you resign from your last position?" If you volunteer the fact that, "We want people who are willing to work long hours," the applicant knows what to say if he wants the job. It's much better to ask, "How long was your normal working day in your last job—how many hours?"

Guard Against Your Prejudices

We all have prejudices. Recognize your own prejudices and guard against them. Don't turn a good person down because of a personal prejudice. The job requirements, not your personal likes and dislikes, should be the criterion.

Ask Personal Questions Naturally

It is impossible to properly interpret the information we get from the interview unless we delve into the applicant's personal affairs. If you show embarrassment or obvious reluctance at asking these questions, fearing that you may be rebuffed, you invite a rebuff. On the other hand, if you ask the question in a normal, natural, conversational manner with an attitude which assumes you fully expect to get this information, chances are you will.

Resistance

If the applicant becomes defensive, you may:

1. Drop the question and come back to it later in the interview.

2. Explain that all applicants are asked these questions because information is necessary in making a decision. Then add: But if you have some reasons for withholding this information, naturally I won't insist. A pause after this statement may induce him to speak. It puts him in a position where he must answer the question or tell why he doesn't want to. If this doesn't work, and the question involved is a significant one, you have no choice but to tell him that you must have an answer and that if he doesn't want to give it, you cannot consider him further for the job.

Let Him Do the Talking
The interview is a fact-finding process. The candidate has the facts. You won't get them if you do most of the talking. Encourage him to talk (that won't be difficult—he's talking about his favorite subject, himself). Listen and evaluate.

Technique of Asking Questions
Don't ask questions in a routine, mechanical way right from the form. While the questions have been phrased so they sound as conversational as possible, their primary purpose is to serve as guides, to remind you of the areas which must be covered. Phrase the questions in your own way.

Record the Answers as You Get Them
You can't possibly remember the answers to all of the questions you are going to ask. You must have a written record of the replies both from the standpoint of reviewing the information later and for its appraisal by others. Will the applicant mind your taking down notes? Experience has shown that he will not. Explain right at the outset what you are doing and why. You will find in most cases that you have created a favorable impression. The applicant is flattered and reassured in the knowledge that you are sufficiently interested in his replies to make a record of them and that you are following a definite procedure which all candidates must go through.

Avoid Moralizing
The purpose of the interview is not to counsel, give advice, suggest, or find fault. It is to obtain information about the candidate's fitness for the job.

Whatever his reply, do not indicate concern or surprise. You should never criticize.

Selling the Job

Don't make the mistake of selling the job to the applicant before you have decided you want him. This doesn't mean you shouldn't explain the job and what it entails. But don't go all out on the sales approach prematurely. If you do a good job in this respect and then have to tell him later that he's not qualified, the problem of rejecting him becomes twice as difficult. Furthermore, in your enthusiasm you may lose sight of the objective appraisal you are trying to make.

Watch the Clock

While you don't want to hurry the interview, neither do you want to spend an overabundance of time at it. A good interview should last approximately 30 minutes. Keep on the track. When you have all the information you need or can get, close the interview tactfully. If you decide at any point in the interview, for any reason, that the applicant should be eliminated from further consideration, terminate the interview right then. Thank him for applying. Graciously explain that his qualifications do not seem to match those necessary for the job. Do not attempt to explain why they don't. (Or if you prefer, tell him you will contact him in a few days by mail.)

End on a Friendly Note

It is important that you send the applicant away with a feeling of goodwill. When the interview has been completed, take a few minutes to write out an interview evaluation.

SUGGESTED INTERVIEW QUESTIONS

Following is a list of general questions to get you started. Your list should include questions pertinent to your particular requirements.

1. I see you worked for the X company. What did you do there?

2. What part of your job did you like best?

3. What part did you like least?

The purpose of questions 1, 2, and 3 is to permit the applicant to talk, thus enabling the interviewer to judge whether he has had the necessary experience and whether the kind of work he likes coincides with the work available. These first three questions, as well as the following two questions, may be asked regarding each previous job:

4. How was X company as a place to work?

5. Do you think the employees there had enough chance for advancement?

The best answers to questions 4 and 5 are brief, noncritical answers. Destructive, bitter criticism may indicate the applicant carries a "chip" on his shoulder and, if hired, will be as critical of your company as he is of the X company.

6. Are you generally lucky?

This may seem a very strange question, but it is a good one. The answers can be surprising. Of course, the expected answer is "yes." Sometimes the answer will be "Lucky at what?" To which the interviewer should say, "Just generally lucky." Sometimes the applicant will contend that luck depends on many factors, which paves the way for discussion. Sometimes he will talk about elements of luck in gambling, explaining the nature of his gambling, time consumed, money lost, and other pertinent facts. On occasion, though only rarely, someone will complain of hard luck and all the things that have gone against him in the world.

7. What was the most monotonous work you ever did?
The purpose of this question is to determine why the particular task was monotonous in order to ascertain whether the applicant would find the job under consideration monotonous also.

8. What are your theories on the best ways to handle people?
Everyone likes to talk about how to handle others. This question provides an opportunity to learn what type of supervision the applicant likes. If he will not find it, employing him might be risky.

9. Do you have any hobbies? (If yes) Tell me about them.
Judgment should be made as to whether or not these interests will tend to inhibit his effectiveness. They may tend to enhance his knowledge of his job and usefulness to the company.

10. For what other jobs are you applying? It's not necessary to give the names of the companies— only the types of jobs.
The response may indicate that the applicant is interested in work which is entirely different from what he would be called upon to do if employed.

Red Flag Factors

A few red flag factors are listed. Other factors should be listed that pertain to a particular job.

1. Appearance. He is obviously unkempt in appearance, shoddy looking, carelessly attired.

2. Earnings. If his most recent earnings exceed by several thousands of dollars annually those which you can offer him, the odds are against him staying very long.

3. Education. At least the minimum education established for the job.

4. Experience. Unless the applicant is specifically outstanding in his other qualifications, a lack of required experience can be a very important deterrent to his success.

5. Salary. Is the starting salary expected far in excess or far below what you are offering?

SUGGESTED INTERVIEW CHECKLIST

The following are items which should be considered and observed during the interview. Some are of a factual nature and can be obtained directly from the application. Some are based entirely on your impressions of the applicant during the interview.

1. Schooling within required range   Yes — No
2. Experience within desired range   Yes — No
3. Past earnings in line with starting salary   Yes — No
4. General appearance. Would you be proud to introduce him to your customers?   Yes — No

5. Personality. Does he seem
friendly, pleasant?   Yes — No
    6. Motivation. Attitude toward work.
Does he believe society owes him
a living? Or is he willing to work
hard for what he wants?   Yes — No
    7. Outlook. Generally optimistic,
or is he a chronic loser?   Yes — No
    8. Attitude toward former job duties.
Does he have a positive attitude
toward the type of duty common
to the job he is applying for?   Yes — No
    9. Overall impression of applicant's
potential.
Rate on a scale of 10.   _____

REJECTION PROCEDURE

If your overall rating is such that the applicant is no longer considered, you may want to end it then and there by tactfully explaining that his background is not exactly what you are looking for. Do not attempt to explain why. To do so only invites what may well develop into a heated discussion. You may find it more practical to tell him that he will be given serious consideration, that you have several other candidates you must interview before making a decision. Assure him you will let him know within a few days. A brief, tactfully phrased letter to the effect that someone has been selected who has a particularly good background in terms of your requirements will let him down easy.

EVALUATION OF INTERVIEW

Character Traits

Basic habit patterns rarely change. We can determine the extent to which the applicant possesses certain basic character traits by noting what these patterns have been. You are not interested in isolated instances—you are interested in the pattern as demonstrated over a long period of time in many areas.

Stability

The extent to which a person has shown the habit of staying with one job, one line of activity for a long period of time.

Industry

The extent to which a person has the habit of working steadily, voluntarily, conscientiously, and productively on whatever job he is given. In other words, will he work conscientiously on the job?

Perseverance

The extent of a person's capacity to persist in an activity despite difficulties and opposition. Has he demonstrated the habit of finishing what he starts whether it be a tough job, his education, or any other endeavor? Or did he quit in the middle of his schooling, or when the going was rough on the job?

Loyalty

The extent of a person's willingness to put the interests of others before his own. The loyal individual is the one who identifies himself closely with the organization and is a member of the team. Does he speak well of others, or does he knock others every chance he gets?

Self Reliance

The extent to which the person has the habit of doing things for himself rather than depending upon others to help him. Has he demonstrated that he can stand on his own two feet, solve his own problems as evidenced by his ability to find his own jobs, support himself and his family, finance his own education, willingness to accept responsibility? Or has he let others carry the burden for him, let others make decisions for him?

Ability to Get Along with Others

The extent to which a person can make and hold friends, maintain good working relations with his supervisors and associates and obtain good personal acceptance by others. Did he get along well with others on past jobs, or is there evidence of difficulty?

Financial Problems

When a person owes more than he can pay out in a year or year and a half from his normal income from the job, he constitutes a risk. This does not refer to legitimate financial obligations which may actually be a spur to greater achievement. The indebtedness referred to is that which necessitates more money than he can find out of income.

FINAL EVALUATION

After considering all aspects of your investigations and interviews, it is helpful to make a final evaluation of each applicant before making a decision. The following factors, supplemented by your own specific qualifications, should be rated on a scale of 4. The total points may help you to select the best of two or more qualified applicants.

1. Appearance 2. Manner 3. Education 4. Experience 5. Mental alertness 6.Ability to get along with other people 7. Industry 8. Stability 9. Motivation 10. Loyalty 11. Perseverance I2. Self-reliance

The Hiring Interview
This interview is an extremely important one. Whereas before you acted in the role of an appraiser, you are now an associate.

This is the time to properly set the stage for the months and years ahead. Your objectives are four-fold:

1. To develop an attitude of respect and confidence.

2. To make him better aware of the conditions and circumstances under which he will operate.

3. To outline more completely the details of the job immediately ahead.

4. To explain briefly the nature of the program to follow—the what, why, who, when, and where of it.

APTITUDE TESTS

Aptitude tests may add a helpful element to the selection procedure. The principal disadvantage is that aptitude test results are too often used as a substitute for sound judgment by the recruiter—judgment based on facts, investigation, and personal interviews. Even intelligence tests can represent little more than the test taker's ability to take a test.

CHAPTER 9

EMPLOYEE
RELATIONSHIPS

EMPLOYEE RELATIONSHIPS
BASIC PROBLEMS

The boss
There are legends about perfect bosses, loved by every employee, but the fact is that few bosses can exercise proper control and make people like it.

Employees need fair and impartial supervision, recognition, and rewards. They need a good boss much more than they need a good buddy. If you aren't genius enough to be both, concentrate on the position you have elevated yourself to — the boss.

The employees
If you have two or more employees, you will have what is often referred to as "office or shop politics." Most of this so-called "politics" is a result of honest differences of opinion, with normal ambition and self-interest complicating the solutions. Your future, and to a lesser degree the future of your employees, depends on how well you handle these differences.

Incentive for employees
There was a time when employee enthusiasm and

loyalty could be successfully fired up with "psychic" compensation and very few hard dollars — security, future opportunity, prestige, lifetime job, etc. — promises, promises, promises — many that were kept. At least enough of the promises were kept to make a good gamble out of it for an employee. When permanent ownership and loyalty to employees disappeared from American business; when owners and controllers of corporations started trading everything for personal benefit, including employee loyalty, the employees wisely decided to get what was coming to them now before it was traded off.

This current attitude has provided small businesses with opportunities never before available. You can hire good employees at the same pay level as big corporations. The call of the corporate sirens is falling on wised-up ears.

You have the best long-term goal to offer — knowledge and experience, that can lead to one's own business. I can hear the disagreement: "Why should I build more competition?" Because if you honestly offer and give this kind of opportunity to employees, the enthusiasm and loyalty you will receive in return will produce effectiveness that no competitor can match. Actually, few employees will take advantage of the opportunities and go into business for themselves, but when one does, rejoice! This is your proof of the pudding. The carrot is really obtainable! The incentive for future employees has been established. Your recruiting job is now much easier. You can make more money in one year with employees with high morale than you can in ten years with drudges.

STARTING COMPENSATION

Hire good people and pay them well! Nothing is more vital to the success of a quick printing shop than this. You can't afford to have an underpaid employee involved in your business in any capacity. You may not always get what you pay for in employees, but for certain you will not get what you don't pay for. How much should you pay? Better than average! But what is average? You can't call your competitor and depend on getting an honest answer. You can, however, telephone quick printers outside of your area of competition and exchange salary information. Don't depend on one call. Check several, and you will have a good idea of the average pay for each of your employees. Revise your information at least on a yearly basis.

RAISES

Most of the people hired by quick printers are already trained to the level required. In order to recruit good people, the starting pay must be above average for their level of experience. Still, raises are almost a must in order to maintain morale. Also, nearly everyone tends to increase his costs of living as his family grows or just as time goes by. The best answer is to explain the problem to the employee. Remind him that the starting pay is above average. Assure him that the pay will remain above average. Tell him how you arrive at an average. Also, assure him that you will review his income on a regular basis and will at least keep it growing at the rate of inflation. Keep base pay raises small and about six months apart.

BONUSES

In order to prevent base pay increases from pricing an employee above what your business can afford, you need to resort to bonuses. The advantage of a bonus is that you can decrease it during bad business cycles. An annual bonus can raise the standard of living of the average employee far more than the same amount added to his regular paycheck. A lump sum that he cannot definitely plan on in advance is often used to purchase something worthwhile instead of being dribbled away weekly.

Another use of bonus money by many employees is to pay off accumulated bills and relieve the pressure these bills have brought about. This helps him on and off the job and can prevent him from looking for another job just for the money. Small, unplanned bonuses can be an effective means of morale building. They should be given in recognition of extra effort that has resulted in extra profit. For maximum effect, these impromptu bonuses should be given at the time of performance.

FRINGE BENEFITS

So-called fringe benefits usually include all benefits of value that are not paid to the employee in the form of money. The cost to you, however, is nearly always money. It is important to convert these benefits to money in the minds of your employees. You are not necessarily doing employees a favor if you enhance their lives and keep it a secret. They enjoy it much more if they know that they are getting something extra.

The most common fringe benefits are holidays and vacation with pay. You can subtly remind employees of the cost of this benefit by showing it on their paycheck stubs. For instance, if you are paying an employee $250 per week and the week has a holiday, list 4 days at $200 and then show "Holiday Pay" $50. The check comes to the same, but you gain employee morale by the reminder. Do the same with vacation pay. Show 0 days worked and "Vacation Pay" $250.

Reminders of cost should be given if you give employees free insurance, sick pay, uniforms, etc.

ENCOURAGEMENT

Many employers refrain from employee praise because they fear that if they tell the employee how good he is, he will want more money. If he is as good as you think he is, he will know or can be convinced that he is being paid enough. You need to be good enough to know what he is worth and to be paying it. Every employee needs to be told how he is doing.

119

MISTAKES

Allow them! More ingenuity and effort is killed by not tolerating mistakes than by any other single cause. When an employee makes an honest mistake

— even a costly one — take the load off of his shoulders. Tell him, "The only way to avoid mistakes is not to do anything." Let him know that you allow mistakes in return for high production. Will this approach cause him to make more mistakes? Absolutely not! He will make less as he will be relaxed. More important, he will enjoy his work. He may even experiment with new ideas or methods that will increase your profit. It's tough to have a slug of money taken out of your pocket and remain tolerant toward the person responsible, but to do otherwise is simply emptying another pocket.

CRITICISM

Don't! Constructive or otherwise! If an employee makes stupid mistakes, if he is lazy, if he is dishonest, if he is dumb, if he is undependable, don't criticize! Fire him if you must. He'll probably understand that you have to fire him, but he will never accept or understand criticism. This does not

mean that you can't point out mistakes. It does not mean that you can't let him know that if the mistakes continue, his job will discontinue. He may accept this, but he will never accept anything that reflects upon his "intent" or upon himself as a person. He will admit he is doing wrong, but he will always rationalize his wrong doing. Every person must preserve his self-respect in order to live with himself. When self-respect is gone, there is no place to go except the booby hatch. Scream and yell if it helps, but watch your words. Don't even "imply" personal criticism. Limit your condemnation to the result, not the cause, if the cause is the action of an individual.

FRATERNIZATION

This is a tough one for many quick printers. There is a close relationship between people working together, and this often expands into a close relationship away from the job. You can get by with it if you are a diplomatic genius, but for the average owner, it creates difficult problems. Five of the most common problems are listed below:

1. Employees are very sensitive to fairness. You are their judge and rewarder. If you fraternize regularly with one employee and not all employees, your fairness on the job will be questioned. If you want to party with employees, it is better practice to invite them all.

2. Most employees gripe about their jobs at home. It is a healthy way of blowing off steam, but they often fail to advise their spouses that things aren't really as bad as they make them sound. In the middle of a friendly outing, you may detect condemnation in the voices and eyes of the spouses. You can't protest because you don't know the causes. It is often better practice to avoid being there.

3. For business reasons, perhaps even for the survival of your business, you may have to cut back on personnel. If times are tough, you need to keep the best employees, and your close friend may not be among the best.

4. When you have the power to give out rewards, your remarks are analyzed and read between the lines. When talking with employees, conversation should be measured. Impromptu utterings can be costly. It is much more pleasant to spend your time away from the business with a friend who could "care less" about analyzing your remarks.

5. The most costly fraternization is between a married male boss and a female employee. More

often than not the price he pays is the loss of the business. If you are so hot-blooded that you are turned on by every goodlooking, shapely female you see, protect yourself by hiring the ugliest woman you can find. You won't be tempted on the job, and she won't be distracted from her work by your amorous advances, which will probably make you enough extra profit so you can afford to "turn on" away from the business.

PRIVILEGES AND ABUSES

Special privileges and abuses are more difficult to handle in a quick printing shop than in a large departmentalized business. A department head only enforces rules. You make and enforce the rules. You can't pass the buck as employees know you can say "yes" if you want to. Excessive telephone use, late arrival, absenteeism, improper dress or grooming, and excessive visiting with fellow employees are some of the problem areas. Unless you control the situation early in the game, the problem will continue to grow until it reaches a point where the cost is a good employee.

The best solution is to put the rules in writing and post them in a prominent place. Keep it simple and with as few rules as possible. For example, a notice posted by the telephone might read, "Emergency calls only. Please ask for permission before making any personal calls." If the abuses continue, harden

the message, such as, "No personal calls." Keep in mind that you are striving for control, not popularity. I have found a simple explanation that cools many situations where employees are getting hot about my rule enforcement. I explain, "I owe you and the others here the obligation to conduct this business in a manner that will allow all of us to continue to make a living from it. If I turn soft, that's when you should really get angry."

UNDERMINING

What is undermining? Usually it takes the form of the deliberate withholding of information or equipment needed by a fellow employee to do his job properly. More obvious and, therefore, less frequently used is the actual placing of obstacles in another's path.

Who does it?
In large business, the greatest underminers are junior and middle management people. Many mediocre people reach this level in large corporations and feel threatened by ambitious underlings. You will, however, find it at the lowest employee level. They will fight for what is available.

They know, for instance, that if business slacks, someone is going to be layed off and if there are only two people in their department — — — —! Mediocre people can hang on for years by undermining every competitor who moves in their direction.

How to cope with it
Your problem is the need to determine the best employee and, at the same time, minimize damage due to undermining. In the absence of other ability measuring devices, the employee who does the least amount of undermining is usually the best.

If you determine that one of your best employees is being undermined, do not ignore it. Few people short of battle-scarred top executives can survive a continuous undermining attack. Firing the underminer is rarely the answer. He may be hard to replace. You can help the problem by reassuring the victim, in private, of his worth to you and by assigning tasks to the underminer that will make it difficult for him to be effective in his undermining efforts. Do not criticize the underminer, threaten him, or lie to him about his future prospects. None of these methods will work. It would be better for you and him to fire him rather than try to reform him.

Who's perfect?
It's easy to concentrate on an employee's shortcomings to a point where his overall worth is misjudged. There are no perfect employees. In fact, there are few, if any, who won't at times drive you "straight up the wall." You're the one who needs to be perfect in order to hire and manage these

puzzling individuals called employees. Since you aren't perfect either (unless you are God), you need to constantly remind yourself to look back at the overall performance and not base your judgment on some current stupidity.

CHAPTER 10

PRICING
PSYCHOLOGY

The psychology of pricing is so important to the success of any quick print shop that I am devoting a special chapter to the subject.

YOU CAN'T "BUY" INSTANT SUCCESS

Most new shop operators believe that business is going to be a lot easier to come by than it proves out to be. They don't take into consideration that people do not change habits easily, and customers who have been getting good or even poor service from one printer aren't likely to try new printers who come along every few months.

Most new owners start out with the bright belief that they will provide quality printing, on time, with friendly service, and at a low price. Potential customers have seen too many bright beliefs quickly tarnished. They will stay away in droves until you prove yourself — the long hard way!

VULTURES PREY UPON THE NEW GUY

Most customers are too involved with their own business to memorize printing prices, so they are not influenced by ads or signs listing prices below normal. There is, however, a class of customer who follows new businesses, knowing that he can talk the new owner into a good deal. He is usually a customer who buys a considerable volume of printing of the type turned out by quick printers. He has found that he can save a great deal of money by taking advantage of the new printer's ignorance. Combine the ignorance with the normal anxiousness of a new business operator, and he has a pigeon. This type of customer is not easy to spot,

and any new operator is rightfully careful not to run off a customer he needs so badly. The real harm done by this type of customer is that the new operator is often convinced that his prices are too high, so he lowers them, and by lowering them, he insures his failure. Your pricing must be based upon a sounder structure than customers' comments.

GET WORTHWHILE BUSINESS

If you believe nothing else you hear from those who have been there, you should believe that very little printing business is placed because of price. This is difficult to believe in the face of the fact that most customers ask about prices, shop prices, and complain about prices. Most customers who ask about prices are simply trying to assure themselves that they are getting a good deal. It is not unusual to see several failing print shops spaced among successful shops with the failures flouting signs listing prices at half the level charged by the successes.

LOW IS ALWAYS LOWER THAN YOU WILL GO

The customers who truly shop prices are either people with time on their hands and too small to waste your time on, or they are customers who have a large volume of low quality business that anyone can handle. Neither type is worth having. You can bet your last dollar that no matter how low you quote, someone is going to quote lower if a large order is shopped around.

KNOW YOUR COSTS

The secret is to know how to figure what a fair price is on every item you sell. You need to know the bottom price below which you will not go. Only then can you stand your ground against price pressures, because only by knowing what your price should be can you state with conviction that you are "competitive."

SHOPPING TIME IS MONEY LOST

The average customer doesn't have the time to shop for business purchases that cost less than four or five hundred dollars. Even if he could save ten or twenty percent, it would be less than he could make by using the time in his own business. If a customer has the time to shop, you don't want him as he's not going to make it in this competitive business world, and sooner or later he will stick you with an unpaid bill when he goes broke.

THE HOBBY SHOPPER

The type of customer who does have time to shop is the housewife or someone playing at business with a lot of time on his hands. This latter type may know the price of every printer in a ten mile area. One remarked to me one time that he knew where every cheapo in town was located. He showed me a list of printers and the items each was low in. He didn't show me the notation he had by my name, but he started me to thinking. After he left, I looked up his invoices for the past several months. Sure enough, I had overlooked charging for a service that all of my competitors were charging for. I was losing money on every order he was placing.

It is often a good warning sign if you are getting business from some customer who seems to know about most of your competitors. Something must be wrong with your pricing of the items he is buying, or you wouldn't be getting his business.

PROFIT IS "YOUR" ONLY PAYCHECK

You must have a good profit to survive and prosper.

If you devote your time and energy to rounding up normal customers and treating them right, you will be making more headway toward the prosperity you are seeking than you will be by catering to the shopper.

You must learn to ignore price cutting competitors. This is a lot easier said than done. It often seems that your competitor is doing a lot better than he really is. Salesmen spread the propaganda he has fed to them in order to better his credit standing. When you see one of your good customers coming out of his shop with a load of printing, it is almost more than you can bear. If you give in and fight on his terms, you will be working for peanuts on your way to bankruptcy.

It seems that some price cutters hang in there an awfully long time, and that is true. There are many reasons for this. He may have come into the business with heavy savings, and it takes time to lose it all. Or he may be working long hours for practically nothing, and by so doing, he can hang on for years. There is, however, no magic formula that will allow a person to sell below a reasonable price and make a reasonable profit. If you are alert and progressive, it is doubtful that a competitor can increase his efficiency to a much greater degree than you.

WORK SMARTER — NOT HARDER

Don't use your time and energy turning out printing for no profit. If you are not busy printing, use the time to plan and secure profitable business.

CHAPTER 11

ARRIVING
AT
SELLING PRICES

THE PRICING PROBLEM

Pricing often means the difference between success and failure in quick printing. However, it is one of the most difficult tasks of shop management. The sheer volume of paperwork and calculating required causes pricing to be put aside in favor of more obvious emergencies.

Even when a shop owner sets aside several hours a week for pricing, he usually is in the dark regarding his costs and competitive practices. So he guesses a lot. Guessing weakens his resolve to stand firm against frequent pressures from valued customers.

There is no easy answer to the problem of pricing. Printing is a complicated manufacturing business. Most retailers simply apply a percentage to their cost of an item. Unprinted paper, for instance, is a breeze to price. But using the paper in a print job involves a great variety of uncertain costs. Commercial printers have long recognized the difficulty of estimating. One of their highest paid employees is the estimator. As quick printing progresses into a greater variety of jobs, shop owners are devoting more and more time to solving the problem of pricing.

METHODS OF PRICING

Copying someone else's price list

Unfortunately, this is the most frequently used method. It has two great shortcomings.

1. The price list you "borrow" from a competitor includes only the few items he has chosen to publish. You are still in the dark regarding the bulk of the items you need pricing for.

2. The list you copy may be secondhand, or even fifth or sixth hand. Alterations and obsolescence may have rendered it more disastrous than guessing.

Building your own price catalog

I recently examined over 100 counter price catalogs obtained from every section of the U.S. These were complete price catalogs used by many of the most successful quick printers in the U.S. In return, we sent them our counter price book. Some of the catalogs we received were masterpieces. However, upon investigation, most were subject to at least one of the following problem areas:

1. Hundreds of hours of shop management time went into the initial preparation of the most elaborate of the price catalogs.These were expensive hours—the boss' time.

2. Few, if any, of the catalogs were properly updated to reflect constantly changing costs. The time was simply not available for this repetitive task.

3. Most admitted that competitive prices were difficult, if not impossible, to come by, especially on nonpublished items.

Computer Pricing

Computer pricing programs for quick printers are finally available. The computer will perform all calculations and apply formulas at the speed of light. Formulas can be designed to develop prices that guarantee a profit on every item. However, the formulas do not always match actual competitive situations. The computer prices must still be compared and weighed against actual prices in the marketplace.

Actual prices currently being charged are essential to a credible pricing program. We found we needed a constant feedback of prices being charged by quick printers. By averaging prices on every item after tossing out the abnormal highs and lows, then checking the results against pricing formulas, we came up with prices we felt were credible.

The problem was how to obtain a sufficient and constant supply of pricing information. Our initial price book swap offer produced the information we needed, but at a cost of over eight hundred man-hours. Our solution was to lease our computer software to other quick printers. In order to continue to receive new revised discs for their computers, subscribers return old discs with actual prices, production times, hourly costs, etc. intact. Our computer analyzes the returned discs and incorporates the changed information into the next revision. This keeps us and our subscribers up-to-date with the computer doing most of the work.

Predesigned Counter Price Book
This is proving to be the answer for many quick printers. Our counter price book is a printout from our computer program. Prices are averaged separately for four geographical regions—East, Central, South, and West. This gives us a regional and national average for every price bracket on every item and service. These averages, along with computerized formulas, form the basis for our counter price book.

Feedback from our computer program and price book subscribers keep the prices current. Subscribers are supplied with the average price actually being charged on every item. This serves as a guide in arriving at their own selling prices.

PRICE FORMULAS

Any price you charge should be spot-checked against your cost. You can't be competitive on every item and make money. Your close competitors may have equipment or techniques that beat your costs. By knowing your costs and applying a formula to each price, you can determine if the item is profitable.

COSTS YOU MUST KNOW BEFORE YOU CAN CONSTRUCT A PRICE LIST

1. Your "fixed" costs

2. Cost of paper used
3. Cost of plates, etc.
4. Cost of typesetting, pasteup, etc.
5. Cost of cutting, folding, binding, etc.
6. Competitors' prices
7. Reasonable profit
8. Efficiency of shop

FIXED COSTS

These are general costs of *being in business.* Each job or item you sell should bear a proportionate share of these costs. Do not include costs that are charged directly to a specific item or job as these costs should be included in the material or labor costs for each job.

RENT *or lease on building or office.*
YOUR DRAW OR SALARY
   The amount you would actually have to pay someone else for doing your job.
REGULAR EMPLOYEE PAYROLL
   Do not include overtime or employees brought in to work on a specific item or job—these extra employee payroll expenses are charged to each specific job.
EMPLOYEE FRINGE BENEFITS
PAYROLL TAXES
GENERAL TAXES
EQUIPMENT RENT OR LEASE
ADVERTISING
OUTSIDE SELLING EXPENSE
DEPRECIATION*of equipment, fixtures, furniture, etc.*

SHORT LIFE TOOLS *and equipment not included in depreciation schedule.*

INSURANCE

VEHICLES — *Lease or depreciation and operating.*

DELIVERY & DISTRIBUTION

OTHER TRANSPORTATION

MAINTENANCE - *Cleaning, trash hauling, painting, etc.*

REPAIRS

SUPPLIES - *All misc. supplies not charged directly to specific job.*

INTEREST ON LOANS

OUTSIDE BOOKKEEPING SERVICE

OUTSIDE MANAGEMENT SERVICE

LEGAL

DUES TO BUSINESS ORGANIZATIONS

BAD CHECKS & DEBTS

UNIFORMS

PETTY CASH ITEMS

BANK SERVICE CHARGES

UTILITIES

TELEPHONE

Plus any other general expense that is not charged to a specific item.

PAPER COSTS

Paper costs will average 20% to 25% of the total cost of the average print job. This is a much lower percentage than experienced by commercial printers. Of course, if you are printing high priced paper such as catalog envelopes, your percentage of paper cost will run much higher.

Paper costs have little variance throughout the U.S. Your main concern should be to guard against being gouged on brackets. Most quick printers buy near the lowest cost end of pricing brackets for cut stock.

PLATE COST

Plate cost can be a significant item in pricing short run printing. However, all too often, the effect cheap plates have on production cost is not considered. An electrostatic paper plate used on an automated press can produce acceptable quality for some short run printing. The cost is much lower than work produced on an A. B. Dick or similar press. However, an electrostatic plate used on an A. B. Dick may result in a much higher cost than a silver-coated plate due to lost production time and lower quality on certain types of jobs.

Platemaking time for electrostatic plates is less (about 20 seconds) compared to slightly over a minute for most silver-coated plates. However, runup and remake time is much greater with electrostatic plates on jobs requiring exact positioning on the page. The thinness of the electrostatic plate often results in wrinkling if much straightening is attempted. Many types of halftone and fine line jobs cannot be produced at a high quality level with electrostatic plates. The difference in platemaking time is negated if a pressman makes his own plates. My observation has been that a pressman will stand and wait the twenty seconds or so for an electrostatic plate. If the wait is a minute or more, as on silver-coated plates, he will use the time to perform other tasks such as cleaning the blanket, loading paper, etc.

Metal plates and negatives, of course, represent additional costs that must be added to each job.

TYPESETTING COST

Typesetting and pasteup are the most subsidized services in quick printing. Very few typesetting departments operate at a profit. The volume of typesetting is rarely sufficient to support a full-time typesetter. Part-time help adds to the unit cost. Also quick printing customers, for the most part, are not sophisticated enough in graphic arts to accept the high cost of good graphic design. Many jobs are so insignificant they won't even pay for the counter discussion time, let alone the typesetting time.

However, even though typesetting is not a profit center, most quick printers are finding it an indispensible department. It is often difficult to pin down exact costs for typesetting due to the fact that the boss and others contribute labor to the department on a part-time basis. Selling prices for typesetting and pasteup are, therefore, based more on competitive practices than on costs.

BINDING COSTS

Time studies are used by many quick printers to determine binding costs. Quick printers do not usually have large investments in binding equipment. Labor is the principal cost. Many use three times labor cost in pricing work done by the binding department.

ARRIVING AT SELLING PRICES

COMPETITORS' PRICES

Quick printers tend to put too much importance on competitors'prices. The price of 100 and 1000 copies of low cost printing is sometimes shopped. 1000 envelopes or NCR two or three part are sometimes compared by shoppers. You should be in line on these and other popular items. The rest need only to be in the "ballpark."

In studying thousands of prices published by highly experienced and successful quick printers, I frequently come across isolated prices at a ridiculous level—high and low. Some are obviously typographical errors. Some are probably wild guesses. If you tried to meet these prices, you would be in trouble. These mistakes were made by the best in the business—consider what you'll find at the other end!

You should study your close competitors' prices, but your costs should be strongly considered before changing your prices.

REASONABLE PROFIT

First, your income should be divided into two categories, salary and profit. Your salary should be based on the amount you would have to pay for comparable help.

Profit is income over and above your salary. It is important that you think of the two as separate sources of income. Your business may not be making a profit because you may be paying yourself too much, or the reverse may be the case.

How Much Profit Should You Figure

A very well run business can expect a return of about 20% on investment. Include "leverage" in figuring your total investment. (The amount you owe plus the amount you have put up.) If you feel you are running your business well, use the 20% figure. If you believe some of the advertisements you will see, you will want to figure 500%. If you go much over the 20% figure, you will be pricing yourself out of business as your investment is a good measure of the type of goods and service you will be able to deliver to your customers. Example: $100,000 total investment, including amount you owe. At 20% your profit would be $20,000. If your salary was $30,000, your total income would be $50,000. With inflation running rampant, the worth of your business should be revalued every year.

EFFICIENCY OF SHOP

% of Efficiency

In order for a business to be 100% efficient, every employee and every machine would need to be producing every minute. A 60% efficiency figure is high— yours may be more, or less. Use *your* percent of efficiency to arrive at fixed cost per hour.

PRICING WORK SHEET

The form reproduced here can serve as a guide in checking your cost and selling price. The formula has been kept as simple as possible to minimize hand calculating time. (Formulas used in our computer programs are more complicated because computing time is insignificant when done on a computer.)

(ORIGINAL SIZE 8½ x 11)

To be printed on press No. _____

PRICING WORK SHEET

ITEM _____

ENTER THESE FIGURES
AT TOP OF COLUMNS NO.

PAPER COST: $_____ per m + 10% waste = $_____ per M ÷ 1000 $_____ Col. 6
BILLED PRICE _TOTAL COST_ _COST PER SHEET_

PRODUCTION RATE: _____ ÷ 60 .... _____ Col. 2
NET COPIES PER HR. _COPIES PER MINUTE_

FIXED PRODUCTION COST FOR THIS PRESS: (See formula below) .... $_____ Col. 3
COST PER MINUTE

DESIRED PROFIT FROM THIS PRESS (See formula below) .... $_____ Col. 8
DESIRED PROFIT PER MINUTE

PRICING FORMULAS

Formula for arriving at fixed cost per minute:

HOURS PER MONTH · · · · · · · · · · · · %· · · · · · · · · · · · · · · · · · HOURS

TOTAL SHOP HOURS PER MONTH **X** % SHOP EFFICIENCY = PRODUCTIVE HOURS PER MONTH

$_____ ÷ $_____ **X** $_____ % = -FIXED COST ÷ 60 = $_____
TOTAL FIXED COST FOR ENTIRE SHOP   PRODUCTIVE HRS. = PER HOUR % OF TOTAL PROFIT   PER HOUR   FIXED COST
GENERATED BY   PER MINUTE
THIS PRESS

Formula for arriving at desired profit per minute:

$_____ PER MO. ÷ _____ = $_____ **X** $_____ % = $_____ ÷ 60 = $_____
TOTAL DESIRED SHOP   PRODUCTIVE HRS. = PROFIT PER HR. % OF TOTAL SHOP DESIRED PROFIT   PROFIT
PROFIT PER MONTH   PER MONTH   PROFIT EARNED BY   PER HOUR   PER MINUTE
(Profit only! Include your salary   THIS PRESS   THIS PRESS
in Fixed Costs above)

1	2	3	4	5	6	7	8	9	10	11
QUANTITY	TIME IN MINUTES @ _____ Copies per MINUTE + _____ MIN. Runup Time	FIXED Production Cost @ $_____ Per Minute	PLATE Cost TIME MIN	Mat'l & MISC	PAPER Cost @ $_____ Per SHEET	DESIRED PROFIT _____ % OF PAPER COST	@ _____ $ PER MINUTE	DESIRED SELLING PRICE One Side Two Sides	COMPETITORS SELLING PRICE One Side Two Sides	BEST JUDGEMENT SELLING PRICE One Side Two Sides
	MINUTES	DOLLARS	DOLLARS	DOLLARS	DOLLARS	DOLLARS	DOLLARS	DOLLARS	DOLLARS	DOLLARS

TIME IN MINUTES =
QUANTITY (col 1) DIVIDED BY
COPIES PER MINUTE =
Then add RUNUP MINUTES to total.

FIXED PRODUCTION COST =
COST PER MINUTE x TIME IN MINUTES =

TIME COST OF PLATE = TIME IN MINUTES
multiplied by FIXED PROD. COST PER MIN.(top col.3)
(Assuming pressman makes plates at your costs)

PLATE COST REMAINS CONSTANT FOR ALL
QUANTITIES.(Except long runs requiring more plates)

PAPER COST =
COST PER SHEET x QUANTITY (col.1)

DESIRED % OF PAPER PROFIT =
% (top of col.7) x PAPER COST (col.6)

DESIRED PROFIT (TIME) =
COST PER MIN (top of col.8) x
TIME IN MINUTES (col.2)

DESIRED SELLING PRICE 1 SIDE =
TOTALS FROM COLs.
3,4,5,6,7,8.

DESIRED SELLING 2 SIDES =
DOUBLE ONE SIDE PRICE
DEDUCT ALL OF PAPER PROFIT (Col.7)
DEDUCT 90% OF PAPER COST (Col.6)

© Wm. Friday
Prudential Publishing Co.
311 California St., Suite 750
San Francisco, CA 94104

142

CHAPTER 12

COUNTER
PRICE BOOK

HORSE TRADING OR PRICE BOOK?

By tradition, we are a nation of "horsetraders." We like the matching of wits over value and price — the head to head competition with an occasional big victory. Horsetrading is exciting and fun.

A counter price book takes away some of the fun, but it adds enough dollars for you to buy a lot more fun than you will lose.

This is not a problem peculiar to small business — it afflicts the very largest corporations in this country. On several occasions, I have had the opportunity to take away the horse trading from major corporations and replace it with a rigid set of published prices. In doing so, I often had to buck not only the sales force, but the top executives.

Many top executives are not satisfied with horse trading entire companies as made popular by the conglomerate movement. They want to make deals with special friends and associates — deals that damage the credibility of pricing at all levels.

My experience has convinced me that when horse trading is eliminated, profits soar and management and legal problems become less complex.

WHY CUSTOMERS WON'T HORSE TRADE

Your customers are also horse traders at heart, but most of them don't have the time to "horse trade" over the many transactions they are required to make. So what do they do? They avoid other horse traders until they have time to play in the game.

You have a choice of the type of customer you want to attract — the "horse trader" who wants to "play" on every order, or the busy buyer. You can't have both! It is not practical to shift hats after you size up your prospect.

Busy Buyers

Most of your quick printing customers are "busy buyers!" They want to have confidence in your prices. They know they aren't getting the lowest price without "horse trading,"but they will settle for a "fair" price. They will not knowingly allow themselves to be gouged.

A well constructed counter price book helps to assure them that they are not being taken. They reason, and rightfully so, that if you are quoting prices from a book — the same prices to every customer — then the prices must be fair or you wouldn't be getting the business. In other words, when prices are printed and openly quoted, a customer assumes that other customers are policing your prices.

TYPES OF PRICE BOOKS

There are several types of counter price books used by quick printers. Some of the most popular are listed below:

1. **A single page**, printed two sides, listing principal items. Most quick printers have outgrown this simplified pricing. The multitude of "principal" items and services offered can no longer be priced on a single sheet.

2. **Formula pricing**. This is where prices are worked out for a few items and tied in by adding, subtracting, dividing, or multiplying. Flexibility is lost in this type of pricing. Some quantities and items are more competitive than others. For example, 100 and 1000 copies of 8½ x 11 twenty pound bond may be priced low to meet competition. There is no reason, however, to give away profit on 200 copies or 2000 copies.

3. **Detailed Complete Price Books**. Most complete counter price books I have seen are computer generated. Hand calculating is too time consuming to be practical. The problem most computer owners have is finding software to run their computer.

Software can cost, in time or money, much more than the total cost of hardware. Then there is the problem of being up-to-date on competitors' practices, press time, etc. on one or two hundred items. Computers will calculate selling prices based on formulas, but the end result needs to be weighed against several other factors such as what competition is doing.

Full blown estimating of complicated jobs is not a counter function. There is some doubt if complicated jobs are even a quick printing function. The traditional, so-called commercial printer estimates all jobs — he maintains no counter price books for fast quoting. If you take complicated jobs, you will probably job them out, and your estimating is done for you before you quote. If you are interested in full blown estimating, courses are regularly conducted by P.I.A. and other big printer organizations.

MAJOR "DO'S"

1. Typeset or type all prices. Changes are easier if the pricing columns are designed for your standard size typing or typesetting without reductions or enlargements. When you run your first copies, save a bunch of extras to use as originals for future changes. If you keep revising your one and only original, it will get shopworn and require frequent major artwork repair.

2. Show an exact dollars and cents price for each category. This allows you to be competitive in a single quantity without affecting other quantities. For instance, you may need to price 100 copies or 1000 copies below your normal markup for

competitive reasons, but you should price the 200 and higher categories or the 2000 and higher categories at normal markups as these quantities are rarely as competitive.

3. Minimums should be listed with each service item.

MAJOR "DON'TS"

1. Do not "pencil" in price changes. When a price is marked through and changed, it loses the credibility and authority of an original printed or typed price.

2. Do not list a price "per 100" or "per M" except perhaps for quantities above 10,000. A "per unit" price will lock you into an inflexible price formula.

EXAMPLES OF PRICE LISTS

The examples shown on the following pages were developed and printed by our computer. At the time of publication, they were the national average prices.

(ORIGINAL SIZE 8½ x 11)

**PRICES ARE NOT CURRENT
IF YOU ARE INTERESTED IN A CURRENT
PRICE BOOK OR COMPUTER PRICING
PROGRAM WRITE TO: Prudential Publishing.**

PRE-COLLATED CARBONLESS

8½ x 11 CARBONLESS SETS 2-PART

QUANTITY	ONE SIDE	TWO SIDES
SETS		
100	22.17	42.07
200	29.30	54.06
300	36.43	66.06
400	43.56	78.05
500	50.69	90.05
600	57.82	102.04
700	64.95	114.04
800	72.09	126.03
900	79.22	138.03
1000	86.35	150.02
2000	157.66	269.97
3000	228.97	389.91
4000	300.28	509.86
5000	371.59	629.81
6000	442.90	749.75
7000	514.22	869.70
8000	585.53	989.64
9000	656.84	1109.59
10000	728.15	1229.54
Add M's	70.63	118.04
A12811676		

8½ x 11 CARBONLESS SETS 3-PART

QUANTITY	ONE SIDE	TWO SIDES
SETS		
100	34.31	64.44
200	37.75	67.75
300	49.10	86.59
400	60.46	105.43
500	71.82	124.27
600	83.17	143.11
700	94.53	161.95
800	105.88	180.79
900	117.24	199.63
1000	128.59	218.46
2000	242.15	406.86
3000	355.71	595.25
4000	469.27	783.64
5000	582.82	972.03
6000	696.38	1160.42
7000	809.94	1348.81
8000	923.49	1537.20
9000	1037.05	1725.60
10000	1150.61	1913.99
Add M's	111.61	183.74
A12812862		

8½ x 11 CARBONLESS SETS 4-PART

QUANTITY	ONE SIDE	TWO SIDES
SETS		
100	40.12	74.34
200	45.29	79.75
300	60.41	104.59
400	75.54	129.43
500	90.67	154.27
600	105.79	179.11
700	120.92	203.95
800	136.04	228.79
900	151.17	253.63
1000	166.30	278.47
2000	317.56	526.87
3000	468.82	775.27
4000	620.08	1023.67
5000	771.34	1272.07
6000	922.60	1520.47
7000	1073.86	1768.87
8000	1225.12	2017.27
9000	1376.38	2265.67
10000	1527.63	2514.07
Add M's	148.18	241.35
A12814000		

8½ x 11 CARBONLESS SETS 5-PART

QUANTITY	ONE SIDE	TWO SIDES
SETS		
100	47.22	86.70
200	53.39	92.76
300	72.57	124.10
400	91.75	155.44
500	110.93	186.78
600	130.11	218.12
700	149.28	249.46
800	168.46	280.80
900	187.64	312.14
1000	206.82	343.48
2000	398.60	656.89
3000	590.38	970.30
4000	782.16	1283.71
5000	973.94	1597.12
6000	1165.72	1910.53
7000	1357.51	2223.94
8000	1549.29	2537.35
9000	1741.07	2850.76
10000	1932.85	3164.17
Add M's	187.49	303.76
A12815185		

(ORIGINAL SIZE 8½ x 11)

**PRICES ARE NOT CURRENT
IF YOU ARE INTERESTED IN A CURRENT
PRICE BOOK OR COMPUTER PRICING
PROGRAM WRITE TO: Prudential Publishing.**

CARD BACKED **CARBONLESS**

8½ x 11
CARD BACKED SETS 2 PART

QUANTITY	ONE SIDE	TWO SIDES
SETS		
100	29.94	54.78
200	41.83	73.46
300	53.72	92.15
400	65.62	110.84
500	77.51	129.53
600	89.40	148.22
700	101.30	166.90
800	113.19	185.59
900	125.08	204.28
1000	136.97	222.97
2000	255.90	409.85
3000	374.83	596.73
4000	493.76	783.61
5000	612.69	970.49
6000	731.62	1157.37
7000	850.55	1344.25
8000	969.48	1531.13
9000	1088.41	1718.01
10000	1207.34	1904.89
Add M's	117.11	182.87

A12813560

8½ x 11
CARD BACKED SETS 3 PART

QUANTITY	ONE SIDE	TWO SIDES
SETS		
100	45.51	83.61
200	51.97	90.36
300	68.93	117.50
400	85.89	144.63
500	102.86	171.77
600	119.82	198.91
700	136.78	226.04
800	153.74	253.18
900	170.71	280.31
1000	187.67	307.45
2000	357.29	578.81
3000	526.92	850.18
4000	696.54	1121.54
5000	866.17	1392.90
6000	1035.79	1664.27
7000	1205.42	1935.63
8000	1375.04	2206.99
9000	1544.67	2478.35
10000	1714.29	2749.72
Add M's	166.29	263.97

A12814842

8½ x 11
CARD BACKED SETS 4 PART

QUANTITY	ONE SIDE	TWO SIDES
SETS		
100	52.58	95.89
200	61.02	105.21
300	82.50	139.78
400	103.99	174.34
500	125.48	208.90
600	146.97	243.46
700	168.45	278.03
800	189.94	312.59
900	211.43	347.15
1000	232.91	381.71
2000	447.78	727.34
3000	662.65	1072.97
4000	877.52	1418.59
5000	1092.38	1764.22
6000	1307.25	2109.84
7000	1522.12	2455.47
8000	1736.99	2801.10
9000	1951.86	3146.72
10000	2166.73	3492.35
Add M's	210.17	335.27

© Wm. Friday 1982

A12816124

8½ x 11
CARD BACKED SETS 5 PART

QUANTITY	ONE SIDE	TWO SIDES
SETS		
100	61.26	111.25
200	70.74	121.29
300	97.09	163.88
400	123.44	206.48
500	149.79	249.08
600	176.14	291.68
700	202.49	334.28
800	228.84	376.88
900	255.19	419.47
1000	281.54	462.07
2000	545.03	888.06
3000	808.53	1314.04
4000	1072.02	1740.03
5000	1335.51	2166.01
6000	1599.01	2591.99
7000	1862.50	3017.98
8000	2126.00	3443.96
9000	2389.49	3869.95
10000	2652.98	4295.93
Add M's	257.34	412.41

A12817406

PRICING TYPESETTING AND PASTEUP

The cost of typesetting and pasteup often represents more than half the cost of quick printing type jobs. Typesetting costs can rarely be "buried" in the total cost of a job. Therefore, it is usually necessary to quote typesetting costs before getting an order.

All agree that the most difficult quick printing services to price are typesetting and pasteup. There are not and never will be any fast, easy formulas for accurately pricing the great variety of typesetting jobs that cross the counter of an average quick printer.

TIME METHOD

My surveys of quick printers have indicated that less than 1% charge customers according to the total time spent on a typesetting or pasteup job. Some trade typesetters can get away with an hourly charge. However, so much depends on talent and equipment that the cost of a single job can vary by 500% or more among typesetters. Few customers are willing to gamble on a time arrangement.

We were once charged $80 for a job that should have been in the $20 range. The typesetter indignantly responded to our complaint that an equipment problem had extended the time. We were reminded that we had agreed to a charge based on an hourly rate. We paid the bill, thankful that the equipment wasn't down for three or four days. Naturally, we found another typesetter.

EXAMPLE METHOD

We use an "example" method of pricing (see examples at end of this chapter). Of course, no matter how many examples we have to compare with, there is always a difference between example and actual job presented for pricing. The examples serve only as a guide.

It was not practical for us to develop this method of pricing until we introduced our national pricing service for quick printers. The time and cost of gathering, updating, and printing price pages were not warranted for use by only a few shops. By spreading the cost among thousands of shops, we are able to enjoy the benefits of accurate, researched, and computerized prices not only for typesetting, but for binding and hundreds of printed items.

The prices shown here, of course, cannot be current. Our service checks and updates prices regularly and mails out new pages. Typesetting pricing pages are issued at four price levels based on difficulty. In addition, each price page is issued in three percentage levels. Pages are numbered 000A, 000B, 000C, and 000D to indicate difficulty levels. Three copies of each page are issued coded A for national average price charged by quick printers, L for 10% below average, and H for 10% above average. This provides a selection of twelve levels for each item or service, taking into consideration difficulty and desired profit.

We also sell computer programs. Our computer software is issued with only one set of prices, the national or regional average. These programs, however, provide for unlimited revisions at the touch of a computer keyboard.

KEYSTROKE METHOD

We also use a character-count method for galley type or straight pages of typesetting. This method requires that copy be presented in typewritten form. It is based on 70 keystrokes per line and a production speed of 7000 keystrokes per hour.

1. Count all typewritten lines. (Count headings as one line.)

2. If copy is to be justified on a stand-alone composer, double the total lines. If automatic justification is used, do not double, but your hourly base cost is increased because of the additional investment, maintenance, and operating difficulty of the equipment.

3. Add difficult copy charges. Do not apply percentages to the doubled for justification total. Use original line count as a base for difficult copy percentage additions.

4. Total all of the above. Estimate each line as 70 keystrokes per line to arrive at total "calculated keystrokes."

5. Figure total hours by dividing "calculated keystrokes" by an estimated production speed of 7000 keystrokes per hour.

6. Multiply number of hours by hourly rate.

DIFFICULTY FACTORS

If all difficulty factors were liberally interpreted, you would turn down or lose 98% of all jobs. The following list and percentages should be used only as a rough estimate. Your application of these charges must be tempered with judgment based on actual experience.

Tabular material: Add 400% to line count if entire job is tabular. Do not charge for justification. If only part of job is tabular, count each tab in each line as an extra line, or as 70 keystrokes.

Handwritten copy: The best method is to have the copy typed and proofed before typesetting. Typesetting directly from handwritten copy should be upcharged 50% to 200%, depending on quality of handwriting.

Technical words, less than "clean" copy, special positioning of words, hard to decipher instructions, etc. — add approximately 30% for each problem.

Font changes: Add ½ line (35 keystrokes) for each change.

Centered or flush right column headings (not including headlines): Add 1 line (70 keystrokes) for each.

Headlines (normally 14 points or larger): Add 1 line (70 keystrokes) for each letter.

Runarounds: Count each line as 3 lines.

Footnotes: Count each line of footnotes as 3 lines.

Narrow column (less than 15 picas): Add 30%.

Wide column (more than 24 picas): Add 30%.

Other factors to consider and estimate are: Math figures, captions, underlining, symbols, accent marks, irregular patterns of columns, close copy fitting, borders, boxes, special lines, etc., etc.

COUNTER PRICE BOOK

The prices shown here have been taken from the Bill Friday Counter Price Book and are not current. Subscribers to the Counter Price Book receive revisions three or four times a year. Revisions are based on computerized national averages. Published by Prudential Publishing Co.

"A" lists the low national average.
"B" lists jobs 133% more difficult.
"C" lists jobs 180% more difficult.
"D" is high level national average.

THE ORIGINAL SIZE OF THIS PRICE BOOK PAGE IS 8½ x 11

88A   TYPESETTING AND PASTEUP   88A

EXAMPLES OF TYPESETTING

SEE DIFFICULTY PAGE FOR CHARGES FOR copy changes, handwritten copy, font changes, special positioning of words, runarounds, boxes, borders, underlining, accent marks, narrow columns, footnotes, math figures, symbols, close copy fitting, and special lines.

Prices are based on typewritten or hand printed copy and do not include "artwork". Also see difficulty factors for possible additional charges.
PRICES ARE FOR ONE SIDE ONLY

TYPESETTING MINIMUM	6.00
TYPESET & PASTEUP	7.50
PASTEUP ONLY	4.00
REPRO'S FOR PASTEUP:	
PAPER PLATE & Print	5.25
STAT size to 3 x 5	4.95
STAT size to 8 x 10	7.45
STAT size to 11 x 16	10.50
HALFTONE size to 3 x 5	7.95
HALFTONE size to 8 x 10	9.95
REDUCE/ENLARGE - Add'l.	3.00
CLIP ART-Ea.-Plus repro.	2.00
LETTERHEAD ONLY (Std.)	9.50
ENVELOPE ONLY (Std.)	7.50
L.H. & ENVELOPE (Std.)	14.50
LETTERHEAD only (Special)	21.00
ENVELOPE only (Special)	18.00
L.H. & Envelope (Special)	35.00
STOCK FORMS	9.50
CUSTOM FORMS (Standard):	
Size to 8½ x 7	18.00
Size to 8½ x 11	26.00
Size to 8½ x 14	34.00
CONTRACTS - 8½ x 11	31.00
8½ x 14	41.00
BUSINESS CARDS (Std.)	9.95
LABELS	10.50
POSTCARDS - Return address	7.50
Message side	12.50
BUSINESS REPLY CARDS:	
Stock - Front side	10.50
Message side	12.50
FLYERS/BROCHURES:	
Size to 5½ x 7	12.00
Size to 8½ x 11	21.00
Size to 8½ x 14	28.00
POSTERS - 11 x 17	23.00
Size to 8½ x 11	15.00
BOOKLET PAGES (Straight)	
8½ x 5½	11.00
8½ x 11	20.00
INVITATIONS - Std.	12.00
MEMO/DESK OF/Etc.	7.50
TICKETS	12.00
RESUME-Typeset-Std.	22.00
Typewritten-Std.	16.00
TYPEWRITING	
8½ x 11	9.50
8½ x 14	13.50

© Wm Friday 1982

FORM (Original size 3½ x 7)

SHIFT REPORT

CONTRACT (Original size 8½ x 11)

Title Insurance and Trust Company

BOOK PAGE (Original size 5½ x 8½)

INVITATION (Original size 7 x 4)

RICHARD G. BURLINGHAM

TICKET (Original size 5 x 2½)

LETTERHEAD (Original size 8½ x 11)

EBRIGHT & TURK INC.
PAVING - GRADING - UNDERGROUND CONSTRUCTION

BUSINESS CARD (Original size 3½ x 2)

LOYAL LUMBER SALES
TAHOE PARADISE, CALIFORNIA 95708

ENVELOPE (Original size 4½ x 9½)

FLYER (Original size 8½ x 11)

NOTICE '10⁰⁰ Haircut
SOFTBALL PLAYERS
THIS IS YOUR CHANCE TO SCORE!
$2.00 Off
ON ALL REGULAR $12.00 HAIRCUTS
TO ANY BALL PLAYER WEARING TEAM CAP OR JERSEY
544-1555
NO APPOINTMENT NECESSARY
THE CLIP JOINT/PINE CONE PLAZA

POSTER (Original size 8½ x 5½)

TURN DOWN HEAT
BEFORE LEAVING
(NOT BELOW 55°)

155

The prices shown here have been taken from the Bill Friday Counter Price Book and are not current. Subscribers to the Counter Price Book receive revisions three or four times a year. Revisions are based on computerized national averages. Published by Prudential Publishing Co.

"A" lists the low national average.
"B" lists jobs 133% more difficult.
"C" lists jobs 180% more difficult.
"D" is high level national average.

THE ORIGINAL SIZE OF THIS PRICE BOOK PAGE IS 8½ x 11

88B   TYPESETTING AND PASTEUP   88B

EXAMPLES OF TYPESETTING

SEE DIFFICULTY PAGE FOR CHARGES FOR copy changes, handwritten copy, font changes, special positioning of words, runarounds, boxes, borders, underlining, accent marks, narrow columns, footnotes, math figures, symbols, close copy fitting, and special lines.

Prices are based on typewritten or hand printed copy and do not include "artwork". Also see difficulty factors for possible additional charges.
PRICES ARE FOR ONE SIDE ONLY

TYPESETTING MINIMUM.....	7.98
TYPESET & PASTEUP	9.97
PASTEUP ONLY	5.32
REPRO'S FOR PASTEUP:	
PAPER PLATE & Print	6.98
STAT size to 3 x 5	6.58
STAT size to 8 x 10........	9.90
STAT size to 11 x 16	13.96
HALFTONE size to 3 x 5 ...	10.57
HALFTONE size to 8 x 10 ...	13.23
REDUCE/ENLARGE - Add'l.	3.99
CLIP ART-Ea.-Plus repro.	2.66
LETTERHEAD ONLY (Std.) ...	12.64
ENVELOPE ONLY (Std.)	9.98
L.H. & ENVELOPE (Std.)	19.28
LETTERHEAD only (Special) ..	27.93
ENVELOPE only (Special)	23.94
L.H. & Envelope (Special) ..	46.55
STOCK FORMS	12.64
CUSTOM FORMS (Standard):	
Size to 8½ x 7	23.94
Size to 8½ x 11	34.58
Size to 8½ x 14	45.22
CONTRACTS - 8½ x 11	41.23
8½ x 14	54.53
BUSINESS CARDS (Std.)	13.23
LABELS......................	13.96
POSTCARDS - Return address	9.98
Message side...............	16.62
BUSINESS REPLY CARDS:	
Stock - Front side	13.97
Message side...............	16.62
FLYERS/BROCHURES:	
Size to 5½ x 7	15.96
Size to 8½ x 11	27.93
Size to 8½ x 14	37.24
POSTERS - 11 x 17	30.59
Size to 8½ x 11	19.95
BOOKLET PAGES (Straight)	
8½ x 5½	14.63
8½ x 11	26.60
INVITATIONS - Std.	15.96
MEMO/DESK OF/Etc..........	9.98
TICKETS....................	15.96
RESUME-Typeset-Std.........	29.26
Typewritten-Std.............	21.28
TYPEWRITING	
8½ x 11	12.63
8½ x 14	17.96

© Wm Friday 1982

FORM (Original size 8½ x 7)
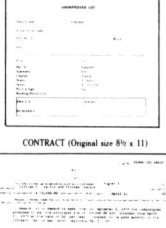

CONTRACT (Original size 8½ x 11)

BOOK PAGE (Original size 5½ x 8½)

INVITATION (Original size 5½ x 4)
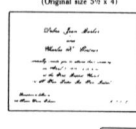

TICKET (Original size 2½ x 4¾)

LETTERHEAD (Original size 8½ x 11)

BUSINESS CARD (Original size 3½ x 2)

ENVELOPE (Original size 4½ x 9½)

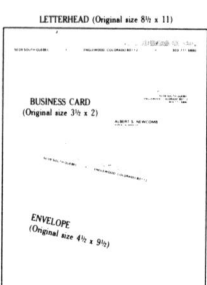

FLYER (Original size 8½ x 11)

POSTER (Original size 11 x 17)

ASK ABOUT OUR EXTENDED SERVICE PROTECTION FOR YOUR CAR

The prices shown here have been taken from the Bill Friday Counter Price Book and are not current. Subscribers to the Counter Price Book receive revisions three or four times a year. Revisions are based on computerized national averages. Published by Prudential Publishing Co.

"A" lists the low national average.
"B" lists jobs 133% more difficult.
"C" lists jobs 180% more difficult.
"D" is high level national average.

THE ORIGINAL SIZE OF THIS PRICE BOOK PAGE IS 8½ x 11

88C TYPESETTING AND PASTEUP 88C

EXAMPLES OF TYPESETTING

SEE DIFFICULTY PAGE FOR CHARGES FOR copy changes, handwritten copy, font changes, special positioning of words, runarounds, boxes, borders, underlining, accent marks, narrow columns, footnotes, math figures, symbols, close copy fitting, and special lines.

Prices are based on typewritten or hand printed copy and do not include "artwork". Also see difficulty factors for possible additional charges.

PRICES ARE FOR ONE SIDE ONLY

TYPESETTING MINIMUM	10.80
TYPESET & PASTEUP	13.50
PASTEUP ONLY	7.20
REPRO'S FOR PASTEUP:	
PAPER PLATE & Print	9.45
STAT size to 3 x 5	8.91
STAT size to 8 x 10	13.41
STAT size to 11 x 16	18.90
HALFTONE size to 3 x 5	14.31
HALFTONE size to 8 x 10	17.91
REDUCE/ENLARGE - Add'l.	5.40
CLIP ART-Ea.-Plus repro.	3.60
LETTERHEAD ONLY (Std.)	17.10
ENVELOPE ONLY (Std.)	13.50
L.H. & ENVELOPE (Std.)	26.10
LETTERHEAD only (Special)	37.80
ENVELOPE only (Special)	32.40
L.H. & Envelope (Special)	63.00
STOCK FORMS	17.10
CUSTOM FORMS (Standard):	
Size to 8½ x 7	32.40
Size to 8½ x 11	46.80
Size to 8½ x 14	61.20
CONTRACTS - 8½ x 11	55.80
8½ x 14	73.80
BUSINESS CARDS (Std.)	17.91
LABELS	18.90
POSTCARDS - Return address	13.50
Message side	22.50
BUSINESS REPLY CARDS:	
Stock - Front side	18.90
Message side	22.50
FLYERS/BROCHURES:	
Size to 5½ x 7	21.60
Size to 8½ x 11	37.80
Size to 8½ x 14	50.40
POSTERS - 11 x 17	41.40
Size to 8½ x 11	27.00
BOOKLET PAGES (Straight)	
8½ x 5½	19.80
8½ x 11	36.80
INVITATIONS - Std.	21.60
MEMO/DESK OF/Etc.	13.50
TICKETS	21.60
RESUME-Typeset-Std.	39.60
Typewritten-Std.	28.80
TYPEWRITING	
8½ x 11	17.10
8½ x 14	24.30

©Wm Friday 1982

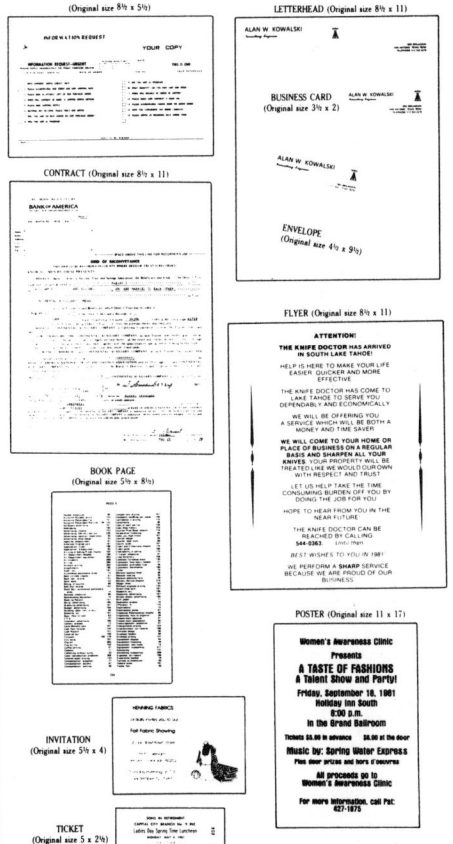

COUNTER PRICE BOOK

The prices shown here have been taken from the Bill Friday Counter Price Book and are not current. Subscribers to the Counter Price Book receive revisions three or four times a year. Revisions are based on computerized national averages. Published by Prudential Publishing Co.

"A" lists the low national average.
"B" lists jobs 133% more difficult.
"C" lists jobs 180% more difficult.
"D" is high level national average.

THE ORIGINAL SIZE OF THIS PRICE BOOK PAGE IS 8½ x 11

88D   TYPESETTING AND PASTEUP   88D

EXAMPLES OF TYPESETTING

SEE DIFFICULTY PAGE FOR CHARGES FOR copy changes, handwritten copy, font changes, special positioning of words, runarounds, boxes, borders, underlining, accent marks, narrow columns, footnotes, math figures, symbols, close copy fitting, and special lines.

Prices are based on typewritten or hand printed copy and do not include "artwork". Also see difficulty factors for possible additional charges.
PRICES ARE FOR ONE SIDE ONLY

TYPESETTING MINIMUM	14.40
TYPESET & PASTEUP	18.00
PASTEUP ONLY	9.60
REPRO'S FOR PASTEUP:	
PAPER PLATE & Print	12.60
STAT size to 3 x 5	11.88
STAT size to 8 x 10	17.88
STAT size to 11 x 16	25.20
HALFTONE size to 3 x 5	19.08
HALFTONE size to 8 x 10	23.88
REDUCE/ENLARGE - Add'l.	7.20
CLIP ART-Ea.-Plus repro.	4.80
LETTERHEAD ONLY (Std.)	22.80
ENVELOPE ONLY (Std.)	18.00
L.H. & ENVELOPE (Std.)	34.88
LETTERHEAD only (Special)	50.40
ENVELOPE only (Special)	43.20
L.H. & Envelope (Special)	84.00
STOCK FORMS	22.80
CUSTOM FORMS (Standard):	
Size to 8½ x 7	43.20
Size to 8½ x 11	62.40
Size to 8½ x 14	81.60
CONTRACTS - 8½ x 11	74.40
8½ x 14	98.40
BUSINESS CARDS (Std.)	23.88
LABELS	25.20
POSTCARDS - Return address	18.00
Message side	30.00
BUSINESS REPLY CARDS:	
Stock - Front side	25.20
Message side	30.00
FLYERS/BROCHURES:	
Size to 5½ x 7	28.80
Size to 8½ x 11	50.40
Size to 8½ x 14	67.20
POSTERS - 11 x 17	55.20
Size to 8½ x 11	36.00
BOOKLET PAGES (Straight)	
8½ x 5½	26.40
8½ x 11	48.00
INVITATIONS - Std.	28.80
MEMO/DESK OF/Etc.	18.00
TICKETS	28.80
RESUME-Typeset-Std.	52.80
Typewritten-Std.	38.40
TYPEWRITING	
8½ x 11	22.80
8½ x 14	32.40

© Wm Friday 1982

FORM (Original size 8½ x 11)

LETTERHEAD (Original size 8½ x 11)

BUSINESS CARD (Original size 3½ x 2)

ENVELOPE (Original size 4½ x 9½)

CONTRACT (Original size 8½ x 11)

FLYER (Original size 8½ x 11)

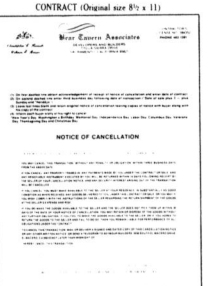

INVITATION (Original size 6 x 9)

BOOK PAGE (Original size 5½ x 8½)

POSTER (Original size 8½ x 11)

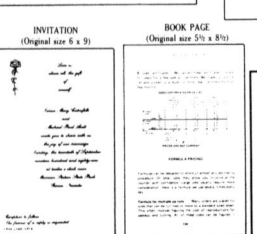

TICKET (Original size 2¼ x 5¾)

CHAPTER 13

RECORD KEEPING

Four basic types of records are needed for most quick printers:

1. Records to convince taxing agencies that you are not "bleeding" into some hidden container and depriving them of their full share.

2. Records to convince banks and other creditors that you are doing so well that you don't really need any more credit — it's just smart business to use their money.

3. Records to convince partners and investors that the future holds rewards worth waiting for.

4. Records needed by you to manage your business.

I am not suggesting that the first three types be anything but truthful. Dishonest records would cost one of the principal benefits of owning your own business — independence! You would lose the freedom to stand by your guns if they try to kick you around. The first three records should, however, present you in the best available light.

The fourth type of records should be brutally frank. You need to know whether you have the bull by the horns or the tail when you look the situation in the face. Some situations are best solved by getting out. Only adequate and completely honest records will tell you which way to jump.

SIMPLE AND MINIMUM

Keep records simple and to a minimum. You can barely live with them, but you can't live without them. Most record systems are designed for "show and tell." This is important for a big business where every move must be explainable and recorded with multiple copies. A quick printing business has only the tax people to account to.

Filing is a chore and can bury you in an avalanche of paper if done incorrectly. Certain tax records must be kept. All other record keeping should be minimized. To do this, weigh the potential value of the record against the cost of keeping it. This is one of the many cost advantages a small business has over its big brothers.

The following is a detailed account of the records we have found vital to our business.

INVOICES & JOB ORDERS

Nothing happens until an order is placed, and then a lot of things must happen fast. We use a combination Invoice and Job Order (copy enclosed) in four part NCR.

(Original size is 8½ x 7)
4 PART NCR

(We do not use the checks at the top but it
is good advertising as it reminds our customers
of some of our services)

Part 1. This goes to the customer only at the time he pays in full or signs for charging at time of delivery. If a deposit is placed, the customer gets the 4th copy until final payment is made, at which time he gets the white (No. 1) copy.

Part 2. This copy stays with the white (No. 1) copy until payment or signing for charging is completed. It then goes to a "hold" file, and it is checked against the No. 3 copy before entering in the charge or cash records.

Part 3. This copy stays at the counter. It is a security copy and is kept in a "hold" file at the counter until it is pulled and checked against the No. 2 copy at the time the No. 2 copy is entered in the records. The No. 3 copy can then be used for other records, or it can be destroyed.

Part 4. This copy is given to the customer when the order is written unless the customer pays in advance. In this case, the customer receives the No. 1 copy, and the No. 4 copy stays with the job until the job is delivered to the customer. The No. 4 copy with a job signifies that the job has been paid in advance. If the customer does not pay in advance and does not take the No. 4 copy, it should be destroyed.

BOOKINGS RECORD

All No. 3 invoice copies are added to get a daily "booking" total, and this figure is recorded on the summary sheet. This becomes an important record as it gives you a current record of the progress of sales. If you depend solely upon the paid records (assuming you are on a "cash" basis), you may be 30 to 120 days behind the actual sale date. If the monthly record is kept, it offers a useful comparison in future years.

DAILY   BOOKING &   CASH RECORD

DATE	AMT. BOOKED	TOTAL TO DATE	CASH AND CHECKS RECEIVED OVER COUNTER.	TOTAL TO DATE

(Original size 8½ x 11)

CASH RECORD

All paid invoices are added to get a daily "receipts" total. This figure is compared against the cash register total and then entered on the summary sheet. We enter the "payments of accounts" and the "cash account" receipts in separate columns as it gives us a separate record of the amount coming in over the counter. At any time we can then figure the percentage of our business that is being charged, which helps us to estimate our cash requirements. The total amount billed is entered at the top of the "accounts receivable" column on the first of each month when statements are mailed. Petty cash receipts are recorded and attached to the paid invoices, and the totals of the petty cash expenses are entered in the check register each month. (See details under TAXES, Expense Record.)

INVENTORY RECORDS

Inventory records are kept to the minimum required for tax purposes. The detailed record keeping needed to keep inventory records current requires more time than the records are worth to most quick printers. The business is too varied and inventory requirements too flexible to establish a normal inventory on anything other than 20 lb. white bond.

SIMPLE BILLS DUE RECORD SYSTEM

We could never find the time to keep a complicated accounts payable record system, so we devised a simple system that works for us.

1. A set of file folders are labeled 1 through 31.

2. Two file folders are labeled "Approved Bills" and "Bills to be Approved."

3. A three page set of 8½ x 14 forms are printed (one set for each month) and marked as follows:

BILLS PAYABLE REGISTER

Page 1. "Bills due 1st to 10th."

DATE DUE   NAME   AMOUNT   NOTES

Numbers 1 through 10 are spaced down the page to allow room for entry of bills due on the 1st through the 10th. Regular monthly bills such as rent or long term leases or notes are printed opposite the date due to save the work of entering them every month.

Page 2 and Page 3. Same as first page except they are numbered 10th to 20th and 21st to 31st.

When bills arrive in the mail, there is often not time to check them, so they are placed in the file folder marked "Bills to be Approved." After they are checked, they are moved to the file folder marked "Approved Bills." When time permits, they are entered in the proper place (opposite the due date) in the "Bills Payable Register" and the bill is placed in the file folder with the same due date.

This system allows the accounts receivables to be worked at odd moments with frequent interruptions. Any bill can be rapidly located prior to payment by scanning the "Bills Payable Register" and noting the number of the file folder where it has been placed for payment. After payment, the bills are filed in a permanent folder under the supplier's name, or in the case of infrequent suppliers, in a miscellaneous folder.

FAST CASH FLOW FORECAST METHOD
(See explanation of item numbers following forms)

CASH ASSETS (Next 30 days)

1. Cash and checks on hand $_____

2. Bank Balance $_____

3. Current daily average cash receipts multiplied by number of working days in month $_____

4. Estimated accounts receivable based on balance still due from last billing plus amount charged already in the current month $_____

5. Other income expected:

_____

_____ $_____

Total estimated receipts next 30 days $_____

Item 3   Add the total cash and checks received across the counter (not including amounts paid on accounts) for the past ten days. Divide by ten for average per day and multiply by total **working days** during the next 30 days.

Item 4   The total billed each month should be recorded and daily receipts from charge accounts listed. The balance is still due. Add this balance to the amount charged in the current month and adjust for known slow pays, etc.

CASH LIABILITIES (Next 30 days)

1. 30 day fixed expense $_____

2. Estimated 30 day variable expense $_____
    (Use ___% of Estimated total volume)

3. Tax reserves

    _____

    _____ $_____

4. Reserves for any large payments

    _____

    _____ $_____

5. Any other unusual expenses due in
    next 30 days

    _____

    _____ $_____

Total Estimated Payments & Reserve
next 30 days $_____

Estimated Net Cash Position in 30 days
(+ or - amount needed) $_____

Item 1   It is imperative that you know your fixed expenses. Once determined, this expense will remain the same until changes are made in personnel, salaries, payments on equipment, etc. It should be reviewed every few months and brought up to date.

We use the following expense items to make up our total "Fixed Expenses:" (These are expenses that remain about the same whether business is good or bad.)

Owner's Draw
Salaries (not including overtime)
Installment Notes
Lease Payments
Shop Rent
Telephone, including classified ad
Trash Removal
Rag Rental
Water & Cooler Rental
Dues
Maintenance Contracts
Insurance

Item 2 These are expenses that will move up and down drastically with business activity. We use the following expense items to make up the total "Variable Expense:"

Overtime Pay
Temporary Help
Job Outs
Auto & Truck Operating
Miscellaneous Shop Supplies
Postage
Repairs
Paper & Other Supplies

The total of these expenses will fall fairly consistently within a regular percentage figure of total volume. Our variable expense ranges from 25% of total volume if our prices are up to par to 35% of total volume if our prices are in need of revision.

Therefore, we arrive at this figure for Item 2 by taking a percentage of our estimated total volume for the next 30 days.

Item 3 Nothing is more sure than taxes, and since taxes come due at irregular periods, a reserve needs to be built before the due date. It is foolish, for instance, to include sales tax deductions when determining the amount of cash you have for business expenditures. Those of us who have made this mistake know the problems of raising this extra amount of cash on the tax due date. Many small print shops have ended up with government padlocks on their doors.

Items 4 & 5 Final lease payoffs (usually 10% of cost) are unusual large payments that can slip up on you. Payments of this type should be anticipated and included when figuring your cash position.

COPY OF EACH JOB
(No clutter, no file, but fast recovery)

If a copy of every job is filed under the customer's name, the filing space needed will soon take up more space than the system is worth. However, a copy of every job should be kept for several reasons. 1. Billing is sometimes questioned by large companies, and unless a copy of the job can be produced, it may be difficult to collect. 2. Reruns are often ordered, and the customer has used the original and all copies. 3. Complaints can be handled more effectively if you have a copy of the job in front of you. 4. Quality control is more effective if copies of every job are kept. 5. Samples are available to show prospective customers the type and quality of work you are producing.

THE FOLLOWING SYSTEM IS SIMPLE AND EFFECTIVE:

Purchase an inexpensive self-inking date stamp for each pressman (different color of ink for each). A copy of every job is date stamped and placed in a carton (we use a regular packing case that we receive our paper in). The date of the first copy is marked on the outside of the carton. When the carton is full, the date of the last copy is marked on the outside of the carton.

The carton is saved for about two years and then disposed of. Copies may be located by referring to the invoice date, which makes the copy easy to locate in the storage boxes. This system is self cleaning and will never grow beyond the space needed to store copies for the past two years. Caution: When going through a box, keep the order of copies in which they were originally placed. If the copies are shuffled, the recovery time is increased considerably.

CATCH-ALL BOX
(Saves thousands of dollars)

There are many pieces of paper that should not be destroyed immediately, but are of questionable value. These include customers' notes, your notes, customers' originals not worthy of filing for rerun, papers left on the counter, miscellaneous receipts not worthy of filing, etc. We have found that a packing carton will hold about a two year supply. By placing each copy on the top of the pile and not shuffling them when looking for something, the file can be cleaned by disposing of the material at the bottom of the box, thereby making room at the top.

This box has saved us thousands of dollars. For instance, customers frequently complain that certain of their directions were not followed. If the scrap of paper the directions were scribbled on can be produced, there is no problem. More often than not, the customer will decide the problem is a minor one he can "live with" when he discovers the error is his.

A good filing system has a place for everything to avoid desk top clutter. The catch-all box offers a place for everything that does not fit into any regular filing category.

ORIGINALS FILE

This is another case where an "easy cleaning" file is needed. We use an A to Z file folder system with all originals of customers whose names start with A going into the A file, etc. Special files are kept only for large customers who have many originals on file.

Even with this limited filing system, your customers' originals files will grow to unwieldy size unless you regularly thin them out. The thinning out process can be accomplished gradually by throwing out obsolete originals each time you go through the file looking for a particular original.

ACCOUNTS RECEIVABLE FILE

For this file, we use an open top file on wheels as it is kept up-to-date and statements are typed by the same person who works the counter. This job can be done during slack periods, and the files can be rolled out of the way when not in use. Individual file folders are a must for this purpose. When a file becomes obsolete, it can be removed from the active file and held for tax purposes in a dead file.

We use a statement in three part NCR. A white copy is mailed to the customer on the first of the month. The yellow and pink copies are placed in the customer's file. If the account is not paid by the fifteenth of the month, the pink copy is mailed to the customer as a reminder. The yellow copy remains in the file as a permanent record. When the account is paid, the yellow copy is moved behind current invoices, and the current statement with the white copy on the front is kept in the front of the file.

With this system, we can thumb through the files and pick out any overdue accounts at a glance. We make a list of accounts over thirty days past due and follow up with a telephone call or other methods. (See chapter on credit and collections.)

CLIP ART FILE

We use large loose-leaf books and a card file. The pages in the books are numbered consecutively, and when new clip art is acquired (we clip newspapers, buy closeouts, etc.), we simply add another page to our book and paste it in. When we have time, we study the new page and make a list at the top of the page of every category we can think of that applies to the clip art on that page. We then list these categories on the appropriate index cards which we have in a rolodex file for easy reference.

OUR LOOSE-LEAF PAGES ARE NEVER CLIPPED! We make a copy of the page with a stat or on the Itek and press. We charge $6.50 for the reproduction. This way we keep our clip art books intact. It is easy for the customer to understand why we need to charge for the use of a cut.

COMPUTER RECORD KEEPING

Computers are beginning to take over some of the record keeping of quick printers. As mentioned in other chapters, we are using a computer for pricing. I expect to soon see a snowball effect regarding computer utilization.

COMPUTER AID FOR BRANCH LOCATIONS

We have started research on a project we hope will make more practical the operation of branch locations.

Our goal is to use computer programs to guide, advise, and check on branch managers. If successful, this should lower the experience (and the cost) needed for profitable branch management. We expect the research and development of these programs to take two to three years.

CHAPTER 14

ADVERTISING

This is where decision making can be a major problem. There are many types of advertising, and we have, unfortunately, tried too many of them. All types of general advertising are costly. Unless you pinpoint your activities for results, you will go broke as you can't live without advertising. It can kill you if it drains your profits without producing results.

A quick printing shop cannot exist without some form of advertising as it is the only practical method of developing new business. The size of the average quick printing sale is nowhere near enough to justify the cost of a sales call, including all of the backup expense needed to support an outside salesman.

This fact promotes advertising to greater importance to the quick printer than it is to a business using outside salesmen.

TYPES OF ADVERTISING

The quick printer is concerned primarily with three forms of advertising:

THE TELEPHONE YELLOW PAGES
SIGNS ON THE FRONT OF HIS BUILDING
FLYERS OR BROCHURES

YELLOW PAGES

This is a necessary evil. The cost is high, but it probably brings in enough profit to at least break even. Unless you have some kind of gimmick going, you should settle for a medium-size ad under the principal category of printing. Keep in mind that you start at the end of the line for the size ad you select and work up to the front many years later. For this reason, you should start out with the size ad you intend to stay with. Otherwise, you may work up toward the front of your size and then start over at the bottom with a different size ad. The most difficult size to work up in is the quarter page (or recently 1/5th page) ad. This is the largest size available and is used by many of the old companies.

For this and cost reasons, you might find it better to start and stay with a smaller ad. If you decide to specialize, it might be profitable for you to utilize small ads (1½ inch) under the section where customers buying your specialty normally look for supplies. These ads are relatively low in cost and can produce some sizeable orders. Another advantage of this type of ad is that you might be the only printer advertising under that particular category.

SIGNS ON THE FRONT OF YOUR BUILDING

You will probably get a larger return for your advertising dollar from this type of advertising than any other you may do. However, like most advertising, if you do too little, you are throwing your money away. This is doubly true in the case of a sign. If you spend a few hundred dollars for a sign, it will do you more harm than good. Unless, of course, the size and style of sign is controlled by your building lease.

A decent sign will cost three thousand dollars and up. In quick printing, unlike conventional printing, the location you select is of prime importance. Customers will be coming to you — not you to them. Every customer you entice to give you some business will see and be influenced by your sign. Also, customers who are attracted by other forms of advertising will be driving in heavy traffic looking for your place of business. Your sign should make it easy for a customer to locate you.

I know of several instances where quick printers have prospered in spite of poor business practices because they have a good sign that people notice when they are driving down the street. I am not suggesting a Las Vegas type sign, but you should have a sign that is easy to spot from a moving car a block or two away.

NEWSPAPERS — RADIO — TELEVISION

You may have special situations where newspapers, radio, or television might benefit you, but most quick printers should avoid this type of advertising.

Your profitable customers will come from a limited type of customer and from a limited geographical area. General advertising costs are based on the number of people reached. Since you are interested in only a very small percentage of the general public in a limited geographical area, you end up paying for a lot of advertising you cannot use.

CUSTOMERS' AD BOOKS

You will be hit often for special ads from customers. For the most part, these are worthless for any purpose except to hold the printing business of the customer soliciting the ad. The value to you should be judged accordingly. It can get out of hand if you do not stay on guard. An answer that most customers will accept is to explain that you do printing for many customers who publish programs and ad books and you must refrain from advertising in any of them since you cannot afford to advertise in all of them. It works! You cannot afford to buy business at unreasonable costs and still remain competitive.

It is good business to buy advertising based only on the return on your investment. If it is charity, then go ahead, but don't deceive yourself by charging the expense to your advertising budget.

FLYERS — BROCHURES

This is YOUR form of advertising. It displays your merchandise (quality of printing), and it conveys your message. You can limit your cost and coverage to customers who offer you the greatest potential.

Most of your customers will come from a few miles around you, depending upon the flow of auto traffic and the convenience of reaching your place of business. You should study this flow, and your coverage should be concentrated in this area. Forget the residences. Your profitable business is with business people. It is true that business people live in houses and some of them may live and work in your area, but you are shotgunning your advertising dollar when you spend it delivering flyers to residences. Everyone buys printing, but a heavy percentage of these buyers of printing are not profitable to handle.

I am assuming that you are going after profitable business which means business organizations. Since you can't go after all businesses, you should limit your coverage to the ones that offer you the greatest potential. Depending upon the area you are in, this usually means the closest two or three thousand businesses.

SELECT A MAILING LIST

You can buy mailing lists, but most lists will cover a lot of areas or types of customers you may not want to cover. If you live in an urban area, your telephone company probably has available for rent a "Street Address Directory," sometimes called a "Cross Directory." Look in your telephone directory under "General Business." In the Street Address Directory, all listings are arranged according to address. Streets are listed alphabetically and addresses numerically. You can turn to any street and find all of the listed telephone subscribers on that particular street or block. These directories are usually renewed every six months and exchanged as long as you pay the rent or lease.

Before making a mailing list from the address directory, it is necessary to mark out the many duplicates caused by one customer having two or more numbers at the same address. You can easily customize this list by selecting certain types of businesses where their name offers a clue, or by selecting certain streets or blocks and eliminating others. You are then in a position to computerize or make address plates for mailing.

MAILING?? Yes, definitely MAILING. Believe me, we've tried all of the less costly methods. The results you get from mailing as compared to other methods of delivery justify the additional cost. You will, of course, want to use a bulk mail permit, and to the thinking of some, this would place your flyer in the category of "junk mail." Even if you put a first class

Bulk Rate
U.S. Postage
PAID
Permit No.

stamp on your mailing, you aren't going to fool anyone for long. Unless you design your flyer to grab the potential customer on first glance, it will end up in the wastebasket — first class or bulk mail.

Few business people throw mail away without giving the contents a glance. They depend on mailings, among other things, to keep them abreast of things. So you can pretty well be assured that your flyer will get a glance before it hits the wastebasket. This is enough to make this type of advertising profitable for you.

MAIL TO OCCUPANT

Why? Because you want to cover the geographical area that is most profitable to you, and customers move often. Customer turnover in some areas is as high as 40% per year. It is costly and time consuming to make new address plates. In fact, it is so costly and time consuming, and there are so many other vital functions requiring your attention, that the odds are that you won't keep a customer list current. After a year or so, a heavy percentage of your mail will not be going into your profitable area.

The person you really want to hit is the business person who has just moved into the neighborhood. He has not yet been tied into another quick printer. Your "occupant" mailing plates will stay current for years. Your list can be updated simply by watching for new buildings and making new plates.

DO YOUR OWN MAILING AND ADDRESSING

I am not suggesting that you go into the mailing and addressing business. This would be a mistake. You could not compete with mailing houses equipped to handle this type of business. You can, however, handle your OWN mailings profitably. Why? Because you can work them into slow periods which every quick printer has. This is a stop and go business. Small mailing equipment is inexpensive, takes up very little space, and can be operated by your lowest paid employee. This also allows you more flexibility in your mailing.

REGULAR MAILINGS ARE A MUST

To get the most from your mailings, they must be regular — not more than two months apart. Keep the same logo, color of paper, etc. Even if all you get is a quick glance, a regular mailing has the effect, in time, of making you known to the customer. When he thinks of printing, there is a good chance he will think of you.

Don't be discouraged with the results you may get from a single mailing. Even high paid advertising people produce duds. There is nothing that is going to boom your business into a success overnight. Keep in mind that advertising is an absolute must for survival. Mailings are your best form of advertising.

TIMING IS IMPORTANT

For some reason that no business person can explain, there are periods when people are energetic and active, and there are dormant periods. Perhaps it's the news, the weather, or the season. About the time you have it figured out, it will be sure to change. In regard to mailings, however, there are a few guideposts that we have found reliable.

Time your mailing to arrive on Tuesday, Wednesday, or Thursday if possible. Mailings arriving on Fridays get the least results, and Monday arrivals are not much better. The reason is fairly simple. Most business people are trying to clean things up on Friday, and on Monday, the mail is loaded and is a bad day in general. Since all you can expect is a quick glance, your mailing should arrive at a time when the "quick glance" has the best chance of producing action.

WHAT TO SAY IN MAILINGS

Everyone likes to hear the words, "Savings," and "Discounted." Put them at the top, but don't be misguided by your own advertising and start believing that the secret of success is discounting. Unwarranted discounts will not keep you in the quick printing business. Your published prices must be competitive with other good operators, and there is no room for costly discounting. In truth, however, your published prices are discounted for volume.

Your principal message should be in large headlines. It should be short and to the point, followed by details in smaller print. If your headline grabs them, they will read the small print, so there is no need to take away from the headline by making the details large too. The details should be fairly complete, giving prices, etc. Don't underestimate the intelligence of your reader. You are going after business people, and your message should be geared accordingly.

Keep in mind that you are going after repeat business. You want to be sure you can do what you claim. Add something for the "readers." There are customers who will read every word of your flyer in search of something that will fit their needs. Reserve a section for them. In fairly small type, list everything you do.

HERE ARE SOME OF THE THINGS WE PRINT
AND SERVICES WE PERFORM:

☐ Letterhead	☐ Invoices	☐ Medical Forms
☐ Stationery	☐ Statements	☐ Dental Forms
☐ Envelopes	☐ Carbonless Forms	☐ Booklets
☐ Business Cards	☐ Office Forms	☐ Book Printing
☐ Quick Printing	☐ N.C.R. Forms	☐ Book Typesetting
☐ Metal Printing Plates	☐ Labels	☐ Book Copy Editing
☐ Plastic Plates	☐ Memo Pads	☐ Catalogs
☐ Paper Plates	☐ From the desk pads	☐ Certificates
☐ Enlargements	☐ Business Forms	☐ Contracts
☐ Reductions	☐ Rubber Stamps	☐ Resumes

☐ Advertising Copy	☐ Bulletins	☐ Binding
☐ Circulars	☐ Announcements	☐ Power Cutting
☐ Brochures	☐ Club Mailings	☐ Folding
☐ Flyers	☐ Directories	☐ Padding
☐ Stats	☐ Invitations	☐ Collating
☐ Graphic Design	☐ Newsletters	☐ Numbering
☐ Pasteup	☐ Programs	☐ Hole Punching
☐ Headlines	☐ Letters	☐ Perforating
☐ Computer Typesetting	☐ Tickets	☐ Mailings
☐ 11 X 17 Printing	☐ Postcards	☐ Plain Paper

COUPONS

Coupons can produce results, but watch out, they can be costly. Coupons tend to attract "shoppers" more than the more profitable type of customer.

If you are starting a new shop and have few customers, a $5.00 discount coupon is usually very effective in bringing in new customers. You, of course, cannot deny old customers the same discount, but if you have few old customers, your cost will be light.

A less costly form of coupon is one that offers to add free copies to an order. "BUY 1000 FLYERS — RECEIVE 1200 — **200 FREE"** etc. The customer gets a 20% discount — you have a 3 or 4% cost.

PRINTING COMPANY
BUY 1000
NCR FORMS
(NO CARBON REQUIRED)
AND RECEIVE 1200
200 FREE
WITH THIS COUPON
CLIP AND SAVE!

WHEN TO INCLUDE A PRICE LIST

This depends on the economic situation and on your particular area. Most people are not familiar with the cost of printing. A limited list of prices on standard items will produce interest and business from people who have never printed before. If, however, several low cost competitors in your area are sending out mailings with price lists, it might be better for you to omit yours.

Your profitable customers will be people who value

and are willing to pay a little extra for service, dependability, courtesy, convenience, etc., and, of course, acceptable quality. This is the message you want to get across. If your appeal is to price, you will attract the "shoppers." There is no long-term profit with this group. Sooner or later some fool will beat your price no matter how low you go and the "shoppers" will live off of his capital for a while.

PROOF IT, INSPECT IT, DESTROY IT

If the mailer is not representative of the type of work you produce, do not send it out — throw it in the wastebasket and reprint it. On the other hand, do not have some other printer turn out a mailer for you that is of a quality you could not produce. You are going after repeat business. The advertising cost is often more than the profit from the first job. If you can give customers more than they expect, you have them hooked. But be ready to duck when they expect rotogravure, and you hand them quick printing.

BUDGET YOUR ADVERTISING

Budget, not because you might do too much advertising, but because you will probably do too little. If you used a salesman, your cost would run 20% or more. Quick printers cannot afford this percentage, but you should spend at least 5% of your gross sales on various forms of advertising. A new quick printing business should budget at least $5,000 for advertising during the first year in addition to the capital expenditure for signs.

BOXES

Don't pass this one up for packaging your jobs. Plain folding boxes will cost about 20 cents each. You can print your own labels on gum stock and have them put on the boxes during slack periods. When you figure that it will cost you at least 20 cents to place a flyer in the office of a prospective customer, you can relate the value of a box on a customer's shelf with your name and telephone number in plain view. Secretaries change jobs, but the boxes remain to remind the new secretary where to purchase replacements when the box is empty.

Large orders, of course, can be packed in the original carton. But even large orders of an item that will be used over a long period of time should be placed in small boxes that can be stored on the customer's stationery room shelf. You will be billboarding your customer's office and assuring yourself of repeat business for years in the future.

The customer likes to receive his order in a letterhead box. The extra cost to you is nil as the cost of wrapping paper and labor is probably more. It is costly labor as the job of wrapping is often performed during rush periods when it could be more profitably used than for package wrapping. Shrink film requires less labor, but still does not give you the advantage of boxes.

DIVIDER SHEETS

Here is a perfect opportunity to get your message repeated over and over again without being obnoxious. Print divider sheets with your advertising and include something useful for the customer, such as a calorie counter or a calendar covering the next few years. These sheets will be passed to secretaries in other offices, often with a personal endorsement of your services. You can't buy this kind of advertising, and it will cost you nothing but a little printing which can be done during slack periods.

CALENDARS

Calendars, printed on 8½ x 5½ twenty pound colors with large squares by every date for writing in reminders of appointments, is an inexpensive way of keeping your name before your customers all year long. The small size fits a desk top or drawer better than an 8½ x 11 size. Try passing out pads of calendars in surrounding offices during December. The reception you will get is great. The new business will more than pay for the cost and effort.

KEEP A RECORD

Memory often makes a poor business record unless it is jogged by recorded facts. Keep a file of all of your advertising efforts. Place notes in the file regarding results, costs, etc. There are so many places for an advertising dollar that the advertising end of your business will always require the best judgment you can muster.

ACROSS THE BOARD DISCOUNTS

One of the costliest forms of advertising is the offer of an across-the-board discount to all customers on all products. To be effective, a discount offer has to be at least 10%. It often takes 30% to 50% to really bring in the bargain hunters. Few quick printing businesses can afford to give up even 10% across the board. If you are going after bargain hunters, it is a much better practice to limit discounts to special purchases, close-out merchandise, or limited coupon type discounts.

EXCERPTS FROM FLYERS THAT PRODUCED WELL
(All copy reduced 50%)

YOU'LL LIKE THE WAY WE DO IT!!

COLLECTIVELY WE'VE BEEN PRINTING FOR OVER 30 YEARS AND WE LIKE IT BETTER EACH YEAR.

WE THINK YOU'LL LIKE:

The care that goes into every job.
The pride that goes with our experience and talent.
Being told when we think a job is beyond our capabilities.
The cheerfulness that comes from liking what we're doing.
Our modest prices, the lowest that our efficiency and
modern equipment can produce.
We hope you'll like us as well as our first customers, most of whom are still
coming back after   years.

WE BELIEVE WE FILL A NEED
ONE THAT FALLS ABOVE THE "COPY HOUSE"
AND BELOW THE "BIG PRESS" PRINTER.

Coupon flyers are best used on potential NEW customers. Not as an introductory offer — they should already know you through regular mailings. The coupons should jar a few loose from their regular printer.

(Reduced 50%)

Co. NAME

JULY
PRINTING
SALE

**SAVE WITH BIG DISCOUNTS
OFF OUR ALREADY LOW PRICES**

JULY COUPONS

PRINTING COMPANY
BUY 1000
NCR FORMS
(NO CARBON REQUIRED)
AND RECEIVE 1200
200 FREE
WITH THIS COUPON
Offer expires July 31, 1981

PRINTING COMPANY
**10% OFF
BUSINESS
CARDS**
WITH THIS COUPON
Offer expires July 31, 1981

PRINTING COMPANY
BUY 1000
ENVELOPES
AND RECEIVE 1200
200 FREE
WITH THIS COUPON
Offer expires July 31, 1981

PRINTING COMPANY
BUY 1000
FLYERS
AND RECEIVE 1200
200 FREE
WITH THIS COUPON
Offer expires July 31, 1981

(Original Size - 8½ x 11)
(A "spoof" flyer that was a success)

NAME ADDRESS, ETC.

Occupant

Why Us?

BECAUSE **WE DO MORE** *THAN INSTANT PRINTING*
WITHOUT
CHARGING MORE !

THE BEST AUTOMATED EQUIPMENT	+	HIGHLY EXPERIENCED AND WELL PAID PRESSMEN
	Equal	
LOW UNIT COST & HIGH QUALITY		

IT'S NOT JUST THE GOOD PAY THAT CAUSES OUR PRESSMEN TO DO **YOUR** *JOB WELL AND FAST.* **IT'S OLD FASHIONED PRIDE!** *YOU'LL FIND THE SAME ATTITUDE AT OUR COUNTER AND IN OUR BINDING AND TYPESETTING ROOMS.*

We're not the world's **LARGEST**

But we are the world's *Best*

(Judging was done by the notoriously unbiased co NAME employees.)

190

CHAPTER 15

SELLING

The term, salesman, means different things to different people. In this book, I am using it in a broad sense to include all forms of direct communication with customers.

Every word, every expression, the appearance of personnel and facilities, and most important, your attitude will communicate meaning to your customers. Unless you control these communicating elements, the message that is received by your customers may not be the message you intended to send. Nothing will bring you greater rewards for effort spent than the time you invest in improving selling skills.

THE SECRET OF SUCCESSFUL SELLING

The secret — buy FOR your customer instead of selling TO your customer. What would YOU buy if you were actually buying for yourself? If you honestly think this way without being influenced by profit or greed, you will be so valuable to your customers that they won't live without you. You will become a rare gem — a trusted salesman.

SELLING QUICK PRINTING

Advertising, referrals, and repeat customers account for most of the people who appear at your counter or who telephone or write. It is a costly procedure to get these people to make such a move in your direction. They are like gold nuggets that you have searched for and laboriously dug from the bed of a stream — unless you skillfully handle the panning operation, the nuggets will not be separated from the common gravel.

COUNTER SELLING

1. Be there! Some quick printers cannot generate the self-discipline needed to open and close on time. Every time they open late or close early, they probably lose a valuable customer or two. This is a prime method of unselling.

2. Be prepared! A heavy percentage of the selling is done before the customer arrives. Unless you have an up-to-date counter price book and paper samples, your selling expertise is wasted.

3. Make it easy for the customer to buy. This is the most neglected tactic in the world of selling. If a customer knows what he is going to get, exactly how much it will cost, when it will be ready, the method of payment, etc., he is much more likely to buy.

4. Smile! An ancient Chinese proverb advises that, "A man without a smiling face must not open a shop." Every entertainer knows the value of a smile. Employees are trained to smile only by a smiling boss. A smile soothes the ruffled feelings of the receiver and sender alike. It reflects strength, confidence, and self-respect. It portrays an image of a person capable of managing his own feelings. Customers will come long distances and pay more for "service with a smile."

5. Remember customers' names. Nothing is more pleasing to a customer than to be recognized and referred to by his correct name. This lets him know that he at least is being thought of as an individual. It is reasonable to assume that if you remember his name, you may also remember some of his individual problems and have a solution for them.

NEVER KNOCK COMPETITORS

Ignore them if possible. Any mention of a competitor raises his status. If your prospect is using a competitor, your condemnation of this competitor is an indirect condemnation of your prospect's judgment. Customers do not expect you to be an unbiased judge, and if you pretend to be, they consider it "sour grapes."

BUILD CREDIBILITY

If challenged, admit your products' weak points. Don't destroy your credibility by trying to defend an obvious shortcoming when compared to competitive offerings. Value is an overall thing. No one product or service is number one on all counts.

If the total adds up in your favor, you have the basis of a convincing sales presentation.

One of the significant values of a product can be the character traits of the person selling the product. A capable salesman has extra worth. Wise buyers often recognize this worth when making decisions.

LISTEN

There is a time for talk, but listening can often be more valuable. When a customer starts talking about his problems in relation to your product or service, button up and listen. Nothing can be more valuable to you in making a sale. He is doing your job for you — all you have to do is listen, and you will know exactly where your product fits into a solution.

As a young salesman, one of my largest sales was to the printing department of Mutual Benefit Insurance Company. They had fifty two Multiliths. I had never before met the printing department manager. I simply walked in and asked his advice about a new line of direct image printing plates we had recently acquired. I explained I had come to him because he managed the largest small-press print shop in the world and should know more about the potential of our new product than anyone else.

After modestly admitting that Ford Motor Company operated 54 presses, two more than he did, he spent an hour telling about the problems of operating a large print shop. All I did was listen. He ended with an offer to test and evaluate our new product which resulted in a large volume of repeat business.

SELLING

TELEPHONE MANNERS

In recent years, salesmanship has been eroded out of the process of answering the telephone. Some quick printers consider incoming telephone calls an irritant. This attitude is reflected in the manner in which incoming calls are handled. This present state-of-the-art of telephone manners offers an opportunity for you to gain an advantage by restoring the element of salesmanship.

Most secretaries are instructed to screen the boss' telephone calls with, "Who may I say is calling?" They may even go further and ask, "What is the nature of your business?" The purpose may be an honest attempt to prevent interruptions from disrupting a busy schedule. The "message" as interpreted by the customer is usually one of the following:

1. "He must be dodging creditors or irate customers."
2. "He considers himself too important to talk to just anyone."
3. "He is a slow thinker and needs a secretary to outline the purpose of the call."

What is lost is the image of an available, accommodating, capable, and straight-forward person who can handle any telephone situation without the protection of screening.

There are times when you cannot afford to be interrupted by a telephone call. Many customers cannot understand why you can't take time to

195

handle their "vital" problem even if they are told you are "tied up." The simplest and most effective message is, "Sorry, he's not in." This, in effect, is a true statement. You are not "in" to telephone calls. This message, of course, should never be preceded with "who's calling" which implies you are in only to certain people.

DO SOMETHING "LATELY"

There is the old story about the salesman reminding a customer of all of the things he had done for the customer, including saving his life, and the customer acknowledging the past favors, but asking, "What have you done for me lately?"

Good salesmanship is never remembering favors you do for someone else and never forgetting the ones they do for you. If you want to drive a customer off, there is no better way than to remind him that he "owes" you. It is much more profitable to forget the past and "do something lately."

CHAPTER 16

CREDIT
AND
COLLECTIONS

The granting of credit and, more important, "collecting" require a lot of common sense administered with kid gloves by a capable manager. Few quick printing businesses can afford a credit manager, so like most other management jobs in small businesses, you are it!

WHY GRANT CREDIT

It is possible to do business on a strictly cash basis, but it may not be good business to do so. The average established quick printer will have about 50% of his business charged, depending upon the type of trade he is catering to. Many customers are simply not equipped to do business on a cash basis. If you intend to have their business, it is necessary to have a credit policy.

HOW TO GRANT CREDIT

A credit application is a must if you plan to grant credit on your own plan. (See Credit Application form at end of this chapter for details.) You can use a standard form, but it is often a good investment to design the form to your particular requirements. If you plan to use a credit bureau to check credit ratings, see section on "How to Judge Good or Bad Risks."

A credit application not only provides information that can be checked over the telephone, it also provides a general picture of the company or individual asking for credit. Most information can be checked over the telephone if you go about it the right way. When you place a call to the bank or to a credit reference, you should identify yourself, your company, and let them know that THEIR customer is asking you for credit.

If the credit reference is a large company, you may run into a clerk who will not give you the time of day without a written request, but most of the time enough information can be obtained over the telephone to help a little. That's about all you can expect from any application — a little help. With common sense and prompt follow through, you can hold your credit losses to a practical level. Our credit losses run between one and two percent.

HOW TOUGH SHOULD CREDIT POLICY BE

This is one of the toughest decisions of a credit manager. Your percentage of loss is about your only guide. If you are not losing anything, you are either the luckiest person in the world or you are being too tough in the granting of new credit. If you are too tough, you are losing a lot of profitable business. If you are too easy, you will go broke. There are few quick printers who can survive with a 5% or higher credit loss, so a good rule-of-thumb is to keep your losses between 1% and 4%.

INVESTMENT NEEDED TO GRANT CREDIT

Many new quick printers overlook this capital investment item. Don't expect all or even most of your customers to pay on time — it simply does not happen that way. With a good credit policy and diligent follow through, you might average 60 days. This means that if you plan to grant $10,000 of credit, you will have at least $20,000 tied up permanently in accounts receivable. It is possible to get loans on accounts receivables, but for the average quick printer, it is rarely practical. Limit the granting of credit to the capital you can afford to invest. As you grow, you can gradually increase your accounts receivable investment.

HOW TO JUDGE GOOD OR BAD RISKS

A credit bureau can be used if you are granting credit to individuals on a volume basis, however, the credit bureau is of little help in judging the financial stability of a business. An individual with a job and salary may have perfect credit of long standing and still fail in a new business venture. (Most do!) The following list is from our experience and may be of some help. A lot depends on the general economic situation and problems that may be peculiar to your particular area, such as an industry that may be going down hill in an area and taking a lot of small businesses with it.

Good risks: (Always check bank and credit references.)

1. Individuals with good credit ratings and steady jobs for the past three years. Not over 2 moves of residence.

2. Businesses that have been in the same location for 3 years or more.

3. Doctors and dentists. (We have had a few losses.)

4. Large established corporations. (We have never had a loss where a purchase order was obtained.)

Poor risks:

1. Individuals with no prior credit accounts or with poor rating. Frequent changes of job or residence.

2. New, small corporations. We will not grant credit without a personal written guarantee from a responsible individual. Even with a personal written guarantee, our losses have been high.

3. Multiple small corporations operated from one location by the same people. Your chances of collecting are about 50-50. Even their checks are risky.

4. Retail stores with less than three years in one location.

The foregoing lists are far from complete. They cover only the areas that are fairly easy to recognize and define. You have to use a lot of common sense and not be taken in by a smooth talker who tempts you with talk about the large amount of business he expects to do with you. Also beware of the customer who tries to bluff you into granting credit. A customer with good credit is proud of his credit standing and will not hesitate to give you adequate credit information.

HOW TO REFUSE CREDIT

For various reasons, you can't grant credit to everyone. The obvious goal is to turn them down and still keep them as customers.

1. Consider using credit cards as an alternative to offer your customers.

2. Use the simple statement, "It's not your credit, but my limited capital." Don't let too much pride stand in your way. Even the largest corporations are often limited on capital or cash flow.

3. Set up a limited amount of credit, assuring the customer that the limit will be increased once a good credit record has been established.

Above all, stand firm in your refusal to grant credit if the facts indicate the risk is greater than the potential gain.

HOW TO HAVE GOOD COLLECTION RESULTS
(Assuming you have selected good risks)

1. Have a definite understanding of your terms from the start.

2. Have every invoice signed upon delivery. This is especially important with companies where several different people are purchasing.

3. Have a rubber stamp made so that terms can be stamped on certain invoices. If you print credit terms on all invoices, you will encourage many customers to apply for credit who you may not be able to accept. This will result in your losing them as

cash customers. Credit terms should be printed on STATEMENTS, but not INVOICES.

4. Send out statements on a regular and prompt basis.

5. Telephone any new customer who is as much as one week late with his first payment unless there is a known reason for the delay.

6. We mail a pink copy of the statement to most customers if they have not paid by the 15th of the month. (Our billings are due on the 10th.) It is important that these pink slips be reviewed before mailing as there may be a good reason for the delay. A pink slip might offend in this case. As a general rule, we have not found any evidence that these pink slips have offended customers, but they do speed up collections.

7. Set up a monthly aging report.

8. We telephone most customers who are 30 days late. A polite call will work wonders. Try to reach the boss and ask him if he will remind his bookkeeping department that your payment has been overlooked. He probably issued the order to hold up payment in the first place, but he won't admit it. This method works well and keeps your relationship good with the boss. Even if he runs a one-person operation, he is flattered by your assumption that some department head handles his accounts payable and will often pay rather than offer an excuse.

9. Make regular polite telephone calls on all accounts over 30 days late until you are ready to start hard collection efforts.

10. Letters can sometimes effectively supplement or replace telephone calls.

HARD COLLECTION EFFORTS

This is mostly wistful thinking, but a few do pay off, so it is worth a small amount of effort. When a customer has reached the point of dodging your phone calls or giving you promises that are broken, your chances of collection are small unless the amount is for several thousand dollars.

If the customer is established in business, you can go to small claims court and collect. But most customers who reach this point are not going to be around for long. Even if you are able to serve them with a subpoena, and this is sometimes practically impossible, they will probably skip before you can obtain and execute a judgment.

You can use a collection agency, but about the most they will do is to write a letter and perhaps make a telephone call. Our experience with collection agencies on accounts under $500 has resulted in a recovery of less than 1%. It is simply not good business for a collection agency to invest the time and money necessary for hard collection efforts of small amounts. Also, new laws and restrictions have made their job more difficult than ever before.

SMALL BALANCE COLLECTIONS

Occasionally you will be stuck with an unpaid balance for twenty or thirty dollars. We have had excellent results with a single mailing of a printed slip on red paper that reads as follows: "Our unpaid accounts are referred to the Credit Bureau and the information may be placed in their computer and be available to members throughout the United States.

Please contact us regarding your overdue balance before your account is referred."

You will need to check your local area regarding regulations or laws, but most credit bureaus will accept accounts for collection from nonmembers, so it is not an idle threat. They won't do any better job of collecting than any other collection agency. They may or may not clutter up their computer with the information you send them, but at least the note prompts most of the delinquents to send a check.

SMALL CLAIMS COURT

In some instances, Small Claims Court can be a satisfactory method of collecting balances of $1,000 or less. (Some courts have limits as low as $300 or less.) If the amount to be collected is slightly over the limit, a credit may be issued to reduce the amount so as to be eligible to use the court.

Disadvantages of
Small Claims Court

The principal disadvantage of Small Claims Court is time. Since you are usually the entire management "team," you may incur substantial business losses as a result of your absence. My experience has been that the average uncontested small claims judgment takes about four hours of my business time. Trying to collect on the judgment can take more time.

Considering that the odds of collecting are rarely as good as 50-50, it is often poor business to use the Small Claims Court. In a few metropolitan areas, companies have been set up to do some of the Small Claims work for you. If this service is available, the costs should be weighed against the cost of your own time.

Advantages of
Small Claims Court

1. Court costs are low — usually $5 to $10.
2. Neither plaintiff or defendant may have counsel representation in court.
3. Earlier hearing date.
4. Minimal time spent in court.

Be prepared to make a decision on the use of Small Claims court by contacting your local court for details before the need occurs.

ATTACHMENTS

Before deciding to use attachment as a means of collection, you should consult a lawyer. There have been many recent changes in the laws, both federal and state, governing attachments. Under certain conditions, you may legally attach property, bank accounts, or salaries. You are usually required to put up a deposit to guarantee the cost of the attachment effort. If the effort to collect is unsuccessful, the cost is deducted from your deposit. As in all other business matters, you must weigh the potential cost against the odds and the amount due and make a decision.

WRITE OFF

After you have made reasonable efforts to collect, write the account off and get on with your business. Keep in mind that you are going to have losses when you grant credit. It makes it easier to take calmly if you look at your losses as a percentage of gross sales over a period of several months instead of isolating on one particular loss. Don't make the mistake of sending good money after bad. Measure the effort required to collect against the amount of money that same effort will produce for your business.

CREDIT CARD COMPANIES AND HOW TO GET SET UP

Major national credit cards, which are available for use by most small businesses, are Visa, MasterCard, American Express, Carte Blanche, and Diners Club.

MasterCard and Visa (Bank of America)

These two are the most popular general charge cards. Set-up arrangements are made through your bank. Most banks can now handle both cards with one plate machine and one deposit slip, so you might as well have both if you are going to have one. There is no interest cost to the customer unless payment is extended past the normal due date.

You get your money immediately. The bank takes all of the risk provided you follow the few simple rules established by the card companies. Your cost for the service is either deducted from the amount of each ticket, or you are billed by the bank at regular intervals.

American Express, Carte Blanche, and Diners Club

By far the most popular is American Express.

Cardholders are charged a substantial annual fee for these cards. Arrangements are made with each card company regarding setup, machine usage, and cost. Unless you have a particular need for one of these three, you are better off with only Visa and MasterCard.

Private store cards,
Gasoline credit cards,
Miscellaneous cards

Few quick printers will find it advantageous to have private charge cards. There are, however, miscellaneous charge cards that may fit into a particular area or business. Gasoline credit cards are usually limited to the issuing companies' stations, but arrangements are sometimes made to extend usage to other companies. Not many quick printers will find these arrangements available or advantageous.

Some small businesses follow the practice of accepting certain cards and then billing the customer direct. This is usually poor business. You are taking the entire risk of granting credit to strangers. Your credit loss will be many times the loss of a normal private credit system.

ADVANTAGES & DISADVANTAGES OF CREDIT CARDS

Many quick printers can get by without their own credit department by using one or more credit cards. You have no risk, and you get your money immediately. The cost for the average quick printing business will run 3 to 4 percent. The exact cost is determined by total and average dollar volume of charges. This is usually higher than the cost of operating your own credit system which is the reason that many businesses offer both — credit cards and private charge accounts. You can offer credit card charges to strangers and low volume or high risk customers and handle your own credit on your best accounts. The principal disadvantage of credit cards is cost and the reluctance of many customers to use credit cards for regular business purchases.

CREDIT APPLICATION

Name of Credit Applicant's Firm _____ Date _____

Address _____ Zone _____ Phone _____

Previous Address _____

Type of Business _____ How Long in Business _____

Name & Address of Bank _____

Corporation ____/____ Partnership ____/____ Sole Owner ____/____

Amount of Credit Desired _____ Terms _____

TRADE REFERENCES

1. _____
   Name   Address   Phone

2. _____

3. _____

Home address and telephone number (Not necessary to fill out if company is
         of Owner or Partner   a corporation)

Applicant's signature attests financial responsibility, ability and willingness to pay our invoices in accordance with our terms.

I agree to be personally responsible in case of non payment. Send billing
to _____, (address)

_____ FIRM NAME _____

By _____
        Title

By _____
        Title

CHAPTER 17

TAXES

Our recorded tax laws, rulings, judgments, and opinions fill enough books to literally make a mountain. No human can understand and interpret these laws with any degree of confidence. Big business and wealthy individuals are spending fortunes on noncreative schemes designed for the sole purpose of saving more taxes than the schemes cost.

Individuals and small businesses, with tax liabilities too small to justify the services of a tax attorney, are paying an unfair, and often crippling, portion of the tax bill.

A quick printer cannot afford the services of a profession al tax avoider. Accountants or C.P.A.'s you may hire part-time are involved with too many different types of business to become experts on your particular problems.

One of your most profitable investments in time and money can be bulletins and books on taxes. Every taxing agency publishes bulletins pertaining to tax interpretations. Books by individuals often give more liberal and detailed explanations of tax laws. You cannot just hand your tax problems to someone else and forget them. You need to manage your taxes the same as any other costly function of your business.

FEDERAL INCOME TAX

When the tax auditor calls and says, "I'd like to make an appointment to come in and examine your records," it can be panic time unless you have prepared for this moment over the years. Here's what they usually want to see in a small business:

1. Daily entries of income.
2. Business expenses listed by category.
3. A diary or some other type of record listing entertainment, travel, and miscellaneous expense with all expenditures over $25 backed up by receipts and business purpose verification on entertainment and travel expense.
4. Canceled checks and bank statements.
5. Lease and purchase contracts.
6. Invoices covering purchases of inventory, supplies, and equipment.

7. Depreciation records.

8. Employee records, including withholding deposit records.

If you do not have records or receipts, the I.R.S. can make a judgment of what they think your tax should be and charge penalties and interest on any unpaid amount. If you don't pay, they can get a court order and padlock your door. Last year over 1,100 persons were convicted of criminal tax fraud with less than half going to jail. Almost all criminal investigations were a result of concealing income.

Do you need a tax advisor to represent you at an I.R.S. audit? If you use an accountant or C.P.A. to keep your records or prepare your returns, he should represent you. A strong-willed C.P.A., if you can find one, might stand off an overzealous I.R.S. agent. On the other hand, the only responsibility any sensible accountant or C.P.A. will take is for arithmetic and interpretation. When it comes to interpretation of business expenditures, you might do better arguing your own case.

FEDERAL WITHHOLDING TAXES

Any federal deductions you make from employees' pay must be deposited on a regular basis. Most quick printers make monthly or semi-monthly deposits with a quarterly accounting. The frequency of deposits is determined by the amount deducted. The government won't let you hold onto very much for very long. For exact details, telephone your local I.R.S. office and ask for a "Small Business Packet."

FEDERAL UNEMPLOYMENT TAX
(In addition to State Unemployment Tax)

This is your expense. It is not covered by employee payroll deductions. This is usually paid annually, but more frequent deposits may be required if the amount is large enough. The amount of this tax is a percentage of your total payroll and is influenced by the amount of unemployment tax your particular state charges you.

HELP ON FEDERAL TAX PROBLEMS

Every community has a toll free number to an I.R.S. office where tax questions are answered. This is a valuable service. You can clear up many problems without so much as giving your name. It is a comfort to have a ruling in advance of taking a deduction. If you think the answer you receive might be questioned by an auditor, it will strengthen your case by recording the date and the name of the I.R.S. telephone adviser.

STATE INCOME TAXES

States that have an income tax require the same basic business records as required for federal taxes. Reporting forms are patterned after the federal. There are, however, important differences in every state.

STATE UNEMPLOYMENT TAX

Here's the way it usually works: You pay it all, with no deductions from employees' salaries. The amount you pay is based on the number of people you lay off or fire. But even if you never fire anyone, you still pay about three fourths as much as the maximum. Under certain conditions such as theft, fraud, misconduct, etc., you can fire someone without having your rate go up.

STATE EMPLOYEE DISABILITY PLANS

This is a tax most often paid by the employee, but deducted by you and remitted to the taxing agency.

SALES TAX

In our area a deposit is required of a new business, with the amount of deposit determined by the estimated dollar volume expected of taxable items. Rules regarding sales tax collections and exemptions are usually tricky. Many quick printers have been required to make payments for uncollected sales taxes or for materials purchased under exemptions that did not qualify for an exemption.

I know of several small printers who have been hit with thousands of dollars of back taxes and penalties as a result of purchasing Itek film as a tax exempt item. (California law does not allow exemptions on material that is used in the process of manufacturing that is not delivered to the customer and invoiced separately to the customer. Ink, for instance, can be purchased as a tax exempt item as it is delivered with the paper, but plates, negs, art work, typesetting, etc. are not exempt.) EACH STATE AND LOCALITY VARIES IN THIS REGARD. CHECK LOCAL REGULATIONS CLOSELY.

Most states and cities publish bulletins detailing the

regulations regarding printers, typesetters, photographers, etc. MOST ACCOUNTANTS ARE NOT AWARE OF THE SALES TAX DETAILS THAT AFFECT QUICK PRINTERS. If you use an accountant, be sure you check the tax details for your area and advise your accountant. I have never known of an instance where an accountant was required to pay penalties and back taxes as a result of not knowing the details of the law.

Some quick printers break all jobs down into the portion that is taxable and the portion that is tax exempt and invoice accordingly. The cost of the additional record keeping is not worth it on the size jobs handled by the average quick printer. Most quick printers keep it simple by charging sales tax on everything except for resale customers or others who have a tax exempt certificate.

CITY, COUNTY, STATE TAX RECORDS

Every city, county, and state has some kind of tax such as personal property tax, business tax, solicitation tax, retail tax, and professional tax.

All equipment and inventory is considered "personal property" in many areas. The quick printer usually gets hit with both retail and professional service tax. He is considered a retailer when he sells printing on his stock and a "service" when he prints on the customer's stock.

Check the requirements and keep detailed records. If you do not have records to back up a claim, you have no chance of fighting and winning any of the unjust tax claims that will be billed to you.

LEASED EQUIPMENT TAXES

On leased equipment, the lessor is required to pay taxes on the equipment. In just about every lease, there is a clause allowing the lessor to bill the lessee (you) for any taxes that may be assessed against the equipment.

The lessor has no incentive to fight or even challenge the amount of tax assessed against his equipment as the bill is passed on to you. If the bill is not right, *you* must challenge the error with the taxing agency. The cost of the challenge can often be more costly than the amount of the tax overcharge.

WATCH "DATE" OF PURCHASE

Most taxes are assessed based on ownership on a certain day of the year (in Los Angeles County, it is March 1). Keep this date in mind when leasing, purchasing, or selling equipment.

The tax on one small press may run six or seven hundred dollars if purchased or leased the day after the tax assessment date. There are also federal tax advantages tied in with dates of purchase. Most new quick printers need not worry about this as they probably won't be paying any federal income tax the first year or two anyway.

EXPENSE RECORD

Keep a record of petty cash or other cash expense involving customer entertainment or any unusual expense. If customers are entertained, list their names, business names, and/or business purpose of entertainment.

Federal regulations regarding business entertainment are constantly changing. Review these regulations carefully each year.

CHAPTER 18

PHOTOCOPIES

SHORT HISTORY OF "COPY SHOP"

In the early days of quick printing, most shops were referred to as "copy shops," meaning Itek type offset copies. Some of the shops installed photocopy machines or Xerox and made a good profit at 10 to 25 cents per copy until the Xerox centers opened with three cent copies, no minimum. This price was based on a Xerox minimum of approximately $900 per month on the meter, which averaged out to about 1.2 cents per copy plus toner, paper, and overhead. Of course, we were never quite sure what the actual Xerox price was as they offered us demonstrators, free toner, meter disconnection for a month or more, free copies, and a billing system that a Philadelphia lawyer would have difficulty deciphering.

Most quick printing shop owners felt they were "hooked" on offering some type of photocopy service, but with the new low, low prices, they were caught between a rock and a hard place. If they continued to charge even as much as 10 cents per copy, customers complained about being robbed. If they lowered the price to meet the Xerox copy centers, they lost money.

WHICH ROUTE

High-volume type copy machines are successfully operated by some shops in combination with offset printing, but the majority end up about 80% copy shop and 20% printing. This poses serious volume-related problems for the printing end of the business.

Most successful shops concentrate on one or the other. Personnel requirements make it difficult to combine the two. A copy shop using only Xerox or similar equipment can be staffed with low cost clerks who can wait on customers and run the machines. If these same low cost clerks wait on printing customers, much of your "profitable" printing business will be lost.

It is possible to operate many types of businesses under one roof, but it is usually more profitable to specialize. The fast "copy" business can be difficult to blend with the current, more complicated brand of so-called "quick printing." I recommend that you start out in either one or the other — not both.

PHOTOCOPY PROBLEMS

1. Suppose two people are working your counter, and it has been slow for a couple of hours. Five photocopy customers walk in the door at the same time, all in a rush. At the end of the line is a potential

customer wanting a quote or information on a $300 job. He watches your two counter people busy themselves for five or ten minutes with customers who are spending from five to 75 cents each and decides he is in the wrong place.

2. A big problem with Xerox or any type of photocopy machine is quality. Unlike printing quality, the quality of photocopies goes up and down rather drastically, depending on the condition of the machine. This is something you have very little control over as many of the problems can only be solved by a serviceman. It often takes a half day or more to get a serviceman, even in the heart of a big city. Also, the quality of most machines gradually declines between major overhauls. Your customers notice the difference — especially if they haven't been making copies on a regular basis and they happen to make copies during a good period and the next during a bad period.

3. The quality problem has always been present in all photocopy machines. The problem is not near as critical when the machine is in a private business. They will accept the copy as usable, or will simply throw the copies away, call a serviceman, and place an out of order sign on the copier. The customer of the commercial shop is paying hard cash for each copy. He doesn't want to pay for bad copies.

4. If you are trying to build a quality image with your quick printing, your efforts are often undermined by the low quality photocopies you are forced to sell. Few customers have the time or desire to listen to

reasons — they want results. If they get poor copy, they remember where they got it.

5. A heavy percentage of your photocopy customers never buy any worthwhile quantities of printing. It is surprising to anyone who has not kept records how large this percentage is. It will vary from shop to shop, but it often runs more than 90%.

Included in this high percentage figure will be secretaries who want to get out of the office and visit. (If you have a friendly person on the counter, you can pick up six or seven daily secretary visitors). Also included will be: elderly men and women who have time on their hands and are willing to pay a few cents for a little attention (as much as they can get for as little as they can spend); closing time emergencies that can run thirty minutes to an hour past your dinner time (two or three a week is about normal); customers who will use your counter, white-out, felt-tip pen, paper, advice, and time, make two copies and complain about the price that is ½ cent more per copy than they have seen advertised elsewhere.

6. Fast moving technology presents a problem. Printing equipment and most of the supporting equipment is usually good for at least five years before it is obsoleted by new technology. Photocopy equipment can often be obsolete a year or two after you buy it. (Most photocopy equipment leases are ironclad 3 to 5 year purchase agreements. The ones that are actual month to month rentals are priced so high that you could own the equipment in

about a year at the cost of the rental.) The rapid rate of depreciation or the high rent needed to cover this problem increases your cost more than is normally estimated. Many quick printers are losing much more on photocopies than they realize.

SELF-SERVICE PHOTOCOPIES

Suppose you decide to solve some of the problems with "self-service." You write out detailed operating instructions. You post signs, saying in effect, "You must pay for all copies — good or bad — unless the machine is at fault." There is no nice way to put such a notice, and very few people will pay any attention to it anyway. A customer will set the dial at 3, not noticing the two 00 behind the 3. After 150 copies are run off, he will ask, "Does this thing ever stop? I

only wanted 3 copies." You might stand your ground and decide that your peace of mind and the customer's goodwill can go to the devil — so you demand payment.

The ones who really get you though are the ones who rush in, ignore your detailed instructions, and make ten fast copies with the dial settings wrong.

When they finally look at their ten copies, they scream about the quality and are indignant when asked to pay the few cents involved. It is a problem to have to get involved in a big argument with a customer over fifty cents, especially if a profitable printing customer is standing by.

Self-service customers will often read each page before putting it in the machine, or they will have many small pieces of paper and will go into long and intricate "puzzle fitting" to get as many pieces as possible on each copy. Potential printing or other photocopy customers are boiling while waiting in line.

The problems with self-service are endless — not the least of which is the desire to get something for nothing. Shops where records have been kept have indicated a loss of from 10% to 15% on self-service photocopies.

CHAPTER 19

DELIVERY SERVICE

Unless limits are placed on delivery area and limits on time of pick up and delivery, the demands of customers will far outstrip the benefits. I recommend one pick up and delivery a day with a limit on free pick ups of five miles. A mileage charge for greater distances will limit the requests for long distance hauls.

No extra charge should be placed on special pick ups or deliveries. A customer can understand an extra charge for mileage, but will rarely accept an extra charge for a special trip within your regular delivery area. The best way to limit special trips is to explain that you use part-time help for drivers, and they are available only long enough to make one regular run per day. You need this or some other good excuse to hold this service to an acceptable cost level.

DO NOT ADVERTISE DELIVERY SERVICE

Watch out for this trap. If you list the service in your yellow page ad, you will get calls from an area much farther than you probably want. Mention of free delivery service should also be left off of your flyers. An offer of free delivery will bring you very little new business, a discovery made by many new operators after spending a large portion of their advertising budget on promoting their free pick up and delivery service.

In fact, the mention of free delivery service will drive many economy-minded customers away as they assume a shop not offering these extra services charges less. Also, it is to your advantage to have major customers come into your shop as often as possible. A much closer relationship is built this way than with an ever changing delivery person. You should have the service, but you should not flaunt it.

PROFIT BUILDER IF MANAGED

Unless this service is carefully planned and managed, it can get out of hand, and the expense can be more than the profit it builds. However, without a pick up and delivery service, a shop is at a big disadvantage. Many of the most profitable jobs are jobs that are placed by busy people who do not have the time to shop or the time to bring the job to you and pick it up.

INSURANCE RATES

A delivery vehicle is often driven by employees who are in the highest insurance bracket. It is often assumed that these high rates also apply to commercial drivers in the same age bracket. Actually, the rates are lower in most states as these drivers are not high risks when they are driving in the daytime, alone, and working. Apparently the risk skyrockets when the same drivers go out "on the town" with a load of their peers.

Rates are usually much higher for a truck (even a very small truck) or a station wagon than they are for a car. A hatchback does not require a commercial license (even with signs) in most states, and the insurance rates are much lower than truck rates.

CHAPTER 20

ART DEPARTMENT
PERSONNEL AND BASIC EQUIPMENT

STAFFING WITH ART STUDENTS

A small art department, staffed by art students on a part-time basis, can be one of the most profitable additions for a quick printing shop. Profitable jobs can be obtained that would not be available if the layout had to be jobbed out.

As in most quick printing, it is important that you know what jobs not to take, and before you accept a job, your customer should know that the work will be done by inexperienced art students. You will stay out of a lot of trouble if you advise them in advance not to expect too much.

You won't get any big corporation jobs or even any small advertising company jobs. What you will get is a lot of small merchant or insurance agency brochures and flyers. Many customers have gotten a taste of the business a flyer can produce by mailing out a few home-made jobs or by stealing a competitor's flyer and putting their name on it, but most have neither the time or talent to design and lay up a professional-looking flyer. The first few jobs they produced they thought were great, and they were excited upon seeing their artistic efforts in print. The excitement soon wears off and they become more conscious of crooked lines and rub-on type that doesn't quite fit.

You can hire good art students for $.50 to $1.00 over the minimum hourly wage, and you can limit their working time to take care of your requirements. At those prices, you can have them doing collating, stapling, or odd jobs when they are not busy doing layups.

HOW MUCH "ART"

Not very much real art work. Mostly typesetting, a little clipart, cutting out customer supplied art, and pasteup. Very few college art students can handle the drawing of pictures or the production of special logos. Also, art students come and go, with a year or two about the most you can expect from any one student. If you get a highly talented student who perhaps can handle complicated art, it is still undesirable to accept this type of business on a regular basis. The reason is that if you develop business that depends upon a short-term employee who cannot be replaced, you will be building for a crash when he leaves.

The safe approach is to accept only jobs that are simple and can be handled by the run-of-the-mill art student. You will find there is a great demand for this level of work, and you can easily get a rate of at least three times your labor cost which is a good rule-of-thumb method of arriving at your selling cost for layup work.

QUALITY OF WORK

It can be simple, but it has to be good. Customers will not accept low quality work even if they know it is art student work. Some art students cannot lay up copy to hairline straightness. Others do not have an eye for good balance. You can determine this the first few hours, and it is a talent you cannot develop if they don't have it. Letters should be spaced properly, and any clipart or pasteups that are used must be professional looking. The finished layout must be clean, and even though it is usually done on an 8 1/2 x 11 sheet of paper instead of a regular artist's board, it should be placed in a plastic bag until ready for use. It is better to use a sheet of paper the size of the actual reproduction as it saves time for the artist and is easier to shoot on a direct image camera-processor. Also, an inexperienced artist can visualize the job better if he is doing the layup on the actual size of the finished job.

RECRUITING ART STUDENTS

Unless you have a college close enough for students to work for you part-time, forget about a student staffed art department as high school art students are not skilled enough to handle the job. If you have a college near, it is a simple matter to list your requirements with the student job placement department. Keep a good working relationship with the placement people as you will be using them often, not only for art students, but for other jobs requiring temporary help. Always report back to the placement office after an interview with a student and when the job is filled. If the job is not filled in a week or so, have the card updated as students, unwisely, do not follow up on a card after it has been on the board for a week or so. They figure that if the job is any good, it is taken in a hurry so they often ignore the older cards.

BASIC EQUIPMENT

This is a department where you can start small and add equipment as the department grows. Keep your investment and fixed costs low as this is a part-time department staffed with temporary help. If your fixed costs are low, you have a lot of flexibility, and never forget that flexibility is the biggest advantage a small business has over a large business.

For instance, you may have a new typesetter or commercial artist start up in your area and offer you prices that are lower than your own production costs. Or you may go through a period where you cannot locate an acceptable student artist. If your overhead is low, you can close the department until you can solve the problems, and in the meantime, you can job out the business. You simply adjust your selling price for art work to take care of any added costs you may have from job outs.

You can start out with a small drawing board and a T-square, however, I recommend the following as a basic starting point:

SMALL TOOLS

Pasteup Boards — 11 3/4" x 15 3/4 - 3/8" Plexiglas or equivalent. Boards should be precision cut with square sides so a T-square can be used in both directions. A job prepared on a clear board can be moved to a light table without removing it from the board. It can be worked on a regular desk top or on a drawing table. You can set it aside in favor of a rush job — even take board and all home for finishing on the kitchen table. Boards can be cut to size by most sheet plastic dealers for about five dollars each.

Short T-Square — For using with above-described boards.

Plastic Triangle — For square corners — can be used in connection with T-square.

Centering Rule — Clear plastic.

Steel Ruler

Scissors — A pair of quality 8" dressmaker's scissors.

X-Acto Knife — Or equivalent with a supply of No. 11 blades.

Tweezers — Regular pointed type. Also the self-closing type that open when squeezed (sometimes called soldering tweezers).

Proportional Wheel — For figuring reductions and enlargements.

Waxer — Regular waxers are expensive (about $350), but a hand waxer (about $35) is adequate for most small art departments.

Graphic White — Used with a brush to cover blobs. Works better than the whiteout used for typing.

6H Pencil — This hard-lead pencil can be used for making light grey lines that will not reproduce. Grey lines are easier to see than blue lines.

Non-reproducing Light Blue Pencil — Eagle No. 761 1/2 or equivalent for guide lines.

Black Ballpoint Pen — (Fine) such as "U.S.A. Illustrator" with india ink — can be used for limited ruling. The Bic Roller pen is also a handy pen to have for heavy lines and patching broken type.

Technical Fountain Set — With point sizes of 00, 0, 1, 2 — for ruling lines.

Felt Tip Pen — With pointed tip - black — for filling in or covering white edges of reverses.

White Glue Stick — Handy for sticking pieces to dummy when the waxer isn't hot. (Not recommended for use on camera-ready art.)

Eraser — Soft white rubber (red will foul up pasteup and tiny specks will photograph.)

Burnishing Roller — About 2" wide teflon roller works well.

Masking Tape Dispenser — For 1/2" masking tape.

Magnifier — Sometimes called linen tester.

Line Gauge — For quickly determining the number of lines of type that will fit into a given area.

Cutting Board — You can buy a fancy board that

seals itself, or use a plain old piece of floor linoleum. Glass will quickly dull your X-acto blades.

Rubylith or Equiv. — If you are preparing halftone work where windows are required or doing multicolor screen work.

Frosted Polyester Film — If you are doing overlay work for two or more overlapping colors. Can also be used for lines that cannot be drawn on rough pasteup.

Pasteup Sheets — You can pasteup camera-ready copy on any clean white paper. Recommended types: high quality, dull-coated enamel for good ruling with india ink pens; 110 lb. white index for general pasteup; 10-point Kromekote or similar — inks and rules well and stays clean from handling; 70 lb. white offset where cost of paper is a factor.

Grid Planning Paper — Preprinted with light blue (nonreproducible) ink. The grid can be designed for any type layout. Pica squares with center line is the most popular.

Clear Plastic Grid — With black lines. Can be placed on top of pasteup to check straightness, or used under pasteup on a light table. If grid planning paper is used, it is helpful to have the same pattern on a plastic grid sheet.

Rubber Cement — Handy to have even if you are using a waxer.

Rubber Cement Thinner — Used for cleaning wax from tools and for removing burnished down waxed copy. Squirt a little around the edge of the paper to help peel it off without tearing.

Ammonia — For cleaning technical pens. Soak point for a few moments, shake, and use.

Windex — For cleaning ink from acetate overlays.

There are many other tools sold for pasteup. Some are useful or essential for special work. Most collect dust after an initial trial. The following is a partial list:

Templates — They come in metal and plastic in every conceivable shape and design. A circle and square templates are the most used designs.

Swivel Knife — An X-acto type knife with a small blade that swivels. Handy if you are cutting out intricate designs.

Scale-O-Graph — A device for framing a section of a photograph and scaling it to the desired reproduction size.

Mechanical Drawing Set

Register Marks and Dowels — For overlays or punch systems.

Tissue Pads — For covering pasteup. May be used to indicate color of ink on various segments of copy.

White Correction Tape

Curved Rulers — For drawing lines.

Screen Finder — For determining screen count on halftones.

Revolving Tool Organizer — Holds small tools and pencils.

Etc., Etc., Etc.

Pasteup Supplies — Sometimes difficult to find locally. There are several good mail order suppliers. One that puts out a regular free catalog is: The Printers Shopper, Box 1056, Chula Vista, CA 92012

Books — The best book I have found on pasteup is: "Complete Guide to Pasteup" by Walter B. Graham, Dot Paste-up Supply Co., P.O. Box 369, Omaha, Nebraska 68101.

LARGER TOOLS

Light Table — Approximately 18" x 24".

Headliner — Strip Printer makes the most popular inexpensive headliner. It is easy to operate and can be handled by most art students. It is difficult to job out headlines. Most customers want to select the headline in advance, and if you are using several outside typesetters (they come and go), it is difficult to know in advance what type styles will be available. With a little practice, a student can turn out professional-looking headlines at a fraction of the cost of job outs. You can buy a processor for the Strip Printer film, but for us, bottles that come with the unit are sufficient. Most students will turn out better work with the bottles as they will develop shorter strips and check the work as they go. A processor is O.K. (we started out with one) if you are doing enough work to use it several hours every day, but that is not the case with an instant print art department. Chemicals will keep for weeks in bottles, but need changing every few days in a processor. Of course, a computerized phototypesetter is better as a great variety of fonts and sizes can be keyboarded. (See typesetting chapter for more details.)

Type Fonts for Headlines — When selecting fonts, choose several sizes of basic fonts, including several script fonts. Stay away from exotic styles. They look fantastic, but few students have the talent to use them properly, so it is better to work with plain vanilla type faces.

Body Copy — Finding an art student who is a good speller, good typist, and who can rapidly learn to efficiently operate a typesetter is harder than finding the proverbial needle in a haystack. I recommend that you either job out all body type or hire a permanent typesetter. See chapter on typesetting.

CHAPTERS "ADVANCED ART" AND "ART PREPARATION AND PASTEUP" ALSO HAVE LISTS OF EQUIPMENT USED IN ART DEPARTMENTS.

CHAPTER 21

ART PREPARATION AND PASTEUP

Most quick print jobs are still produced from camera ready copy supplied by the customer. The trend, however, is toward more complicated jobs involving planning and layout. As quick printers gain experience, they tend to move in this direction.

Complicated jobs are not only more profitable, but they add security against a new competitor cutting into your business with price cutting. This type of business is harder to acquire — and harder to lose.

MAKING A LAYOUT OR DUMMY

A rough layout is generally sufficient for a small job, but booklets or pamphlets sometimes require that a dummy be prepared to show the page by page content in rough visual form. A dummy is a book of blank pages showing the position of type and illustrations. In quick printing, a very rough layout is ample if the different departments work closely together.

There are several ways of indicating type areas on the layout or dummy. One of the simplest methods is to rule a square or rectangle on the page to show where the type is to go. Another method is to rule in a series of lines. Wide lines are used for large type and narrow lines for small type.

When proofs or reproductions of illustrations are available, a photocopy may be pasted in the proper positions on the layout or dummy. However, it is generally sufficient to rule in an outline and indicate the photograph or illustration that is to go there.

PRESS LAYOUT SHEET

A press layout sheet, sometimes called a dummy, consists of a blank sheet of stock of the same kind and size as the sheet to be used in printing the job. It is folded just as it will be in the bindery after printing, and the pages are numbered in the proper sequence to show the arrangement of the pages on the plate. It sometimes shows the location of the printed matter and provides other information, such as margins, cut marks, backup, signature marks, and so on.

TIPS ON PREPARING COPY

1. The graphic camera sees dust specks, smears, and dirt spots. Keep originals protected with some kind of cover.

2. Best Colors: The camera sees black and red better than any other colors. If black is overprinted on red, the camera will not see the two colors separately. The best originals are black on white paper or red on white paper. Dark inks such as deep blue, dark brown, orange, or purple can also be seen by the camera.

3. Impossible Colors: Light blue, light yellow, and light green inks are almost impossible for a camera to see.

4. Difficult Colors: Medium green or medium blue can sometimes be photographed by using special filters.

5. Paper Colors: Originals should be on white paper if possible. Light blue, light yellow, or light green paper with black or red ink is O.K., but red, purple, tangerine, and orange papers are usually impossible. Pink and goldenrod with solid black or red ink can usually be photographed.

6. Typewritten Copy: Always use a fresh black ribbon with clean typefaces. Cloth ribbons that are not new will not produce sharp copy. Strike each letter firmly. A carbon ribbon gives much better results than a cloth ribbon.

7. Typeset Copy: Watch for smearing, misalignment, round corners on letters, gray letters, off-white background, nicks, or light spots.

KINDS OF COPY

All artwork falls into one of three general classifications: line, tone, or combination.

Line copy consists of typewritten material, reproduction proofs, clippings, lettering, pen-and-ink drawings, and any other artwork which will appear as lines or solid blocks of color without gradations in tone.

Tone copy (sometimes called "continuous tone") consists of watercolor drawings, oil paintings, photographs, and other types of work composed of a series of tones that blend together without clear-cut divisions. In order to preserve the shadows and tones found in this type of copy, the cameraman must photograph it through a ruled screen. The screen breaks up the image into a series of tiny dots. These dots are so small that they blend together to give the appearance of continuous tone. This process is known as "halftoning."

Combination copy, as the name implies, is art that consists of both tone and line work, as for example, a photograph to which lettering and arrows have been applied. To reproduce the photograph as tone and the lettering and arrows as line, the cameraman must make two negatives or stats — one for the line and one for the tone. These negatives or stats are then stripped or fitted together to produce a combination image when the plate is printed.

LINE WORK

Line drawings ordinarily print only as lines and solid blacks, but if shading is required, you can supply it by such methods as crosshatching with pen and ink or by sticking a sheet of patterned acetate over the area that is to be shaded. (See Fig. A.)

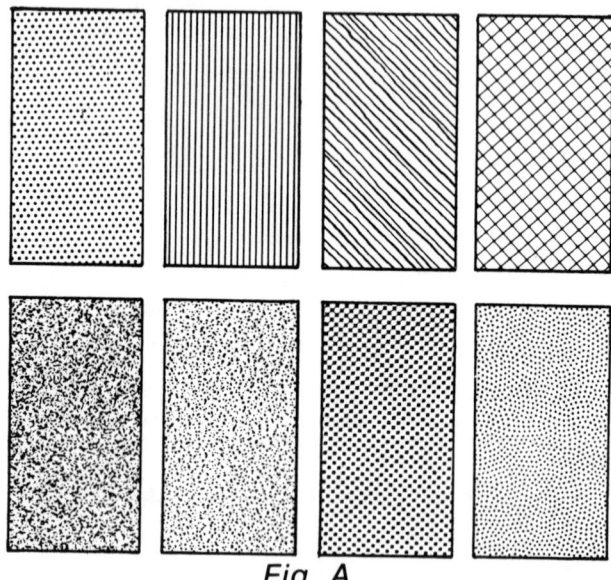

Fig. A

TIPS ON USING SHADING FILM

1. Surface where benday is to be applied must be clean — free of specks.

2. Edges of pasteups will often create a reproducible shadow when overlayed with shading film. To avoid this, make a stat of the pasteup and place the shading film on the smooth surface of the stat.

3. Avoid wrinkles and bubbles in the shading film by

lightly rubbing the overlayed copy with your fingers. Eliminate bubbles with a pin — then finish with a light burnishing.

PREPARING LINE DRAWINGS

Line drawings are generally done on white paper with black india ink. Glossy paper, such as Kromekote or Lusterkote, provide an advantage when ruling lines with india ink.

Dark blue and red ink will also reproduce fairly well, but pale colors such as light blue, gray, or yellow should not be used. Nor should you prepare original drawings on colored papers. Some colors photograph as black or gray, making it difficult for the cameraman to separate the drawing from the background when he makes the negative, stat, or direct image offset plate.

Most line copy is shot same size or smaller. Enlargement magnifies defects and gives line work a crude appearance.

PASTEUP CORRECTIONS

Corrections are usually made by **over-mounting.** If wax is used, small pieces may be pasted over incorrect copy without the need to clean the edges. Rubber cement must be cleaned from the edges of the pasteup or the exposed cement may photograph as a line around the pasteup area. Cleaning away rubber cement can pose a problem with small pieces. The gum eraser or "pickup" pulls the rubber cement out from under a small piece when the edges are cleaned. If overmounting pasteups are done on galleys of phototype or other thin paper, a light table can be used to line up the new copy.

Mortised corrections must be used when correcting film and is used by some pasteup artists for all insert type corrections. Mortising is accomplished by cutting through both the original and the corrected copy with an exacto knife or razor blade. A window is thereby created in the original. The correct copy is placed in the window and held in place with a clear piece of tape on the back of the original.

Computer typesetting corrections. Many quick printers are now using computerized typesetters. They will often rerun a new corrected section of a galley from the computer memory rather than make time-consuming pasteup corrections.

ILLUSTRATION BOARD OR PAPER

Camera-ready copy prepared for film negatives and metal plates is usually mounted on heavy illustration board with tick marks showing where corners are located. (See illustration B.) If more than one plate is to be shot, as with multiple color work, registration marks are placed outside of the copy area.

The heavy board protects the copy from stretch, wrinkles, and bending that may cause small pieces of copy to flip off. A sheet of tissue protects the copy from dirt and allows notations to be made indicating changes or camera procedures.

Cardboard mounted copy presents a problem with photo-direct plates. A film negative is straightened when it is stripped onto a goldenrod sheet. Photo-direct copy must be placed on the copyboard straight or it will be out of line on the plate, causing a loss of press time. Therefore, it is advantageous to prepare photo-direct copy on a sheet of paper or thin board cut to the size of the reproduction. This makes it much easier for the camerman to place the copy on the camera-platemaker in the correct position.

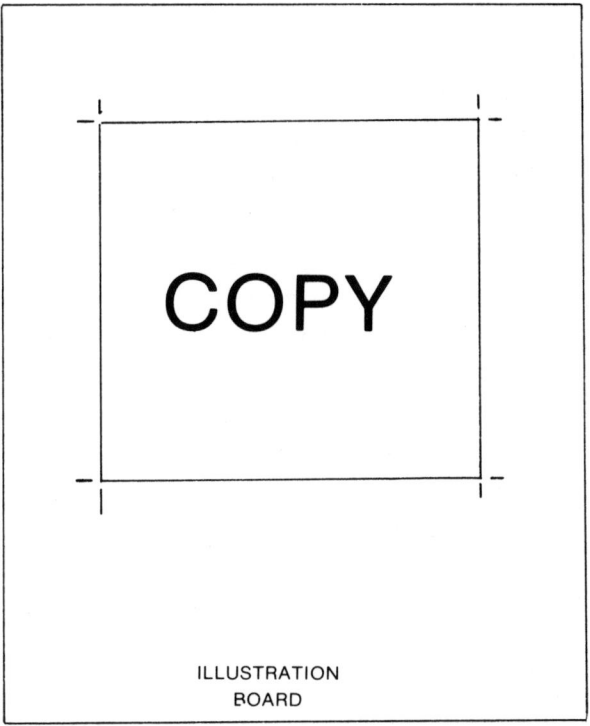

COPY

ILLUSTRATION
BOARD

Figure B

CLIPPINGS AND PHOTOGRAPHIC PRINTS

When original artwork is not available, you can use clippings of previously printed line drawings as copy. However, if the clippings have been printed in color or if they are printed on colored paper, you should consult your cameraman before submitting them. He can sometimes reproduce color by photographing it through a filter. A filter is a disk (or square) of colored glass, gelatin, or acetate which makes some colors photograph darker and others lighter than the original copy. In some cases, the filter will cancel out the background color, making it photograph as white. In other cases, it will not be possible for the filter to separate the background from the copy, and it will be necessary for you to make a new drawing in black and white.

You can also use sharp, glossy photographic prints of original line drawings or clippings as copy. You may retouch these photographic prints with ink or with black and white watercolors. Smudge marks and fuzziness may be painted out with chinese white, and broken or grayed areas may be sharpened and filled in with india ink.

PRODUCTION SHORTCUTS

You can produce a line drawing by tracing over a photograph with pen and ink and then having the photographic image bleached out so that only the inked lines remain.

RULING FORMS

Regular drafting tools are used for ruling forms with pen and ink. These tools include such items as a drawing board or drafting table, a T-square, plastic triangles and curves, a line gauge, a metal ruler, pencils and erasers, drawing and tracing paper, a compass, dividers, knives, razor blades, scissors, and rubber cement or hot adhesive wax.

DRAFTING TOOLS

Drawing boards are generally made of pine or some other soft wood, however, many quick printers prefer a 3/8" thick **Plexiglas board,** square cut to approximately 11" x 16."

The **T-square** consists of a long strip called the "blade" and a cross strip called the "head." (See Fig. C.) When the head is butted against the side of the drawing board, the blade is squared (at right angles) with the edge of the board. You can use the T-square for drawing lines and for squaring up work on the sheet. You can also use it as a base for the triangle when you are drawing vertical and slanted lines.

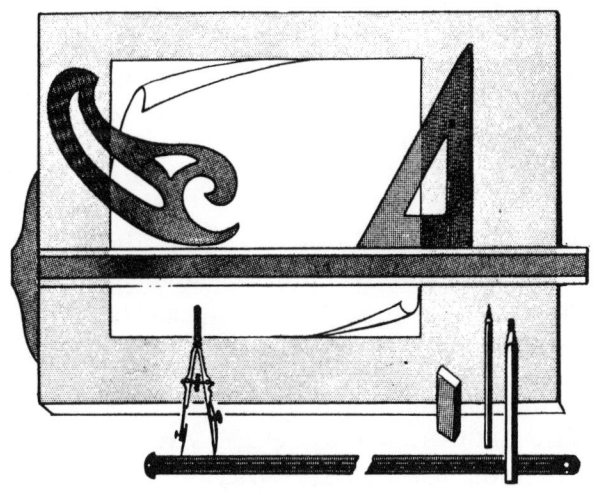

Figure C

Another useful device is the **steel straightedge.** It is essentially the same as the T-square, except that it has no head. You may use it for drawing long, straight lines, but it is primarily intended as a guide when you are cutting with a knife.

You should never use a knife or razor blade with plastic drafting tools.

Plastic triangles, like the one shown in Fig. C, are used for drawing vertical and slanted lines. To draw vertical lines, you simply move the T-square to the proper horizontal position and then place the base of the triangle against the blade. You can then draw the vertical line along the side of the triangle.

French curves are used for drawing all sorts of noncircular curves. Actually the french curve is composed of a series of curved sections. Occasionally one of these sections will exactly match the curved line that you wish to use, and you can draw your line by simply tracing around the curved area. But more often, you will have to fashion your curve by shifting the guide as you go along.

You can use the **compass** for drawing circles and arcs. Some compasses have interchangeable parts so that you can use the same instrument for either pencil or ink drawings. Ink compasses are handled much the same as a ruling pen.

Dividers are similar to compasses except that both legs of the dividers are provided with needle points. They are used for transferring measurements and for dividing lines into equal parts. In layout work, you will find them especially useful in centering headings and checking margins.

Drawing pencils range from 6B (soft and black) through HB (medium) to 9H (very hard). You can use soft pencils, such as 2B or 3B for making heavy, thick lines, but hard pencils should be used for making guide lines and writing in instructions. Drawing pencils do not have erasers. **Art gum** or kneaded gum erasers are generally used for making corrections and for cleaning smudges and dirt from the surface of the drawing paper.

Most artists use **light blue pencils** for preliminary and base drawings. It is not necessary to erase blue lines after the sketch has been inked in as they will drop out during the photographing operation if they have been applied with a light touch. This is especially important when preparing camera-ready art for a photo-direct camera/platemaker.Even the lightest blue pencil will reproduce if applied with a heavy hand. Red lines photograph as black; other colors vary.

Tracing paper is a thin, tough, semitransparent paper which is available in pads or rolls of varying sizes. Artists generally prepare rough layouts on tracing paper and then transfer them to the regular drawing paper where they are used as a basis for the finished art.

Ruling pens are used for ruling lines of uniform widths. They should be used with T-squares, triangles, and other guides; they should never be used for freehand work. A ruling pen, like that shown in Fig. D will produce lines of various widths, depending on the set of the thumbscrew which separates or brings the blades of the pen together.

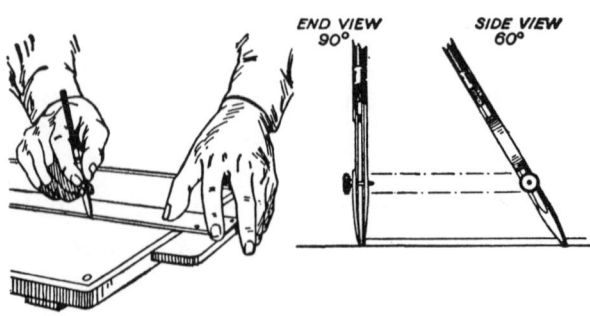

Figure D — Ruling pen. Setscrew regulates the width of the line.

Do not place the ruling pen into the bottle of ink. To fill the pen, you should use the dropper in the top of the bottle.

Put ink between the two points of the pen and keep the outside wiped clean to prevent the ink from running. Always keep your ruling pen clean when it is not in use. A dirty pen will produce a ragged line.

You should hold the ruling pen so that the setscrew is away from you. The pen should be almost upright with a slight tilt in the direction you are drawing.

You should square the sheet on the drawing board or table with the T-square. Then fasten the paper to the board with draftsman's masking tape, a brown crinkly paper that peels off readily without injuring the surface of the drawing paper.

Pencil in outlines lightly, using the T-square for all horizontal lines and the triangle for all vertical lines. After the outline has been carefully laid out in pencil, go over it with the ruling pen. Once the form has been inked in, you can remove the sheet and type in the copy. Of course, if you prefer, you can type the copy on a separate sheet of paper and cut it out and paste it into place after the boxes have been inked in. You may also type the copy on the sheet before you rule in the form.

KEEP IT CLEAN

Line drawings are not as critical as tone copy. In halftone work, every smudge, brush stroke, pasteup shadow, or even a fingerprint may show up on the printed sheet. But in line work, only the blacks will print. Shadows and other defects may be burned out during photographing, or they may be painted out afterwards on the negative, provided they do not fall within tone areas.

SCALING

The same system that you use to scale copy for reduction may be used for scaling photographs. When the width of a photograph is increased or decreased, the height is also increased or decreased proportionately. Customers often specify both height and width that are not in proportion with each other. This can be accomplished to a degree with a distortion lens which is not standard equipment in the quick printing business.

Scaling is usually done with a scaling wheel (circular slide rule), or any one of many patented devices available. Instructions for the use of these devices are usually printed on the face of the dials.

TONE DRAWINGS

Tone drawings are generally prepared for one-half or one-third reduction. In preparing them, you should use the same rules for scaling, marking, and so on, that you use in working with photographs.

Tone drawings should be crisp and sharp. If they are flat and lacking in strength, they will not reproduce properly. Wash drawings are generally done with lampblack and water on a white drawing paper having a slight tooth.

It is better not to do drawings for black-and-white reproduction in colors—especially showcard colors, because these colors usually appear muddy and photograph as either too dark or too light.

It is difficult to copy colored photographs, oil paintings, and pastel drawings for black-and-white reproduction because the colors do not photograph true. Film emulsions are more sensitive to some colors than they are to others, and consequently some colors photograph too dark while the others photograph too light. To help balance the colors, the cameraman often photographs colored copy through a filter. Filters alter color values making some colors photograph darker and others lighter than the original copy.

Crayon drawings generally give good reproduction. Charcoal and pencil drawings are sometimes difficult to copy.

CLIPPINGS

When original drawings or photographs are not

available, good glossy photographs of original drawings may be used as copy. Clippings or photographs of clippings of previously screened halftones may also be used. If the halftone dots in the clipping are coarse, the cameraman may be able to copy the clipping as a line shot. But if the original screen was fine and the dots are indistinct, the clippings must be rescreened and the copy should be marked "halftone." Clippings never reproduce as well as the original copy. When clippings are rescreened, the dots from the old screen often overlap the new dot formation to form a disturbing pattern called moire.

TRANSPARENCIES

A transparency is a photograph printed on glass or film, sometimes in color and sometimes in black and white. Transparencies have wide use in color separation work, but they are used less often as copy for black-and-white reproduction. To make a negative from a transparency, the cameraman places it in direct contact with the emulsion side of a piece of film and exposes the two to a weak, diffuse light. Transparencies may also be placed in a light box and copied with the camera.

SPECIAL EFFECTS

You may inject additional interest into a page by the use of oversize or bleed illustrations, insets, or combinations of tone and line.

BLEED ILLUSTRATIONS

A bleed illustration is one that has no margin of

white space between it and the edge of the paper. In other words, it runs off the page. An illustration may bleed on all sides or it may bleed only on one, two, or three sides.

When an illustration is to bleed, it must be marked so that after reduction, it will be at least 1/8" wider and higher than it is to appear after the page has been trimmed. Since some of it will be cut off when the page is trimmed, you must see that nothing important comes too close to the edge of the copy.

Since bleed illustrations usually require larger paper stock and need considerably more care in production, they are more costly and are seldom used by quick printers.

INSETS

An inset is a small picture inserted into a larger one. To accomplish this on a film negative, you should crop the inset and indicate the area on the larger photograph where it is to go by rubber cementing a piece of black paper (the size of the inset) to the larger photograph. This will produce a transparent area in the negative of the larger photograph which will enable the stripper to position the inset visually. If the inset is to be enlarged or reduced in size, you must scale it accurately so that it will fit the space allotted. Attach a tissue overlay sheet to the photograph and write in on the overlay exact instructions for the cameraman and stripper.

Quick printers often use prescreened stats, in which case the smaller prescreened photo is trimmed and pasted onto the larger prescreened photo.

COMBINATION COPY

When lettering or other line work is to be combined with a photograph (or any kind of tone drawing), the photograph should be mounted first on a piece of cardboard. You can then cut out the type and paste it directly on the photograph or you can attach an acetate overlay to the photograph and paste the type on the overlay.

Pasting the type directly on the photograph is more economical than the overlay method because it enables the cameraman to shoot the entire job as a straight halftone. However, it has two disadvantages.

1. The lettering in the finished cut is likely to be fuzzy and indistinct since it will be broken up by the halftone screen.
2. Shadow lines may appear in the finished illustration around the pasted-up areas, and there is no way to remove these shadows.

Therefore, when you are looking for quality, you should prepare your line copy on the acetate overlay and mark the job "surprint."

When lettering or artwork is done on an overlay, the overlay should be keyed to the photograph (master) with register marks to aid in proper positioning.

REVERSE COMBINATIONS

When you wish to reverse the type so that it will print white against a black background, you should mount a good reproduction proof or a line of paste-up lettering of the desired type face on a sheet of stiff drawing paper and draw a border in red ink to indicate the dimensions of the black area. Then instruct the cameraman to make a positive from the type.

Reverse lettering is available on some models of phototypesetters.

COLOR WORK

(See chapter on "Color Printing" for more details.)

A simple black-and-white drawing is all that is required if the colors do not overlap. To guide the cameraman in making the color separation, you should attach a tissue overlay to the original drawing and fill in on the tissue with colored pencils all the areas that are to be in color.

The cameraman will then shoot as many negatives from the original as necessary to reproduce the number of colors desired. Then, using the overlay as a guide, he will make his color separations by masking out on each negative all but the areas that are to print in one particular color. From these masked-out negatives, he will make the plates for each color.

Photo-direct separations are made by cutting a mask out of a sheet of white paper.

CENTERING RULE

The Graham color coded centering rule has color patches in relative position on each side of zero. Three picas to the left of zero and three picas to the right, the color is blue; the next three picas the color is yellow, then red, then green. When you place the rule under a line of type, merely adjust the color patches and you quickly find the center.

The Graham rule is sold by graphic supply houses, and we have found it to be one of our most useful pasteup tools. We made a second one out of a clear plastic ruler with a pica grid on it. Black marks placed on the ruler 4 1/4" from both sides of center speeds centering on the often used 8 1/2" wide paper.

GRIDS AND PLEXIGLAS BOARDS

One of the handiest devices for pasteup is a clear plastic grid ruled with vertical and horizontal lines spaced one pica apart.a grid can be used throughout the shop for positioning copy or checking alignment before making a negative or plate. Some pressmen use grids to check press alignment of copy and plates. A grid fastened to a hand cutter can be used to check the straightness of copy on photo-direct plates. The cutter trims the end of the plate square with the copy, speeding press alignment.

We use several grids permanently hinged with tape to a 3/8" thick 12" x 16" square cut Plexiglas board (or similar plastic). The grid is taped square with the edges of the board and the copy is lined up with the grid so a T-square can be used when the grid is hinged back. The Plexiglas board can be used on a light table, eliminating the necessity of removing and replacing the copy. Board, grid, and job can be used at a regular desk or carried home and used at a kitchen table. An 8 1/2 x 11 outline on the grid allows fast placement of a base sheet of paper for pasteup.

The base sheet, on which pasteup pieces are placed, can be taped in place. We find it handier to keep a patch of wax on the board under the area where the base sheet will be placed. A small amount of wax will adhere to the base sheet, but not enough to cause problems. We use a thin sheet of clear plastic to cover the wax patch on the Plexiglas board when the wax is not needed.

On repetitive jobs, such as lining up copy for book pages, small pieces of masking tape placed next to lines on the grid will guide and speed the positioning of copy.

ROUNDING CORNERS OF BORDERS

Draw your border with the usual 90° corners. Use the same pen point to draw a circle (use a template or compass). Cut the circle into four equal parts and paste on each corner. The lines will match and be undetectable when printed. (See illustration E.)

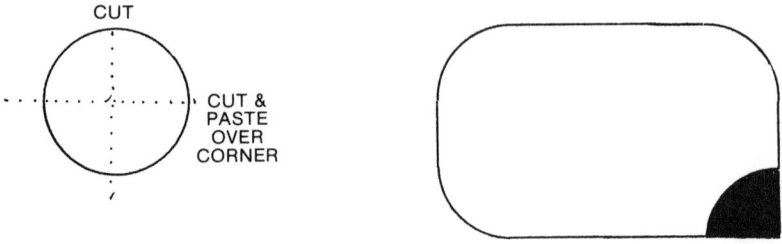

Figure E

SPREADS AND CHOKES

Hairline register is difficult to maintain on most models of quick printing type presses. Occasionally, however, you may want to print color inside of an open outline letter. By "spreading" the inside color so it will overlap the outside color (or "choking" the outside color), you simplify the problem of register.

A spread can be made on film and metal plates by making a contact positive from the original negative. A clear sheet of film placed between the negative and the new film will cause the image to spread. The new negative is then used to produce the color plate. Any contact printer or vacuum frame with a constant light source can be used.

A choke is made in the same manner, but a film positive is first made from the negative. A clear sheet of film between the positive and unexposed film will cause the image to shrink, or "choke."

PMT TYPE STATS

PMT (Photo Mechanical Transfer) is the trade name for Kodak diffusion-transfer material. Diffusion transfer prints (PMT and other brands) can be pasted up and photographed onto printing plates with camera/processors.

A darkroom, simple process camera and an inexpensive one-chemical processor is required. Running water is useful, but not essential. The stat will yellow if not rinsed, but a tray of water or even a squirt bottle will do the job.

The principal uses of PMT are for precise copies (enlargements or reductions) of originals and for halftoning stats that can be used in pasteups. Photo-direct plates can be made from halftoned stats, eliminating the dependence on film negatives and metal plates.

RUBBER CEMENT AND WAX

Always use rubber cement or wax for pasting up copy—never use glue. Rubber cement, which is actually rubber dissolved in a solvent, should be of the proper consistency to adhere to the paper surface without penetrating or staining it. If the cement is too thick, you can thin it with cement thinner. It is needless to add that rubber cement is flammable, so don't try to dry it by holding a match under the copy.

Rubber cement has certain characteristics that make it especially suitable for pasteup work. It is tacky enough to hold the copy in place, yet it doesn't set hard like glue. You can peel the copy up and remove it if necessary without a great deal of damage or effort.

You can apply rubber cement to the back of the copy and position the copy on the illustration board before the cement dries, or you can apply the cement to both the copy and the drawing paper and allow both to dry before positioning the copy. You will find that dried rubber cement surfaces still have an affinity for each other. Attach one corner of your copy to the illustration board and then align it with the T-square before pasting it down.

After the copy has been mounted on the drawing paper, you should clean up the layout with a ball of dried rubber cement and an art gum eraser. The ball will pick up the excess rubber cement and the eraser will remove smudges and dirt.

WAXING MACHINE

A waxing machine should be turned on at the beginning of each day and turned off at the end of the day. As soon as it heats sufficiently to melt the wax, it is ready for use. Copy is fed face up through two rollers on the machine. The lower roller carries the wax and waxes the bottom of the copy.

Wax has several advantages over rubber cement. It is quicker to apply and it is easier to move the copy in case you mount it in the wrong place on the layout and later have to move it to another area.

Most quick printers use hand waxers which are adequate for small quantities of work.

PROOFING

Most quick printing proofing is done with photocopies. If original pasteups are given to customers, they will often damage elements that are costly to reproduce.

Silver prints, sometimes called "brown prints," require a film negative. The negative is exposed to silver print paper and developed to produce a print (blue line paper is often used).

3M makes a "color key" which is a colored negative material. A film negative is contacted onto the color key, providing a film positive in color. Basic colors are available. Color key is also available in "process" colors. Overlapped colors are used for proofing process color jobs, avoiding the cost of press proofs.

CHAPTER 22

ADVANCED ART

Quick Printers with special art talents are finding profitable markets for these talents within the scope of quick printing. Most commercial artists prefer to work with customers who require a large volume of complicated printing. They often specify exotic papers, close register multiple colors or process color, matching inks, bleeds, large solids, and other requirements beyond the normal range of quick printing. That's the only market where an artist can sell his talent for an adequate price.

There is, however, a great demand for complicated drawings and designs that can be printed on normal quick printing equipment. An artist who is an owner or manager of a quick printing shop can benefit by adapting complicated art to quick printing requirements. He may not be able to make a living on art alone, but his art can greatly increase the profit of his quick printing business.

Quick printers with even a "flare" for art can attract customers who will pay extra for layups that have a bit of imagination, balance, and attractive use of type styles and sizes.

This chapter is intended as a guide to quick printers interested in doing more advanced pasteup and design.

TYPES OF LAYOUTS

The tenor of the copy enters into the picture when you are planning your design. Work of a serious or dignified nature generally calls for a formal layout, but you can use informal layouts for other types of work.

Formal layouts follow the simple rules of good composition involving harmony, balance, proportion, and contrast. They utilize type set in inverted pyramids, rectangular blocks, and fluctuating-line arrangements. They give the job a pleasingly balanced, though static quality. It is their beauty and symmetry that attract the eye.

Informal layouts make use of off-centered arrangements, geometric contours, and mixed typefaces. They depend for interest on freshness and motion. (See Fig. A.)

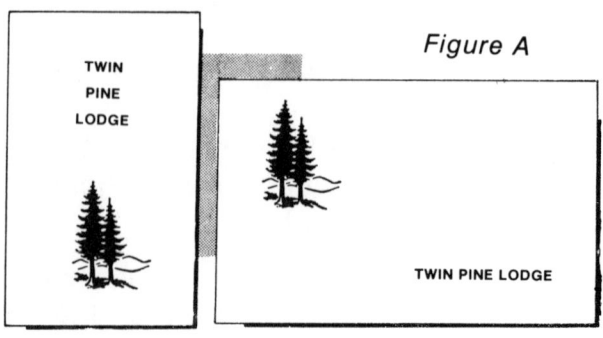

Figure A

BALANCE

Balance is a factor in both formal and informal layouts. It is controlled by the size and shape of the elements, their tone (lightness or boldness), and their placement in relation to the optical center of the job. The optical center rather than the actual center is used in printing because the eye normally strikes the page about two-fifths of the way down and slightly to the left of center. Any element placed in the optical center of the page will receive the maximum of attention and will be pleasingly positioned, while an element placed in the exact center will look as if it were below the center of the page. (See Fig. B.)

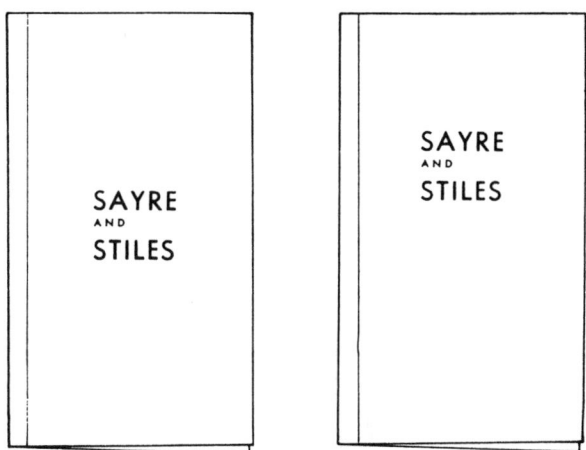

Figure B. Note how copy in the center of page looks like it is below center.

PROPORTION

Balancing the layout is not enough. A good printing job, like a pretty girl, must have pleasing proportions if it is to attract and hold the attention of the eye. The proportions (relation of width to depth) of a page are more interesting when the page is laid out in a rectangular form. The various elements of the job, such as blocks of type, cuts, and white space, should also follow these same general proportions.

Any job will lack interest if you use two main elements that are equal in size and shape. Such a job not only lacks variety, but it also forces the eye to compare the two areas. The example in Figure B₁ shows how the design is improved when one of the elements is made smaller, say two-thirds the size of the other.

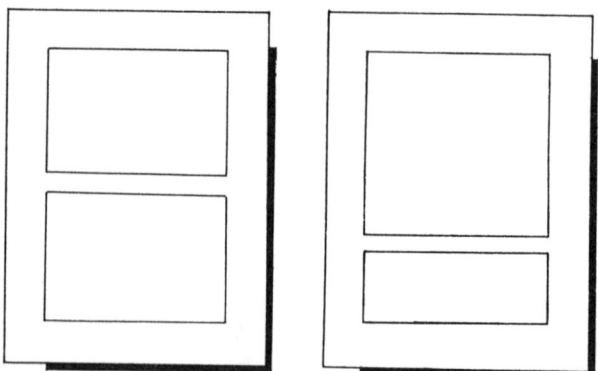

Figure B₁ The same size rectangles on the left forces the eye to compare the two areas.

Similarly, if the layout contains three elements, one should be large, one small, and one somewhere in between. But none of them should be of a size that is a simple multiple of either of the others.

These same principles of proportion apply to the spacing between the border and type and to the distribution of white space between the various elements of the job.

CONTRAST

Contrast is the element that makes some of the tones, shapes, and sizes stand out from the others.

You can obtain contrast through the use of large and small typefaces and light and dark faces. The use of italics with upright type will also provide a form of contrast, and so will a variety of shapes.

Contrast is achieved by grouping related lines into type blocks. Grouping the lines in this manner relieves monotony and sets up a contrast between the type and white space.

Variations in contour also add punch to the design. Contrast in the length of lines is almost as important as grouping. If the lines are nearly all the same length, it will be difficult for the eye to pick out the most important elements even though they are set in a bolder type.

HARMONY

In printing, if every heading is set in a different style of type and if every element has its own unique style and shape, the results are certain to be displeasing.

Proportions of the blocks of type should harmonize with the proportions of the page. But harmony goes farther than that. It also enters into the choice of typefaces, cuts, and borders. In selecting a typeface, you should try to pick one that will match the subject matter of your copy. And in addition, you should select faces that look good together and match the weight of the lines in the illustrations.

Always choose borders that follow the tone values of the type and illustrations. Don't use a heavy border with a lightface type, and vice versa. Certain borders are designed to go with certain styles of type, and you will get better results if you try to match them.

TECHNIQUES

Some of the techniques used by artists, in addition to ordinary pen and ink work, in preparing line drawings are:
1. Brush and ink.
2. Dry brush drawing — the artist works on rough paper and uses very little ink in his brush.
3. Crayon and ink on a special type of drawing board which has a pebbled surface. Little dots provide a shaded effect similar to that produced by the acetate shading sheets. Ross board is the trade name for the paper. Drawings done on Coquille board are similar in appearance.
4. Scratchboard drawing. Scratchboard is a type of drawing paper which has a smooth, clay surface. The artist first coats the paper with ink and then scratches highlights in the clay surface with a knife. This produces a woodcut effect.

5. Craft-tint. The surface of this paper is chemically impregnated with an invisible line or dot pattern. The artist first makes a black-and-white line drawing on it in the regular manner and then brushes the areas that are to go in tone with an acid developing solution. This solution brings out the patterns or tones. Craft-tint papers come in single-tone or double-tone patterns. The double-tone patterns require two developers.

6. Acetate shading sheets. These sheets are available in various patterns. They are waxed on one side so that they can be applied directly to the drawing paper. After positioning the sheets, the artist cuts along the edge of the tone areas with a knife and removes the trim. This process of applying the tone is generally referred to as "applying benday." Benday is a generic term used for all tone effects. It is named after Ben Day, the man who developed the process for applying shading to letterpress cuts. Some of these mechanical shading sheets are known by such trade names as Zip-a-tone, Paratone, Art Type, and Visi-type.

Shading sheets should not be applied to areas where the copy is dirty or patched over, because dirty or patched copy sometimes produces shadows or other defects when it is photographed.

The cameraman can produce tone on film by photographing a sheet of white paper through a halftone screen. These tone negatives are then superimposed on or stripped into the master negative in the areas indicated on the overlay.

TONE COPY

The artist can introduce flat, gray tones into his line drawings by the use of shading sheets. The shading sheet dots or lines print as solid and are just as black as the darkest portions of the copy. But since they have white space around them, they look gray. (The eye mixes the white with the black and subdues its color.) Printers rely on this optical illusion for producing tints and tones in single-color printing.

Benday shading process generally produces flat, gray tones because the dots are all the same size. (See Fig. C.) As you can see in the illustration, if some of the dots are made larger than the others, they will appear darker. This is because the larger dots cover more of the paper and there is less white space between them. The halftone process is based on this principle.

BENDAY - All dots are same size.

HALFTONE- Small and large dots.

Figure C.

You cannot accurately reproduce the many half shades and tones found in photographs with solid blacks and flat, gray benday shadings. To reproduce a photograph accurately, you must break the entire copy into a series of dots. And the dots must be of varying sizes so that some will appear darker than the others and thus produce an uneven or graduated tone like that found in the original.

The cameraman breaks the copy into dots by photographing it through a screen having a series of crosslines. These crosslines form a pattern that breaks up the light as it passes through the camera, causing it to register on the film as a series of small individual dots, each varying in size according to the amount of light being reflected from the copy at that particular point. Like the benday shadings, these dots blend together to produce an overall gray tone. But since these dots are of varying sizes, they produce a series of tones ranging from light gray to black.

Tone copy includes, besides photographs, drawings rendered in pencil, crayon, charcoal, wash, watercolor, tempera, oil, and airbrush.

PHOTOGRAPHS

The requirements for tone drawings and photographs are similar. They should be crisp, sharp, and clear. Glossy photographic prints are better for reproduction purposes than dull (matte-finished) prints. Blurred and faded prints will not reproduce properly and should not be used.

RETOUCHING

It is often necessary to retouch photographs to bring out the details desired, to paint out objectionable backgrounds, or to heighten contrast between blacks and whites.

Retouching is generally done with a regular watercolor brush and retouch watercolors, which consist of seven shades of gray as well as chinese white and lampblack. You can mix them to match the color of the photograph. The colors should tend toward brownish rather than bluish tones.

If the surface of the photograph is not receptive to watercolors, you should rub it with a piece of cotton and a powder called fuller's earth.

Retouching must be done with the process of reproduction in mind, since coarse halftone screens necessitate greater contrasts of light and shade. If the cameraman uses a fairly coarse screen when he copies the original, the dots will be large and part of the detail will be lost. Therefore, you needn't worry about faint brush marks as they will be lost in screening. But if the screen is fine, the brush marks may show up in the finished job. With a little experience, you will be able to tell what will reproduce and what will not.

RETOUCHING WITH THE AIRBRUSH

Perfectly smooth backgrounds may be had through the use of an airbrush, a delicate watercolor spray gun about the size of a fountain pen. (See Fig. D.)

Thinned retouch color is placed in the color cup of the airbrush which is attached to a hose from an air compressor. When the air-control lever is depressed, the air escapes through the point, siphoning the color from the color cup, and with the aid of the needle, shooting it out in a fine spray, like an atomizer.

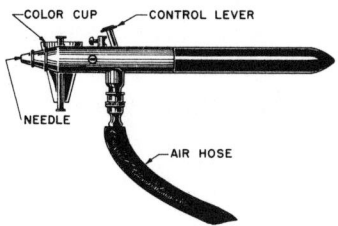

Figure D. Air brush is a very delicate spray gun used for illustrations and photograph retouching.

Airbrushing is particularly useful for retouch work on photographs having a cracked or damaged emulsion. The airbrush is also useful in preparing photomontage work. A photomontage is a group of separate photographs pasted together to produce a single picture. After they have been pasted up, they are rephotographed and the new print is retouched with the airbrush to blend them all together.

PHOTOGRAPHS SHOULD BE MOUNTED

Photographs should never be rolled or folded. They should be mounted on stiff cardboard. Polaroid photographs should not be mounted with rubber cement, as it is liable to damage the photograph. Some types of glue will also damage photographs after a period of time. You can use wax to mount all types of photographs provided you are equipped with a waxing machine.

Halftones are generally designated as square finish or outline. Square finish halftones are the conventional square or rectangular forms that you see used every day. Outline halftones are those in which the background has been cut away or eliminated. (See Fig. E.) The vignette is another type of finish which has soft, feathered outlines that blend into the surrounding white space of the page. Although they were once very popular, vignettes are seldom used today.

Square finish

Outline

Vignette

Figure E. Methods of printing halftones.

CROPPING

When you want to reproduce only a portion of a photograph, you should crop (mark off) the unessential parts. You can mark the margins of glossy prints with grease pencil or ink. Some cameramen prefer copy that has been marked with ink since the grease pencil tends to come off on the glass of the copyboard when the job is photographed. Grease pencil marks may be removed later with a dry cloth or eraser. It is difficult to completely remove the ink marks, but you can lighten them with a damp cloth or eraser.

When a section of a valuable photograph or of a dull, matte-finish print is to be reproduced, you may mask it off by covering the whole picture with a sheet of paper and cutting a window to expose the desired area. If the photograph is to be reduced or enlarged, the exact width should be marked in picas in the margin of the copy. Same-size photographs should be marked "S/S" in the margin.

WHEN COLORS OVERLAP

If the colors are to overlap, you should make a key drawing in black (the main color) on a sheet of white illustration board. Then attach an acetate overlay to the key drawing and draw on the acetate the parts that are to print in the second color. If the job is to be run in more than two colors, use a separate acetate overlay for the artwork for each additional color. Tracing paper may be used as an overlay if acetate is not available, however, it is not as suitable for this purpose because it tends to wrinkle when ink is applied to it.

HALFTONE COLOR SEPARATION

Halftone color separation negatives may be made from copy consisting of color photographs, color film transparencies, watercolor drawings, drawings done in showcard colors or tempera, pastel drawings, and oil paintings.

As a rule, you should not attempt to separate the colors when you prepare tone copy for color reproduction. You can simply furnish the cameraman with full-color drawings and photographs and leave the job of color separation entirely up to him.

COLOR BLOCKS AND TINT AREAS

Background color generally consists of color blocks or tints. These color areas may be filled in with india ink on the original drawing or you may simply indicate where they are to go by outlining the area on the original drawing with red ink. You should then block in the area on a tissue overlay.

The cameraman will then make two negatives and mask out parts of each to produce the color separation plates. When asking the cameraman to supply a tint, you must always indicate on the overlay or on the original art, the tone value required. A 25 percent tint means 25 percent of the paper will be covered by dots and 75 percent will be left as white space. As a rule, anything below 25 percent is rather light for color work, especially if the tint is to be printed in a light color of ink.

CHAPTER 23

TYPESETTING

TYPESETTING

Over half of all quick printers now have typesetting departments. Most are using strike-on equipment, but purchases of the new, low-cost ($10,000 and up) phototypesetting equipment are increasing.

OPERATOR SKILLS

Good, accurate typing skill - not necessarily speed - is needed. Good spelling ability is an absolute must and the hardest ability to find. Do not depend on any operator being able to turn out typesetting all day long. Most typesetting jobs grind at nerves and eyes and about four or five hours of usable production is all you will probably get in a day. Frequent breaks for other duties relieves the eye strain of typesetting.

HAZARDS TO AVOID

Technology in typesetting equipment is moving so fast that equipment can be obsoleted in a few years. This is especially hazardous for trade typesetters who must update equipment to remain competitive. A typesetting department can be an asset to a quick printer because of convenience, speed, quality control, cost control, prestige, and dependability. These pluses can bring in a lot of printing business and can make the department worthwhile, even with somewhat obsoleted equipment. The greatest problem is finding a good operator. In spite of the problems, quick printing shops are finding a typesetting department to be a profitable addition.

STRIKE-ON OR PHOTOTYPESETTING

The principal reason more quick printers have selected strike-on over phototypesetting equipment is the lower initial cost. Good used strike-on equipment is available at a fraction of the cost of a phototypesetter.

The best strike-on equipment is the IBM selectric composer which is readily available on the used equipment market (not to be confused with the IBM selectric typewriter). This machine is ideal for setting letterheads and envelopes and for low-volume typesetting. The largest type is 11 pt., but reasonably sharp headlines as large as 33 pt. can be made with a stat camera. To achieve sharpness, a clay-coated paper should be used and pressure adjustments set for a sharp initial image.

SELECTING A PHOTOTYPESETTER

The most recent trend by quick printers is toward the use of electronic computerized typesetters. Most users of this type of equipment have mixed feelings — sort of a love-hate attitude. They love the speed, the automatic justification, the flexibility, the great variety of fonts and sizes, the storage of data, and the ease of keyboarding. They hate the "secret" codes, the foul ups when they strike a wrong key, the inability to self-service the electronic innards, and the high cost of maintenance and repair. (Service policies on a $12,000 phototypesetter may run as high as $1600 a year — or service calls at $150 for the first hour and $50 each additional hour.)

We selected the AM Comp/Set because of readily

available service and features that fit our particular needs. Many quick printers are using Compugraphic equipment. The features listed here are based on our Comp/Set experience and on interviews with quick printers using various other brands of typesetters. Like current computerized typesetters, this information may well be obsolete before this book gets into print.

The operator of a computerized typesetter should have initial instruction, considerable study time, practice time, the ability to visualize numbers and codes into a printed image, patience, and tolerance. The potential rewards, however, are great. Customer-pleasing work can be produced in a fraction of the time required with other typesetting methods — and "time" is the scarcest and most valuable commodity in a quick print shop.

Price Range

Most quick printers settle for phototypesetters in the $10,000 to $20,000 price range. It's a fast developing field that requires current investigation before making a choice. Some important things to look for are listed here.

1. Storage of jobs. Our Comp/Set stores jobs on a floppy disc. Other models and makes use punched or magnetic tape to store information. This storage feature is almost a necessity. We temporarily store every sizeable job on a floppy disc. After the job is finalized, we can reuse the disc. If something goes wrong, like a paper jam, bad chemicals, wrong font or size, etc., etc., we have the job recorded. We can rerun a job from a disc a lot faster than we can rekeyboard. Corrections can be made in the process. A problem area in a frequently used disc is wear. The disc spins inside a sleeve and reuse can, in time, result in lost data.

Another reason for temporarily storing each job is the difficulty of visualizing the finished job before seeing it in print. After the photo paper is developed, improvements are often obvious. If the job has been stored, a few changes and another printout can produce a more professional result with a minimum of effort.

Floppy discs or tape can be used to produce repetitive copy such as four-up business cards. The stored copy is simply played back several times, producing the multiple copies needed for pasteup. This can be a big time-saver, particularly if the original copy involves complicated copy fitting, symbols, codes, etc. It's a lot less costly in time and material than duplication with stats.

2. Data or tab storage. This is a feature that is usually separate from disc or tape storage. It is a memory built into the electronics of the typesetter. However, it is a temporary memory that is lost when the typesetter is turned off. It can save time by temporarily storing repetitive tab information. Other repetitive data, such as special symbols, often requires time-consuming keyboarding of codes, fonts, or size changes. With data storage, numerous bits of copy can be placed in memory and recalled by number when needed.

3. Availability of service. Unless you are an electronic expert equipped with special testing equipment and programs developed for servicing your particular equipment, you are at the mercy of the manufacturer's service department. Prompt service by qualified experts is an extremely valuable consideration.

4. Multiple font selection. Just about every new phototypesetter has at least four fonts on line that can be instantly changed by a simple keyboard command. It is handy, but not essential, to have more fonts on line.

AM makes a model that will hold several discs that can be moved into position with a keyboard command. This is a costly extra. Simpler machines require manual changing of discs. If a job is replayed from a disc, the playback must be stopped at every point where a type disc change is required. However, by carefully selecting the variety of fonts on each disc, you can produce most jobs without a disc change. The use of more than three type styles on a single job is rarely eye pleasing. Type should convey a message — not show off the typefaces. A good advertising piece, like a good salesman, should be dressed in a manner that will not attract attention away from the message.

5. A two-disc drive system offers the advantage of transferring stored data from one disc to another. With a two-disc system, you can make a backup disc as insurance against losing important data. A backup disc provides peace of mind and may save days of rekeyboarding if a data filled disc is damaged.

SELECTING TYPE STYLES

Some type faces seem to fit almost any kind of job while others are suitable only for special types of work. There are no hard and fast rules. The use of type is governed entirely by good taste and association. But to choose type wisely, you must be able to recognize the different typefaces and to know something of their general usage.

Selecting Display Typefaces

When you choose typefaces for display work, you should select styles that are appropriate and that seem to match the mood expressed by the copy. Typefaces reflect certain characteristics, such as refinement, dignity, boldness, and strength; and you can use them to emphasize or suggest the thoughts expressed by the copy.

Take the specimens shown in Figure A for example. When you see the word "Playbill" set in old-fashioned type, you immediately think of the days of

Figure A.

PLAYBILL   **FUTURA**

Trafton Script

STYMIE   **FRANKLIN Gothic**

Garamond

gaslights, the iron horse, the gold rush, and nickel cigars. The Futura reminds you of the severity of our modern architecture and the hustle and bustle of everyday living in our streamlined generation. The line of Stymie Bold reminds you of power and strength. You think of the steel girders that support our skyscrapers or of the tremendous horsepower created by our modern engines.

Similarly, the line of script reminds you of fashion and feminine allure. The line of Franklin Gothic reminds you of the standard bread-and-butter items, such as the tools and commodities that we use. The line of Garamond suggests stability and dignity. It is one of the typefaces of tradition.

How to Select Body Type — The agreement of the type style with the subject matter of the copy is less important in the selection of body typefaces. In selecting a typeface for the text or body of a job, you need simply select a style that is legible and pleasing in design.

Legibility — The factors that help you attain legibility are the style of letter you use, the size of the type, the length of the line, the indentions, the margins around the job, and the spacing you use between words and lines.

Style of Letter — Roman faces or simple Sans Serif faces are generally used for body type because they are the easiest to read. Unusual faces such as Old English and Script are difficult to follow and are generally used only for headings and display work.

Type Size — The size of the type also affects its legibility. Twelve and fourteen point are the most legible sizes. They are often used for textbooks that must be read under adverse conditions. Ten-point type may be used to conserve space. It is large enough for comfortable casual reading. Eight-point type is less legible than 10 point, but it is used in some cases where space is an important factor. Six-point type is rather difficult to read, and sizes smaller than 6 point are very tiring on the eye.

Sizes above 12 point are used mainly for display work; they are too large and barny to be used for text.

Additional Legibility Factors — Other factors which affect legibility are:

1. Caps and lowercase letters are more legible than lines set in all caps. Words set in all caps in a script or text typeface are almost illegible.
2. Medium faces are more legible than condensed or expanded faces, particularly in the smaller sizes.
3. Expanded faces are more readable than condensed faces, but they take up more room and are sometimes not worth the difference.
4. Condensed faces are more practical than expanded type for display work because more characters can be placed in a line and the type is large enough that there is no appreciable loss of legibility.

BASIC CLASSES OF TYPE

Type is generally divided into six groups: Roman, Gothic, Script, Text, Italic, and Contemporary. All authorities do not agree on this grouping, but for practical purposes, this book will discuss typefaces under these six main categories. (See Fig. B.)

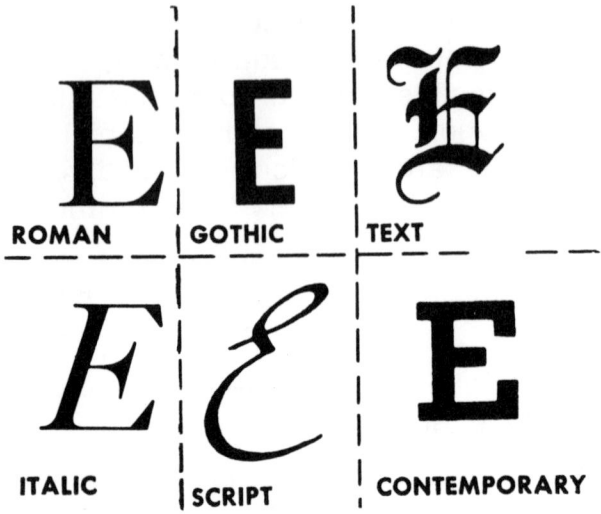

Figure B. The six main classes of type

Roman — Roman is the type most used for the text of magazines, newspapers, and books. It is chosen because everyone is familiar with it and because it is the easiest to read in the smaller sizes, especially when a small amount of leading is used.

Text and reference books are often set in a simple sans serif type. Good legibility depends on adequate size and leading so sans serif types are rarely chosen where space saving is of prime importance. This book is set in 12 pt. Megaron with two points of leading. While not providing the fastest reading, this style type and leading makes it easier to locate isolated reference points. (See Gothic and Sans Serif headings for more details.)

Roman types are divided into two classifications: modern and oldstyle. The chief difference between modern and oldstyle Roman is found in the serifs. (Serifs are the little cross-strokes at the ends of the main lines.) Compare the two letters shown in Fig. C. The oldstyle letter has soft, rounded serifs, while the modern letter has heavier shadings and thin,

Oldstyle   Modern

Figure C. Comparison of oldstyle and modern roman letters.

clean-cut hairlines. Bodoni is typical of modern Roman and Caslon is a good example of the oldstyle faces. (See Fig. D.) Roman faces can be used for any kind of work, but printers generally try to avoid mixing the oldstyle faces with the modern.

BODONI Bold
BODONI Book
BODONI   Bodoni
CASLON, True-Cut
CASLON Old Style
CASLON Bold
CASLON No. 113, Condensed
CASLON Bold Condensed
CASLON   Caslon

Figure D. Oldstyle

Gothic — Study the difference between the Roman letter and the Gothic letter shown in Fig. B. The Roman letter is composed of a series of thick and thin lines. The Gothic letter is constructed of lines of even weight. It has no serifs; it is perfectly plain. It might be called a block letter. Fig. E shows some of the Gothic types. The sans serif included in the illustration is an up-to-date style of Gothic. However, because of its modern design, it is generally grouped, not with the Gothics, but with the contemporary typefaces.

There are several kinds of Gothic typefaces. Each has its place in modern printing. Copperplate Gothic, for example, is generally used for letterheads, envelopes, cards, announcements, and many kinds of office forms.

BANK GOTHIC CONDENSED BOLD

FRANKLIN Gothic Extra Condensed

POSTER GOTHIC

NEWS Gothic

SANS Serif Bold

COPPERPLATE GOTHIC BOLD NO. 132

COPPERPLATE GOTHIC EXTENDED

GOTHIC No. 32   (LIGHT COPPERPLATE)

GOTHIC No. 31   (BOLD COPPERPLATE)

ALTERNATE Gothic No. 2

Figure E. A few gothic type faces.

News Gothic is another serviceable face. It may be used as a body type, and it is equally serviceable for titles and headings. Franklin Gothic, Alternate

286

Gothic, and Poster Gothic are used chiefly for display work. They are very popular for posters and headings.

Script — Script and cursive typefaces are generally grouped together. Scripts have little connecting links or kerns that combine the letters and give them the appearance of handwriting; cursive letters do not have these kerns. Actually, the scripts are an imitation of the old Spencerian handwriting, and the cursives are patterned after old-fashioned hand lettering.

Script faces are suitable for announcements and invitations. They may also be used to impart an air of elegance and charm to display work.

Fig. F shows a few of the script typefaces. Some of the faces shown are contemporary styles used in modern display work.

Bernhard Cursive Bold　　*Kaufmann Bold*

Commercial Script　　*Helanna Script*

Signal Medium　　*Bulletin*

Repro Script　　*Brush*

Figure F. Some Script Styles.

Text — Samples of text typefaces are shown in Fig. G. You may know this type simply as "Old English." Text was among the first type styles used. In fact, Gutenberg worked almost exclusively with this style of type. Although it is still used frequently, it is generally limited to a few lines of copy. You should

Figure G. Text examples.

save it for something religious or formal, such as prayer books, programs, and invitations.

Italics — Italics are slanting letters like those shown in Fig. H. They are made to match almost every Roman, Gothic, and contemporary type style in use

Figure H. Italics are made to match many type faces.

today. They are used in text matter to show emphasis and in display work to create contrast and to add interest to the job. Although italics were originally used for text, they were rather hard to read in lengthy articles, and so they have been used less and less for this purpose until today they are used rather sparingly.

Swash letters are similar to italics, but they are embellished by additional swirls and curves known as swashes. You can sometimes use them with italics to dress up a page which otherwise might be bare and unattractive.

Contemporary Faces — The past fifty years have been significant in typographical history. The old Gothics have had their faces lifted, and everywhere new streamlined faces have appeared. Many of these modern faces are fads. Their style and usefulness will be short-lived. Out of it all, however, have come a few serviceable typefaces that will take their place alongside the old standbys.

Leading the contemporary field are two distinct styles: the square serif and the sans serif.

Sans serif is actually a kind of Gothic type. It has the same even strokes as the Gothic, and it has no serifs. But unlike its Gothic ancestors, it has such perfect geometric proportions that it is generally classified with the contemporary typefaces.

The Futura typefaces shown in Fig. I seem to be constructed from squares, rectangles, and other geometric forms.

FUTURA Bold Oblique   Megaron Medium
FUTURA Display   *Megaron Medium Italic*
FUTURA Bold   **Megaron Bold**
FUTURA Demibold   **Megaron Extra Bold**
FUTURA Bold Condensed
FUTURA Medium   SANS Serif Medium
20th CENTURY Bold   20th CENTURY Medium

Figure I. San Serif type faces.

289

The Futura and Megaron faces are the last word in simplicity, yet they are among the most serviceable of all the typefaces. They can be used almost anywhere.

Square serif is little more than sans serif with serifs added. It has the same even strokes and the same perfect geometric proportions. Square serif type

STYMIE Light   **BAUER Beton Bold**

STYMIE Bold   **GIRDER Heavy**

STYMIE Medium   **KARNAK Medium**

Figure J. Square Serif type faces.

originated in Europe shortly after the sans serif faces made their appearance. It became popular in the United States in the early thirties. Some people think it is an offspring of the old Egyptian alphabet. Others believe it was inspired by typewriter type which was widely employed by advertisers of that period. Stymie is a typical example of this type. (See Fig. J.)

Contemporary display faces is a classification which includes hundreds of modern typefaces used in display work. There are so many of them that it would be difficult to try to list them all. There are a number of scripts and italics, for example, which can be identified by their streamlined appearance. The Kaufman shown in Fig. F is one of these modern scripts. Others include Brush and Gilles Gothic.

There are also a number of tall, condensed types

290

such as Onyx and Valiant. (FIG. K.) Then there are wide, bold faces, such as Venus Extrabold Extended. And in between, there are medium faces, such as Lydian and Studio. These types are used chiefly for display composition.

Venus X-B Extend. *Studio*

Lydian Cursive **LYDIAN Bold**

Dom Casual **CARTOON BOLD**

Figure K. Comtemporary display type faces.

ORNAMENTATION AND BORDERS

Ornaments, such as stars (called dingbats) and dots (called bullets), are used to add interest and beauty to a job. When you use ornaments, you should always select something that goes well with the style of type that you are using. Above all, don't overdo them. Fancy types and decorations should be used only if they make the word more effective. Decoration just for decoration's sake was abandoned at the turn of the century in favor of simple harmony and balance. (See Fig. L.)

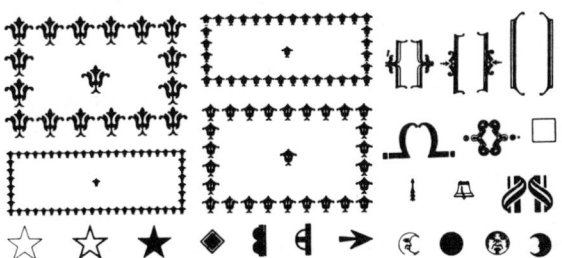

Figure L. Ornaments and borders.

Borders and Rules — Borders should be selected with the same care that is used in selecting a typeface because the same general principles of typography apply. Different borders go with different typefaces just as certain typefaces go together. One type of border, called a scotch rule, is made up of one heavy line and one thin line. The scotch rule is ideally used with the Bodoni typeface because their elements are the same—a heavy and a thin line.

The various lines used within a printed page are called rules. Rules may be used to separate sections of a page, to guide the reader's eye, or serve as writing lines.

A rule primarily used for a writing line is called a hairline rule. A medium rule is used for dividing sections of a form. A heavy rule is used to add special emphasis to a section and is generally used for the first and last lines of a form. Figure M illustrates the various rule sizes, which are referred to as line weights.

The selection of rules is important to the overall legibility of your work. Too many rules, or rules which are too heavy, tend to make a printed page or form difficult to read.

——————————————————— HAIRLINE RULE

——————————————————— MEDIUM RULE (1/2 POINT)

——————————————————— HEAVY RULE (1 POINT)

Figure M

COPYFITTING

There are several methods of copy fitting. Some of these, such as the words-per-square-inch-method, are rather inaccurate and should be used only for rough calculations. For accurate calculations, you may use another method based on the number of typewritten characters in the manuscript. This is known as the character-count method.

Words Per Square Inch — When exact copy figuring is not required, the words-per-square-inch method will do very well. Fig. N shows the approximate number of words per square inch for different sizes of type.

Size of type	Words per square inch	Size of type	Words per square inch
6 pt., solid	47	12 pt., solid	14
6 pt., 2 pt. leaded	34	12 pt., 2 pt. leaded	11
8 pt., solid	32	14 pt., solid	11
8 pt., 2 pt. leaded	23	14 pt., 2 pt. leaded	7
10 pt., solid	21	18 pt., solid	7
10 pt., 2 pt. leaded	16	18 pt., 2 pt. leaded	5

Figure N. Words per square inch.

Suppose you have 750 words of copy to be set 10 point, solid. If you divide the 750 by 21 (the number of words to the square inch for that size of type), you will find that the copy will require approximately 36 square inches of space. So you can set it 4" x 9" or 3" x 12," or in any other combination of width and depth that will make up the 36 square inches.

NUMBER OF WORDS THAT WILL FIT IN A GIVEN SPACE

You can also use this table to find the number of

words that will fit into a given space. Suppose you have a space 24 picas (4 inches) wide and 8 inches deep to be filled with 10-point type with 2-point leading.

From the table you will see that there are approximately 16 words to the square inch when the copy is set 10-point leaded. Your space is 4 inches wide and 8 inches deep, which is a total of 32 square inches. Multiplying 32 by 16 gives you 512 words as the approximate number that will fit into the space.

Actually, you could get closer to 530 words in this amount of space. Therefore, you should keep in mind that the words-per-square-inch method of copy casting does not give you a completely accurate estimate.

CHARACTER COUNT

The character-count method is the best system for determining the amount of space your printed material will fill. To use it, you must determine the number of typewritten characters (and spaces) contained in the manuscript. In addition, you must know how many characters (and spaces) will go into a line set to the proper width in the size and style of type desired, and how many lines of this size of type will be required to fill a column inch.

ESTIMATING THE NUMBER OF MANUSCRIPT CHARACTERS

To determine the number of characters in the manuscript, you must count every character and space on each page. If the typewritten lines are fairly even in length, you may use the following system for making computations:

ESTIMATING THE NUMBER OF
MANUSCRIPT CHARACTERS

To determine the number of characters in the manuscript, you must count every character and space on each page. If the typewritten lines are fairly even in length, you may use the following system for making computations:

1. Draw a light pencil line down the right side of the copy at a point where the majority of the lines seem to end.

2. Count the number of characters (and spaces) between the left margin and the line. This will give you the number of characters to the average line.

3. Multiply this number by the number of lines on the page.

4. You will notice that some lines run over the pencil mark and some lines stop short of it. Proper allowance must be made for these long and short lines. Go back and count the number of characters (and spaces) that run over on the right side of the pencil mark. Add these to your total in step 3.

5. Then count the number of spaces that some lines are short of the pencil line and subtract this number from the total in step 4. The adjusted total will be the number of characters on the page. (Omit steps 4 and 5 unless very accurate calculations are required.)

6. Following this procedure, find the number of characters for each page in the manuscript and add them together. The sum will be the total number of characters (and spaces) in the manuscript.

MEASURING THE COPY

You can vary the process just described by measuring the typewritten copy with a ruler. (The standard "elite" typewriter has a 10-point face and types 12 characters to the inch; while the standard "pica" typewriter has a 12-point face and types 10 characters to the inch.) Measure off a distance from the left margin of your copy and draw a line down the right side, as was shown.

If your typewriter types 10 characters to the inch, and if your pencil line is 5 inches from the left margin of the copy, your average line will contain 50 characters.

COPYFITTING AIDS

There are still other methods of copy fitting involving the use of slide rules, circular rules, line gauges, and typewriter scales. Manufacturers of typesetting machines also put out copy-fitting manuals.

CHAPTER 24

PAPER

Most quick printers buy paper in precut sizes, ream wrapped. Paper problems are generally solved by changing suppliers. We have found, however, that a basic knowledge of the makeup of paper helps us to solve some problems. If nothing else, it helps us to sound more professional when talking with customers.

PAPERMAKING

Paper is a thin layer of vegetable fibers. Most papers are composed of wood fibers, although cotton, flax, hemp, bamboo, grass, and other vegetable fibers may be used.

Essential to papermaking for this modern age is the continuous papermaking machine. A widely used machine, it is called the Fourdrinier machine, after its inventors. The wood fibers, diluted to about one-half of one percent, are flowed onto an endless wire screen. The screen is agitated as it travels, causing the fibers to align parallel to the direction of travel. As the water drains from the paper, the web (as it is called) is capable of being lifted.

The web is passed under felts to remove more water, then over drying rolls to remove almost all of the remaining water. The paper is then treated and smoothed and wound on rolls. These master rolls are later slit and rewound on rolls or cut into sheets.

COATED PAPER

Uncoated paper consists of the stock just as it comes from the papermaking machine; coated stock is paper that has received a fine layer of mineral substances or a synthetic, plastic-like covering. Coatings are applied by passing the web through vats, or through rollers or blades (similar to the ink fountain blade). The coating may be applied to both sides of the paper, as in the case of paper used for quality pictorial magazines, or to only one side of the paper, as in the case of paper used for labels.

Coated paper presents the smoothest possible surface for printing fine halftones. The surface may be highly polished or it may be matte or semi-matte. Some paper manufacturers refer to their coated papers as "enameled" stocks, but this term has no precise technical meaning.

FINISHES

The term "finish" refers to the last paper-making operation. This operation affects the appearance and the texture, or "feel," of the paper. Since a smooth surface is important in fine halftone reproduction, most full-color printing is done on coated paper which has been finished to a high polish. The smoothing is done after the web has passed through the drying drums in the paper machine.

"Antique" paper is an example of stock which is used just as it comes from the paper machine. For a smoother surface, the paper is passed through a series of calender rollers on the paper machine. This stock is known as "machine finish" (MF) paper. It is possible to produce an even smoother surface by passing the paper one or more times through supercalenders. This paper is known as "supercalendered" (SC) or "super," and is one of the more frequently used printing surfaces.

Special finishes are applied to the paper in a number of ways. Papers used for better stationery are often given a "laid" or "wove" finish. These patterns are impressed into the wet web on the paper machine by a "dandy roll." Evenly spaced wires across the roll produce the ladder or laid effect, while a woven screen of wires produces the wove finish.

The dandy roll is also used to produce watermarks on paper. After the paper web has been dried, other finishes such as leather, pebble-grain, linen and so on, may be produced by passing it through a rotary embossing machine.

PAPER GRAIN

The grain of paper refers to the position of the fibers.

Diluted pulp is flowed onto a screen in the paper machine. As the screen moves forward, it is agitated and the fibers align in a direction parallel to the length of the machine.

Paper grain is of particular importance to printers. First, paper is stiffer in the grain direction. This is important in the case of books and pamphlets which are to be folded. The grain direction of the stock should be parallel to the binding edge; if it is not, the pages may be difficult to turn. Second, paper changes (stretch or shrinkage) due to the humidity, are greater across the grain than with it. Third, paper is more easily torn in the grain direction than against it.

Paper Face
Except for a few special papers, all papers have two distinct sides or "faces." The paper pulp is formed on a moving wire screen in the paper machine. The surface in contact with this screen is impressed with the pattern of the wire and is called the "wire side" or bottom of the sheet. The other surface is pressed against a series of felt rollers in removing water and is known as the "felt side" or top of the sheet.

In the paper machine, there is a tendency for finer fibers and filler materials to float on the surface of the diluted pulp. Therefore, the felt side is a better printing surface. Printing should be done on the felt side if there is a choice (letterheads, for example). Many fine commercial papers are marked or tagged to show the felt side. In the case of watermarked papers, the watermark reads properly (left to right) when viewed from the felt side.

Although calendering removes most of the wire marks, you can determine the "faces" of an uncoated sheet by observing the surface with the light striking it at a 45° angle. The typical screen pattern may then be seen. Sometimes it may be necessary to dampen the sheet on both sides to swell the fibers, making the pattern more discernable.

BASIC SIZE AND BASIS WEIGHT

Size and weight in relation to printing papers are the basis of much confusion. For you to make calculations regarding paper, two kinds of data are necessary. You must know the "basic size" and "basis weight."

Basic size refers to the established standard size for a stock sheet of a specific type of paper. The basic sizes are related to the uses of the different papers and the presses on which the different products are printed. For instance, the basic size for business papers such as bond and other types of writing paper is 17" x 22". Most commercial stationery is 8½" x 11", and this can be cut four-out of a 17" x 22" sheet. Therefore, 17" x 22" is used as the basic size for all business papers. Publications work is generally run on 38-inch presses, so 25" x 38" is the accepted basic size for book papers. Basic sizes for various papers are given in Figure A.

Figure A

Sizes of "parent" sheets of paper

Kind of paper	Basic size (inches)
Business papers bond, ledger manifold, mimeo, writing, map)	17 x 22
Blotting	19 x 24
Cover	20 x 26
Bristols, postcard, tag and blanks	22½ x 28½
Index	25½ x 30½
Newsprint, tissues, wrapping	24 x 36
Book papers (including offset and coated)	25 x 38

Basis weight is the second factor to consider in working with paper. It is the weight of a quantity of paper of the basic size. The quantity is generally a ream (500 sheets). For example, 500 sheets of 17" x 22" 20 lb. bond should weigh 20 pounds, and 500 sheets of 25" x 38" 70 lb. offset should weigh 70 pounds. Confusing, but not likely to change.

BULK AND CALIPER

The "bulk" of a paper stock is a term relating to the thickness of the paper. It should not be confused with the basis weight. Papers are said to "bulk at 320 to the inch," for instance, indicating that a stack 320 sheets high would measure one inch. Some book papers, for example, are made in 60-pound basis weights and bulk at from 320 to 720 to the inch. The one which bulks at 320 to the inch is said to be "high bulk" paper as opposed to that which bulks 720 to the inch.

Thickness of paper is called "caliper" and is expressed in thousandths of an inch. The paper should be "miked" at several places to obtain an average reading.

Cardboard was traditionally measured by the number of plies, or layers of paper used in its manufacture, such as 4-ply, 8-ply, 14-ply, and so on. Most of the paperboard today is measured in thousandths, the same as other papers.

Cardboards are sometimes referred to by "points," which is derived from the caliper: .030" board would be called 30 point board.

KINDS OF PRINTING PAPERS

There are three divisions of paper stock used in the printing industry. These are (1) commercial and book papers; (2) newspapers; and (3) packaging papers and boards. Of these three, quick printers are most concerned with the first.

OFFSET BOOK PAPERS

Papers are usually named for the purpose for which they were originally made. This is the case with book paper, the largest class of printing papers. Book papers are made in a great variety of finishes, colors, and basis weights. Their basic size is 25" x 38".

Offset book papers are those which have received special sizing to prevent rapid absorption of moisture during the press run. The term "offset book" paper is generally accepted to mean an uncoated, wove finish paper. Offset papers may be run on letterpress equipment, but not all letterpress papers may be printed by the offset process. This is due to the lack of sizing in letterpress papers.

Coated papers are the "elite" of the book papers. The base stock is most often tub-sized, then surface-sized, dried and supercalendered. The coatings are then applied to one or both sides, and the stock is then supercalendered again to provide a very smooth surface.

Coated papers may be finished to a high gloss or they may have a matte or semi-matte finish as required. Although all coated papers are sized, the soluble binders used with some coatings make them unsuitable for offset printing. Most letterpress reproduction proofs (repros) are pulled on coated stock.

BUSINESS PAPERS

The broad classification "business papers" covers

those which are used for stationery items and business forms, rather than publications work or promotional or advertising printing. The basic size for all such papers is 17" x 22".

The paper of this class which quick printers use most often is called "bond." The name refers to its original purpose, that of printing such legal documents as bonds and stock certificates. Some bond papers are made from chemical wood pulp; the better grades contain rag fibers. All bond papers are sized to accept writing inks without feathering; some receive special coatings to make erasures easy. Business forms are usually printed on sulfite bond papers.

A heavier paper with similar characteristics is known as "ledger." It was originally designed for the printing of accounting records. In addition to ready acceptance of inks and long life, ledger has extremely good folding endurance, which means it may be repeatedly folded without cracking or tearing along the fold. Ledger also has good erasure tolerance.

At the other end of the scale, lighter-than-bond papers are known as "manifold." These lightweight papers are used in typing carbon copies. Rag content manifold papers are often referred to as "onionskin" from their texture and are often used as airmail stationery.

A specially sized, soft-textured paper is required for stencil process (mimeograph) duplicating. This is known as "mimeo." Some mimeo stock contains rag fibers, but most is made of chemical wood pulp. For hectograph processes (such as Ditto), a differently sized, smooth-surface paper known as "duplicator" is used. Neither of these stocks is particularly suited for offset printing.

Another specially treated business paper is used for checks, receipts, and similar documents which must be protected against alteration. Such papers are called "safety papers." They usually have watermarks consisting of geometric designs or similar protective devices.

CARBONLESS PAPERS

These papers are coated with certain chemicals which react under contact and pressure of a pen, pencil, or typewriter key to produce a duplicate image on successive sheets. Like little capsules, when crushed, the two chemicals blend together to form color. As many as ten legible copies may be made with an electric typewriter using some of these papers, but the normal quantity is five.

To effect the image transfer, chemicals from the back of one sheet combine with chemicals on the front of the next. Top sheets (originals) are coated on the back only (CB), and the bottom sheets need to be coated on the front only (CF), while intermediate sheets need coating on both front and back (CFB).

Carbonless papers are not compatible with one another, so they cannot be used interchangeably. Another word of caution: *the system will not work if the printing is on the wrong side.* Determine the proper surface before printing. Generally, the coated side of carbonless paper has a gritty feel to it, while the uncoated side is smoother. A test may be made by placing two sheets together and marking the top. If the mark is transferred to the bottom sheet, the proper printing surface is on top.

Problems can be eliminated by allowing the paper to condition itself in the pressroom area. This conditioning period permits the paper to adjust to the humidity and temperature of the pressroom gradually, thereby reducing the possibility of the sheets curling or wrinkling as they are run through the press. (This is true of all papers, but is most important when the paper is carbonless.)

The pressure setting between the blanket cylinder and the impression cylinder must be adjusted to a minimum that will produce an even impression on the sheet without "toning" it.

When cutting carbonless papers, place scrap pieces of chipboard or index paper on the top and bottom of the paper lift to eliminate pressure marks from the paper clamp. Also use a minimum amount of clamp pressure.

BRISTOLS AND CARDS

Bristols are lightweight cardboards and are of three types: (1) index; (2) mill bristol; and (3) wedding bristol. Index is a heavyweight writing paper, sized to accept writing inks and permit easy erasure. The basic size of index is 25½" x 30½".

Mill bristols are made for advertising materials

which require a stiff sheet with a good printing surface. Wedding bristol is made of plies of white boards, with a surface which will accept writing inks and is used for invitations and other social items. Basic size for mill and wedding bristols is 22½" x 28½".

Tagboard is another lightweight cardboard, most often made of sulphate pulp and hard-sized and supercalendered. It is an especially tough board, made for rough use such as baggage tags and so on. Since the use of computing machines has become so widespread, special papers have been developed for the punched cards used in these computer systems. Tagboard, made to close tolerances with extra resistance to curl and of exceptional dimensional stability, is used for these cards. It is known as "tabulating board." The basic size for all tagboards is 22½" x 28½".

COVERS

A broad range of cover papers is available. They come in a great variety of colors — bold and pastel, with embossed or plain finishes, coated and uncoated, gloss or matte, and some even have one color on the front and a different color on the back. Cover papers may be used for purposes other than book covers. Programs and menus are two applications to which cover papers are especially suited.

There are instances where exceptionally hard use will be given to a publication, a telephone book for instance. In this case, it may be advisable to use an index or tagboard cover.

The basic size for all cover papers is 20″ x 26″.

ENVELOPES

Envelopes are made in a great variety of sizes and shapes with papers of almost every conceivable type. Envelopes are made of sulfite and rag content papers to match letterhead stationery. They are made of rag content stock or the cheaper grades of sulfite or sulfate papers, usually with a wove finish for general mailing. They may be made of lightweight cover papers for advertising mail and are made of lightweight rag and sulphite stock for airmail.

For heavier usage, envelopes are made of kraft and manila sulphate stocks. Kraft stocks are brown; manila papers are tan or cream colored. Still stronger envelopes are made of lightweight tagboard or ledger papers.

Illustrations of commonly used envelopes and their sizes are shown in Figure B.

PAPER STORAGE

Paper is composed of fibers that are easily affected by moisture. Because of this, paper is dimensionally unstable. A sheet of paper will gain moisture and expand in a moist atmosphere, or it will lose moisture and shrink in a dry atmosphere. When paper is piled, the changes affect the edges of the sheets first and most noticeably.

Dry paper in a humid area absorbs moisture along the exposed edges, expands, and develops wavy

Figure B.
Common types of envelopes

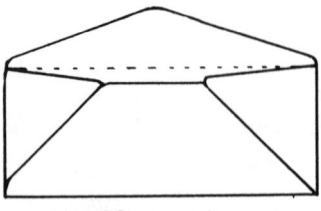

No. 10 Bond *(Long)*
Business envelope
4-1/8 x 9-1/2

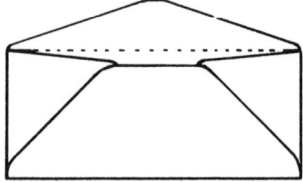

No. 9 Bond envelope fits
inside No. 10
3-7/8 x 8-7/8

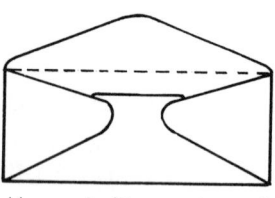

Monarch *(Special size)*
Bond stationery
3-7/8 x 7-1/2

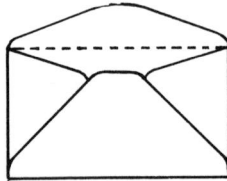

No. 6-3/4 Bond
regular business
3-5/8 x 6-1/2

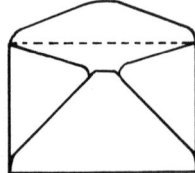

No. 6-1/4 Bond
return envelope
3-1/2 x 6

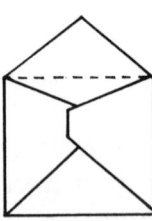

Baronial
Envelope for
invitations

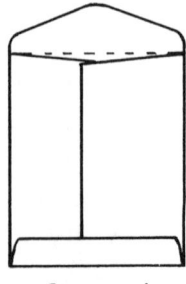

Open end
catalog envelope

Window envelope

PAPER

edges, particularly across the grain. Paper that has a high moisture content, when left in a dry atmosphere, loses moisture, shrinks, and develops tight edges. These changes are also more severe across the grain. This is because the paper fibers expand and contract more readily in their diameter than in their length.

Whether the problem is a wavy edge or a tight edge, paper that has been altered by moisture will no longer be flat. When such a sheet is subjected to the continuous, equalized squeeze of offset printing, distortion, misregister, and wrinkling are likely to occur.

When paper is brought into the pressroom from storage areas, it should remain in its sealed wrappers until it has reached stability with the shop atmosphere. This is particularly important when the difference is pronounced, such as would be the the case if the paper were just brought in from a cold warehouse to a warm shop.

The ideal condition for the paper for offset printing is to have a moisture content at or slightly above that of the pressroom. Allowing the paper to remain in its sealed packages until moisture balance is reached is called "seasoning" or "conditioning." Seasoning is the most effective preventive for paper problems.

STATIC

Rubbing two unlike surfaces together generates static electricity. Running your comb through your hair will create such a charge. You may have noticed how small pieces of paper will cling to the comb. A

311

similar condition exists when paper passes through the press.

If the proper humidity balance has been attained, the moisture in the paper will act as a ground and dissipate the electrical charge. If the moisture content of the paper is low (and this is often the case in cold weather), static may cause the paper to cling to the blanket or impression cylinder of the press. Sheets charged with static electricity may cling together, causing the ink to offset.

Static eliminators are attached to many larger presses, and tinsel is often used on duplicator type presses for this purpose. The most effective means of static control is proper moisture balance. Even a little water sprinkled on the floor in the press area will help when static is a problem.

CHAPTER 25

INK

All printing inks consist of pigments or coloring matter, vehicles which carry the pigment and additives which modify the other two. These materials are blended together in varying amounts to produce the many types of ink required for today's printing industry.

Vehicles
Lithographic varnish is the most commonly used vehicle. It is composed largely of boiled linseed oil. Linseed oil is derived from flax seeds. In addition to flax seeds, vehicles for printing inks may be made of other vegetable oils, such as tung (also called China wood oil) and soybeans. Some types of fish oils are also used to make varnishes.

Sometimes vehicles are made of combinations of oils and resins. Either or both the oil and the resin may be natural or synthetic. The heat-set inks are an example of resinous-vehicle inks. Other specialized vehicles are used in other phases of the printing industry.

Pigments

The coloring matter of ink is provided by a substance known as the "pigment." There are two broad classifications of pigments: inorganic or mineral pigments (mostly metallic), and organic or synthetic pigments (mostly derived from petroleum or coal tars).

Black pigments are used in the greatest quantity. The most common of these is carbon black, which is made by partial combustion of natural gas.

White pigments also have wide usage. The most common of these is titanium dioxide. It is made from a natural ore, ilmenite, which is, ironically, jet black. White pigments serve to reduce highly concentrated organic pigments and improve their working qualities.

The rainbow of colors used in printing inks is produced by a variety of pigments, ranging from simple mineral salts to complex synthetic dyestuffs. Some are relatively opaque while others are almost transparent.

Additives

Substances used to modify the vehicle or pigments are called "additives" and are used in very small proportions. Included in this group are such materials as metallic driers, waxes, anti-skinning agents, and retarders — even perfumes.

The most important of the additives is drier. Driers are metallic compounds which act as catalysts. Metals such as cobalt, lead, and manganese are the most commonly used. Driers are added to inks in small amounts, a little at a time. The rule of thumb is 1 ounce to 1 pound, but up to 1½ ounces may be added if required. Larger quantities of drier do not cause faster drying; in fact, they may even retard it. This is especially so in the case of liquid driers. Less drier is used in colored inks than in black.

Waxes of various types are sometimes added to provide a special surface to the dried ink. Anti-skinning agents and retarders are used to prevent drying of the ink in the fountain or on the press rollers. Perfumes are used to cover odors in the ink which might be objectionable, or to give a scent to inks compounded for advertising materials.

BODY

An ink with a heavy body is called "short" or "stiff." Its consistency is much like shortening or waterpump grease. A small amount placed between the thumb and forefinger will break readily when the fingers are separated. As the body of the ink becomes thinner, it becomes "long" or "soft." Its consistency is like molasses or motor oil.

TACK

Tack is related to the body of the ink. It refers to its stickiness, or the force required to split an ink film between two surfaces. Tack is necessary to transfer the ink from roller to roller, to the plate, to the blanket, and to the stock. Tack is also necessary to ensure that the ink adheres only to the image areas and does not flow to nonimage areas of the plate. There must be a sharp break between the two.

Excessive tack is a serious ink problem. The most common symptom of excess tack is "picking" of the paper, in which the ink tears off particles of the paper surface.

DRYING OF INKS

Drying occurs in two stages: "setting," when the sheets can be handled without smearing; and "hardening," when final drying has taken place. Ink that has set up properly can be handled without damage in successive operations.

The first type of drying action is that of "oxidation," in which the vehicle absorbs oxygen from the air. The second drying action is known as "polymerization," in which smaller molecules of the vehicle combine into larger, more complex molecules. Most lithographic inks dry by a combination of oxidation and polymerization. The third drying action is that of "penetration."

Rubber-base ink will not dry properly on slick-coated paper stocks. A chalking condition will occur. Oil-based inks should be used when printing slick-coated stocks.

INK PROBLEMS

Back off refers to ink which does not follow the roller in the fountain. It may occur over the entire length of the roller or just in spots. **Chalking** occurs when the vehicle does not form a bond between the pigment and the paper and allows the pigment to powder or rub off the sheet. Inks **crystallize** by drying from the top down, forming a crust which repels other inks. **Embossing** of the blanket occurs when inks are so stiff that they impress the image into the surface of the blanket.

Emulsification occurs when water emulsifies in the ink, and small droplets of water are carried up into the film of ink on the rollers. Generally, this is not a serious problem. In some cases, the image will become grayed, however, and the pressman may increase the ink flow, thus causing fill-in. In an effort to remedy this, the pressman may then increase the water flow and a vicious circle has begun.

Filling-in of the image is most noticeable in halftones and reverse images. Ink spreads from the image areas into the nonimage areas, giving a muddy appearance to the halftones and plugging up the fine lines and serifs in reverses. **Roller glaze** is an overall glossy appearance on rubber and composition rollers. It consists primarily of dried varnish. When inking properly, the rollers should have a velvet-like sheen. **Hickies** are small doughnut-shaped spots in the image areas, caused by dried ink, paper dust, or other dirt.

Livering is a generally uncorrectable condition of the ink, caused by a reaction between additives and the vehicle. It is characterized by a gelatine or liver-like appearance of the ink. **Misting** refers to the action of a soft ink in breaking away from the rollers and spraying about the pressroom. **Mottling** is a term used to describe an uneven appearance of the printed image. It is most often seen in large solid areas.

Offsetting describes the transfer of fresh ink from the front of one sheet to the back of another when they are stacked together. It is sometimes called "setoff" to distinguish the problem from the printing process. **Picking** is a condition in which the surface of the paper is broken or torn due to the stiffness of the ink. It occurs most often with cheaper grades of coated stock. **Piling** occurs when the ink does not transfer from the plate to the blanket, or from the blanket to the paper. As the ink builds up, it will emboss the blanket and possibly ruin the plate.

Ink is being poorly **distributed** when it does not flow evenly over the roller surfaces. **Poor trapping** refers to the inability of the first colors printed in multicolor work to accept the successive inks. **Scum** is a localized condition of the plate in which the ink adheres to nonimage areas of the plate in certain spots. **Show-through** refers to a condition in which some of the pigment and vehicle are absorbed by the paper to create a reverse image on the back of the sheet. It is often confused with offset; but it is always in register, whereas offset is generally not in register.

Smudging is similar to chalking, but the pigment is not completely rubbed off; it is transferred or smeared over another portion of the sheet in the partially dried vehicle. **Stripping** is the refusal of the rollers to take ink. It occurs on the rubber or composition rollers that have become glazed, and on steel rollers that have become desensitized to ink. It may be an overall condition or it may be spotty. The printed image may be **scratched** after the ink has dried. The condition may be confused with chalking, but it is only the surface of the image that is affected. It is primarily a problem in package printing.

Tinting is the overall deposit of ink in the nonimage areas. The tint may be wiped from the plate with a light touch of a sponge or fingertip, but it will probably reappear when the dampeners are dropped on the plate. It differs from scum in that scum cannot be wiped off easily and generally does not reappear.

COLORED INK (See chapter "Color in Quick Printing)

CHAPTER 26

RUNNING COLOR

RUNNING COLOR

COLOR IN QUICK PRINTING

Today, single color jobs are standard in most quick printing shops. Two color printing is routinely offered by many. Improvements in inks, plates, chemicals and knowhow have eased the problems that prevented most early quick printers from offering color.

A large percentage of the two color work is done with a T51 color head attachment. Registration problems are minimized with the T51 because of the unique arrangement of using the same blanket for both colors. With two colors on the blanket at the same time, the register is correct even if the paper alignment is not perfect.

Metal plates, of course, still run color better, or at least with less problems than paper plates. Most long run two color jobs, even on a T51 head, are run with metal plates because of the stretch factor of paper plates.

MULTICOLOR PRESSES

The multicolor press consists simply of a series of single printing units combined into one machine. Each has its own inking and dampening system and each has its own plate, blanket, and impression cylinders. The chief difference between color printing and regular black-and-white work is in the problem of register and the characteristics of the inks. If the inks for the first colors dry too hard between the runs on a single color press, they will lose their affinity or ability to trap the inks for the succeeding colors. Multicolor presses have a special trapping problem, too, because the inks do not have time to dry between impressions, and there is always the risk that the ink from the first impression will mix with the ink in the second unit and adulterate its color. To prevent this from happening, pressmen generally run a stiff ink in the first unit and use progressively softer inks in each of the other units. Since stiff inks have more tack, they tend to pull the softer inks to them and resist fusing with the subsequent colors.

Besides knowing the characteristics of the inks and the mechanical problems involved in obtaining register, pressmen must also know how to mix inks at the press when it is necessary to run a color that they do not have in stock or when it is necessary to match a color used in a previous job or a piece of artwork. On the surface this sounds like a simple problem, but actually there is more to it than meets the eye.

WHAT IS COLOR

Color is nothing more than waves or rays of light which your eye records just as your ear records tones. The longest rays that you can see are those which produce the sensation of red. There are longer ones, called infrared, but they cannot be seen. The shortest rays that can be seen by the eye are violet. The ultraviolet rays are too short to be detected by the human eye.

When all the wave lengths are combined, the eye receives the sensation of white. And if white light is passed through a prism, it is broken into its component parts: (1) the violet, the indigo, and some of the blue; (2) the remainder of the blue, the green, and some of the yellow; and (3) the remainder of the yellow, the orange, and the red.

Whether you see an object as white or colored depends on the light it receives, the amount of light it absorbs and reflects, and the color sensitivity of your eyes.

A colored object always reflects the rays of its own color and absorbs all the others. It will appear black if it absorbs all the colors or if the light striking it does not include its particular color. That is why green objects look black under the red light in the darkroom. The red light contains no green light waves and there is no green light for the green objects to reflect.

COLOR RELATIONSHIP

In printing, you can produce an almost endless variety of colors by mixing pigments or dyes. This is known as the subtractive process of producing color because the pigments absorb or subtract from the light all but the desired color. For example, when you print on white paper with blue ink, you are covering the paper with a mixture that absorbs the red and green light and reflects the blue. The diagram shows what is commonly known as the primary and secondary colors. The primary colors,

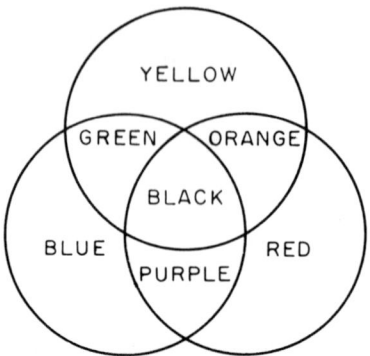

SUBSTRACTIVE COMBINATION RESULTING FROM SUPERIMPOSED DYED LAYERS (COLOR FILM), OVERLAPPING COLOR FILTERS, OR OVERLAPPING TRANSPARENT COLORED PRINTING INKS.

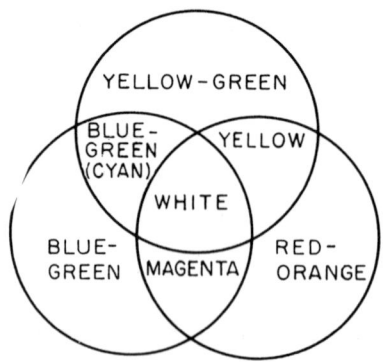

ADDITIVE COMBINATION RESULTING FROM PRO-JECTION OF COLORED LIGHTS OR APPEARANCE OF ADJACENT COLORED HALFTONE DOTS.

red, yellow, and blue, are basic; they cannot be produced by mixing pigments of other colors. If you mix or overprint equal amounts of two of these primary colors, you will get a secondary color. You will notice in the diagram, for example, that when blue and yellow are overprinted or mixed together, you will get green. If all the primary colors are overlapped or mixed together, you will get black (or a muddy gray). When two of the primary colors are overlapped or mixed, the resulting color is always complementary to the third primary color. Thus, red and green, yellow and purple,and orange and blue are complementary to each other.

You can also produce colors by overlapping colored lights. This is known as the additive process, because the colors in this case are produced by adding light instead of absorbing it. Again a complementary color is formed when two primary colors overlap, but in this case, if you overlap the lights of all three of the primary colors, you will get a white light. Furthermore, if you compare the diagram in the lower part with that at the top, you will see that the color combinations are reversed. The primary colors for additive combinations consist of blue-violet, yellow-green, and red-orange, and the secondary colors consist of blue-green (cyan), yellow, and magenta. Scientists consider these secondary light colors to be the true primary pigment colors instead of the traditional red, blue, and yellow, shown in the diagram, and these colors are used by printers as the basis for mixing colored inks. This is also why magenta, cyan, and yellow are used instead of bright reds, blues, and yellows in printing halftones in color. In halftone color work, you have both subtractive and additive color combinations. Additive combinations are produced when the halftone dots do not overlap but print side by side and tend to blend together; subtractive color combinations are formed in areas where one dot overlaps another. Colored inks and films cannot reproduce all the color hues seen by the eye, so colored halftone reproduction is never completely accurate.

COLOR TERMS

Color is divided into hues, such as red, yellow, blue, and so on. The chroma of the color is the measure of brilliancy; and the value of the color is the measure of its lightness or darkness. You can change the value of the color by adding white or black. White will make any color lighter without changing the identity of the color, and black will make it darker. When the color is mixed with white, the result is said to be a tint; and when it is mixed with black, a shade results. The strength of colored ink has to do with their covering power. Strong inks have greater covering power and produce more impressions because it is not necessary to carry as much ink on the rollers to obtain the desired results.

Colors may also be classified as warm or cool. Red, yellow, and orange are the warm colors; blue, green, and violet are the cool ones. Warm colors, like red and orange, excite the eye and are excellent attention-getters. But some blues and violets are so cool that they tend to repel the eye rather than attract it. Yellow is the best attention-getter of all.

A touch of red will make any color warmer; a touch of yellow will make it brighter; and a touch of white will make it cooler and lighter. Blue will make it cooler and less compelling to the eye.

As a general rule, the warm colors should be used sparingly because they are so strong that they are likely to attract attention to themselves. But the cooler colors can be used more profusely and in larger blocks.

COLOR COMBINATIONS

If you will study the diagram, you will see that directly opposite the yellow is the purple; opposite the red is the green; and opposite the blue is the orange. As you have already seen, these colors are said to be complementary to each other.

When used together in printing, complementary colors always produce harmonious combinations. The cool color should always be predominant, however. Warm colors should be used sparingly in printing, just as they are in dress, interior decoration, and art.

Black goes well with any color, but when a cool color is used with black, it is often mixed with a touch of one of the warmer colors to make it more appealing. When printing with colored ink, you should lean toward heavier, bolder typefaces, because colored inks tend to show up lighter on white paper. This is especially true when the color is used in combination with black ink.

MONOCHROME COMBINATIONS

You may also use monochrome combinations in printing. That is, you may print part of the job in a dark color, such as dark green and part of it in a tint of the same color (light green). Monochrome effects are also achieved by printing on a colored stock, as for example, with dark blue ink on a light blue stock. Other pleasing effects may be obtained by printing with brown or blue ink on buff paper, and so on.

WHY COLOR IS USED

Color is used to direct attention. Colors also give additional meaning to illustrations. In advertising and publications, it is used not only as an attention-getter, but also to add realism to the illustrations. For example, advertisements for food products are far more effective and appetizing when they are printed in color.

Color is also used to create a mood of light heartedness in advertisements for amusements. And it has a similar use for children's books, comics, movie magazines, and so on.

Sometimes color is used to suggest abstract ideas. For example, one might use a block of light green as a background color for a window-card advertising spring fashions, or a warm brown and orange for a poster advertising a football game in the fall. People often associate red with danger (red lanterns, red stoplights, and so on) and with passion (seeing red) just as they connect orange with the pumpkins in the fall or the cheery fire on a winter's night. Green suggests springtime and brightness; light blue suggests coldness and repose; dark blue, quality and courage; yellow, life and gaiety; purple, royalty and formality, as well as sorrow and remorse; warm brown suggests fall; and gold suggests riches.

COLORED INKS

Ink is perhaps the least expensive part of any offset job; therefore, it is a good idea to use the best inks available. This is particularly important when you are working with colored inks or presensitized or direct image plates. A poor ink has a grinding effect on the image and may shorten the life of the plate by as much as 50 percent.

In most cases, the color is specified by the person who originates the job, and it is then up to the printer to select or mix the inks to supply the color desired.

It is not necessary to match colors exactly for run-of-the-mill work, and you can use the ink just as it comes from the can as long as it has the covering and working qualities required. But occasionally, it will be necessary for you to duplicate a certain color.

If the color is to be used frequently or for long runs, it is generally better to order the ink already mixed by the manufacturer. But if the run is short and the color is seldom used, you can produce it yourself by mixing together the inks you have in stock.

MATCHING COLORS

Books and charts are available which show

standard colors which the customer can refer to when ordering the job and you can refer to when making a color match. Many of these systems show in what proportion the base colors are to be used in producing the desired blends.

The Pantone Matching System (PMS) is very popular because almost all printing ink manufacturers now subscribe to the system and distribute Pantone color charts in addition to their own individual ink color books. The Pantone system is widely used for specifying colors throughout the printing industry.

Pantone, Inc. has published a book of over 500 colors (blends) that can be produced by mixing 9 basic pantone colors (plus transparent white) in various combinations. In addition, free Pantone color charts are available from a number of ink suppliers which show the 9 basic colors and 51 most popular blends based on art directors' recommendations, the most frequently used papers, and manufacturing and ordering frequency records. These charts are useful in ordering colored inks and in mixing inks in the shop. The base inks and the 51 blends are available commercially as stock inks. Other blends selected from the Speed-Match Pantone book are also available from suppliers, but they must be custom mixed.

As useful as color matching systems are, they are not entirely fool proof. The color may darken or lighten, for example, if the ink feed varies during the run, and the color may also change slightly with a change in the strength of the fountain solution. Color may also vary with the speed and temperature of the press, the setting of the rollers and cylinders, and with the reflecting qualities of the paper. You must also remember that inks are deceptive. They often dry lighter than they appear when they are placed in the fountain, and they sometimes dry darker. So, if you want to turn out top-quality work, you must have a good understanding of the properties of the inks and know how they will react under varying conditions.

MIXING INKS

In small shops, inks are generally mixed in the pressroom on a slab of stone, a piece of plate glass, or the back of a used press plate. Large shops often have a separate room or laboratory for ink storage and mixing.

If your shop is engaged in color work, you should have a good selection of basic inks, both transparent and opaque. This selection should include a set of three-color process inks in addition to opaque reds, blues, and yellows. You should also have transparent and opaque oranges, purples, and greens; halftone and job black; a transparent white or tint base; and an opaque white. All of the inks should be of regular strength for good offset work without the need for reducers or driers, inasmuch as the addition of these items affects the ultimate color strength of the inks.

In addition to the inks, your shop should be equipped with an ink slab, approximately 24" square, which may consist of stone, glass, or plexiglass. You should have an assortment of spatulas and ink knives, including two 8" spatulas, one or more 4" spatulas, an ink knife 1-1/2" wide and one or more 4" knives.

You should also have an accurate scale and a balance. A balance (sensitive to 1/10 of a gram) can be used for small trial mixes, and a scale of at least 5 pounds capacity (sensitive to 1/4 of an ounce) can be used for final batch mixes. The scale and balance will enable you to weigh out all ingredients so that you can keep a record of them and duplicate the mixture again if necessary. It is always better to mix the inks in small quantities working slowly until the desired color is reached. Then if you have kept an accurate record of the amount of each color used, you can simply increase each amount proportionately when you are preparing the final batch of ink for the run.

If your shop is small and color is seldom used, you may not have all the items mentioned. In a small shop, for example, you may mix the ink at the press with an ordinary galley spatula or a putty knife.If an exact match is not required, you may measure out the portions of ink instead of weighing them. Even if your stock of colored inks is limited, you will find that you can produce dozens of colors and tints by mixing the few basic inks you have on hand.

TAPPING OUT THE INK

Since the color of the ink may vary with its thickness, some tints and pastel colors look much darker on the mixing slab than they do after they have been spread thin on white paper. Therefore, you should tap the ink out with your finger onto a sheet of white paper, as shown, to find its true color. Then match the "tap out" with the sample to be duplicated. If time permits, you may allow the ink to stand until it dries on the paper. This will not only give you a more accurate idea of the finished color, but will also furnish you with a clue to the drying qualities of the ink.

Pressmen generally keep a notebook or a file of cards listing all pertinent information about the colors mixed for each job. Besides including the ink formulas and notes on the drying and working qualities of the inks, they often attach a color swatch from the printed job or a swatch showing the ink as it was tapped out on the sheet during mixing. Although inks sometimes dry dark or light and fade or change color over a period of time, if the formulas are correct, it will not be too difficult to repeat the color when the job comes up again.

In matching colors, you will find that appearances are often deceiving when you place two colors side by side. A color may appear warm when placed beside a colder color, for example, and cold when placed beside a warmer color. You will also find that if you attempt to match a color from memory, you will generally come up with a color that is darker and brighter than the original.

CHARACTERISTICS OF THE BASIC INKS

Inks are classified as transparent, semitransparent, or opaque, depending on the nature of the pigment or dye and the extender used. The opaque inks are generally used for printing down first colors or where good opacity is required, as on colored stock. The transparent colors are used in process color printing and in other types of work where the subsequent impressions must not block out the previous colors.

Inks are also classified as organic and inorganic. The pigments used in inorganic inks are generally made from minerals, such as mercury or iron. They are fast driers and have good color permanency. The pigments used in organic inks are made from coal tar dyes. They are generally more brilliant than inorganic pigments, but they dry more slowly and are also more fugitive (more apt to fade in the sunlight)."Lake" colors are typical examples of organic inks. They are made from metallic dye compounds and are available in a variety of colors.

YELLOWS

Some yellow inks are transparent; others are

opaque or semiopaque. Yellow lakes are transparent and somewhat fugitive. They have reasonably good drying and working qualities.

Benzidine yellows are also organic and transparent. They are brilliant in color, but are extremely fugitive. (As a rule, the brighter colors are more fugitive than the others.)

Chrome yellows are inorganic. Since they are made from lead chromates, they are natural driers and are semiopaque. They are reasonably permanent, but tend to have poor working qualities because they are so heavy.

Cadmium yellows are inorganic and opaque and similar to chrome yellows in drying and working qualities.

Many of these inks come in a variety of shades ranging from cool (greenish) yellow to warm (reddish) yellow. Warm yellows are better for the average run of work than the cool ones, because they have more eye appeal. That is why lemon yellows are generally selected for process printing—cool yellow would give the job an overall greenish tinge.

If the yellow is to be printed first down, and the other colors are to be printed over it, you may use an opaque or semiopaque ink, but you should always use transparent ink if the yellow is to overprint the other colors. A transparent yellow over black will enhance the black, but an opaque yellow will make the black look muddy and greenish.

REDS

Transparent or semitransparent lake reds are clean working and reasonably strong, but they tend to be fugitive. They are often used to add warmth to cold reds when permanent, warm colors are needed. Cold reds can also be made warmer with a touch of orange, but the results are not as good. You can produce a cold red by mixing warm red with a cooler red or a touch of blue. Opaque reds generally have a good permanence, but they are more difficult to work and often dry dark on the paper.

BLUES

Most blues are transparent or semitransparent, and most of them have good working qualities. Peacock blue (made from coal tar dyes) is generally used for process work. It is transparent and brilliant in color, but rather fugitive unless it is mixed with another color, such as milori blue.

Milori blue (iron blue) is semitransparent and a fast drier. It is reasonably permanent, but tends to darken as it dries, and the prints sometimes change color with age. It is a good working ink and requires little acid in the fountain solution. Too much acid may cause the rollers to strip when milori blue is on the press.

Like peacock blue, alkali blue is an organic lake. It is transparent and has reasonably clean working qualities. However, it tends to darken as it dries and is also slow drying and fugitive.

There are many other types of blue, but you can derive almost any shade from the colors just mentioned. Besides mixing cool blues with warm blues, you can also make blues warmer by adding a touch of red; or you can make them cooler by adding green. You can increase the brilliancy of dark blues by printing them over a light blue.

GREENS

You can provide a bright green by mixing milori blue with lemon yellow or chrome yellow. The blue is stronger than the yellow, of course, so don't use too much of it. One part of blue to two parts of yellow is generally sufficient for this purpose, but you can add more blue if a blue green is required or use slightly less blue if you want a yellow green. Use the pure colors if possible. A reddish blue will give the green an olive tinge. Use a touch of black to darken the color and a touch of white to lighten it. The chrome greens supplied by manufacturers are fast driers and reasonably permanent. The lake greens are brilliant, but they are extremely fugitive.

PURPLES

The purple inks supplied by manufacturers are generally made from coal tar dyes, but you can produce purple in the shop by mixing 2 parts of cold red with 1 part of warm blue. Do not use warm reds or greenish blues, because they contain traces of yellow that distort the color.

To form maroon, mix cold red with cold blue, and then add orange or black until you have reached the desired hue.

ORANGES

To form orange, you should mix 1 part of warm red with 2 parts of reddish yellow ink. The transparent lake orange inks supplied by manufacturers are fugitive and tend to bleed. Semitransparent (permanent) lake oranges are somewhat stronger and less fugitive. Inorganic oranges, such as chrome orange, are opaque, permanent, and fast drying.

BROWNS

To form a brown ink, you should mix green and red together and add yellow, black, or blue as necessary. You can also add black to orange or mix yellow, red, and black together. Yellow will brighten the resulting color; black or blue will darken it; and white will lighten it.

OTHER COLORS

Although the colors just discussed are the ones you are most likely to use, there may be occasions when you will be called on to produce off-shade colors, such as rust or olive green. This should not be too difficult if you will learn to recognize the basic colors and then mix them together and modify them as necessary until you obtain the desired results.

You cannot mix colors to produce gold and silver inks. Special metallic inks must be used when these colors are required.

WHITE INKS

Although opaque white inks are available for printing on colored stocks, white inks (both opaque and transparent) are used chiefly in preparing tints. Transparent whites or reducers, such as laketine, alumina hydrate, and magnesia are generally used for producing the tints when the job is to be printed on white or light-colored stocks. Opaque whites are used to provide the covering qualities required for dark stock.

When you are mixing a tint, you should always add the color to the white; not white to the color. If you add the white to the color, you may find that it will take more white than you had anticipated, and you will end up with more ink than is required.

If you have a manufacturer's ink chart, you can use it in preparing tints. These charts generally show each color printed solid and also show various (screened) tints of the color. As you know, a 25-percent screened tint means that 25 percent of the paper is covered by dots and 75 percent is left as white space. So if the ink chart shows that the color desired is a 25-percent value or tint of the solid color, you can approximate it when you mix the inks by using 1 part of the color and 3 parts of white. Further modifications may be necessary of course, but this will give you a starting point. Remember that you should mix the inks in small quantities until you hit on the correct amount of each ingredient.

Remember, too that pastel colors are tricky. They often change shades as they dry. Some colors also tend to become fugitive when they are reduced. Above all, don't cut the ink so far that it will be necessary to carry an excess amount on the rollers in order to maintain the proper color. This may lead to scumming, filling in, mottling, and other press troubles.

BLACK INKS

Some lithographic shops carry only one black ink— an all-purpose black—which they use for all jobs. Others carry a toned black in addition to the regular black, because toned blacks add sparkle to the work. You can add tone to black ink, of course, by mixing it with a touch of dark blue ink.

GLOSS INKS AND VARNISHES

Although gloss inks are available, pressmen sometimes overprint color work with a transparent varnish to give it a gloss finish. Gloss varnishes applied on the offset press not only supply a glossy finish, but also impart a degree of durability to the paper. You should not confuse overprint varnishes with the varnishes used for mixing inks. Overprint varnish is handled much the same as ink on the press, and it may be run solid (without dampeners) or run only on the image areas on the paper. Besides providing a gloss, it is also useful as a sealer for jobs that chalk.

The luster of the varnish varies, of course, with its rosin content and with the absorbency of the paper. Absorbent stocks naturally have less gloss.

If the stock has a tendency to pick, pressmen sometimes run it through the press to coat it with a wax-free varnish before the job is begun. Although this means an extra run, pressmen consider it worthwhile because it waterproofs the paper and gives it a good working surface.

Gloss inks add brilliance to the job, but they also offset easily and the stack should be removed from the delivery pile frequently if sprays or other drying devices are not in use.

PROCESS INKS

Yellow, magenta (red) and cyan (blue) are the inks most commonly used for printing halftones in color. These inks are transparent so that one can be printed over the other to produce the secondary colors, such as orange, purple, and green.If a solid block of magenta is printed over a solid block of yellow, the result will be a bright red, but if the red consists of a 60 percent screened tint rather than a solid, the result will be orange. A flesh color will result if a 20 percent red dot is printed over a 20 percent yellow dot.

The color of the paper is important when process inks are used. Since these inks are transparent and allow the paper to show through, coated stocks produce the best results in this type of work. When printed on white paper, each of the process colors absorbs one-third of the light and reflects the rest. When one color is printed over another, the secondary color thus formed absorbs approximately two-thirds of the light.

Since process inks vary according to the pigments used in making them, progressive (color) proofs should be made with the same stocks and same inks as those which will be used for the actual run.

In proofing, the yellow plate is generally printed first, and the blue plate is printed next. The red plate and black plate then follow. This order is used because the red and black plates generally require more corrections than the others, and if corrections are necessary, the red or black plate can be remade without the necessity of reproofing the yellow and blue plates.

3M COLOR KEY

The Minnesota Mining and Manufacturing Company produces thin, light-sensitive, color-coated acetate sheets which may be used in proofing color jobs. The colored coatings on these sheets match standard process colors. The sheets are exposed to light through the proper separation negatives and are then developed with a chemical which dissolves the unexposed areas of the coating, leaving a colored image on the acetate. Since the colors are transparent, when sheets with a magenta, cyan, yellow, and black image are registered one over another, a full-color proof results.

DRIERS

As you know, cobalt is a surface drier and is used when hard drying is desired. It is generally used with black inks in single-color printing. But in multicolor work, where one color is to overprint another, paste driers are often used with the black as well as with the colored inks to prevent the first color from drying too hard.

If the first down color dries too hard or if you wait too long before you run the next one, the first color may lose its affinity or ability to receive (trap) the next color. An excess of drier or too much wax in the ink may also cause the ink to crystallize and fail to trap the succeeding colors properly.

COLOR SEQUENCE

Although other factors may enter the picture, the sequence in which the colors are to be run depends to a large extent on the following things:

1. The type of press to be used—whether it is single or multicolor.
2. The characteristics of the inks.
3. The image area on each of the color plates.

On multicolor presses, the first down color is overprinted by one or more of the other colors while it is still wet. Therefore, the pressman generally prints the light colors first so that the wet ink from the first colors will not degrade the colors in the succeeding units if it happens to backtrap. If he is operating a two-color press, he may run the yellow and red during the first run and the blue and the black during the second. And on a four-color press, he may run the yellow on the first cylinder and follow it with red, blue, and black, using a slightly softer ink and more drier for each succeeding color.

There are times when this sequence must be altered, of course. For example, if the red in the second unit tends to build up or pile on the blankets in the third and fourth units, it may be necessary to run the red last. Other factors may also necessitate a change in the sequence of the colors in order to effect quality production.

Color sequence is not as important if the job is to be printed on a single-color press. In this case, pressmen generally follow the sequence that best fits the job. Some pressmen run the color plate with the smallest image area first, but others print the key plate first and then build over it with the succeeding colors.

You may print the black first down when you are using transparent colors. The black will print sharp and clean and the other colors will enhance it, giving it a luster in the areas where they overlap. If you attempt to overprint black with opaque colors, the result will be discolored and muddy, of course.

When large black solids are used in combination with halftones, in process printing, printers sometimes run an extra plate carrying the solids and type, because it is difficult to ink the solids properly without degrading the halftones when they are printed in the same run. In many cases, pressmen use a weaker black for process work.

If yellow is printed first down in process printing, the pressman generally uses a blue glass for viewing the impression. The blue glass acts as a filter and makes it easier for him to tell how the yellow tints are printing.

Color sequence may also be influenced by the flow of work in the shop. For example, if you have been running red on the press, it may be simpler to run the red first. You must clean the fountain and rollers thoroughly when you switch from a dark color to a light one, of course. Some pressmen run laketine or Burnishine Putz Pomade on the press for a few minutes after they clean the rollers to allow all the dark ink to work out of the rollers before they give it the final washup.

FLUORESCENT INKS

X-rays, light waves, and radio waves are the same kind of electromagnetic energy; however, they vary in frequency and wave length. The frequency of visible light waves, for example, is millions of times greater than that of radio waves. The waves that produce the sensation of red are longer than those which produce the sensation of blue or green, and the waves which produce the sensation of violet are the shortest of all.

When you print with ink on a piece of paper, you are simply applying a pigment to the paper that absorbs some of the light waves and reflects others. The ink will appear white if it reflects all the colors and it will appear black if it absorbs them all. On the other hand, the ink will appear colored if it absorbs part of the light and reflects a portion of it. The color depends on the length of the reflected light wave.

Fluorescent color pigments differ from those found in ordinary inks in that their molecules pick up energy from the light at a short wave length and emit it at a longer wave length. For example, if you are printing with red fluorescent ink, the pigment reflects not only the red rays but also converts the violet, blue, yellow, and green into visible energy in the red wave length. This causes the red to fluoresce. Normal reds waste this energy.

You can print fluorescent inks on the offset press; however, it is necessary to lay down a heavier film of ink when using these colors than it is when conventional inks are run. Any type of metal plate can be used, but deep-etch plates seem to work best because they can carry more ink. If the image consists of reverse type or fine lines, it is recommended that you use a medium or coarse grained plate to provide the pressman with additional water. If he is using presensitized direct-image plates, the pressman may find it necessary to increase the strength of the fountain solution since these plates do not carry as much water as grained plates. Pressmen sometimes run the dried sheets through the press a second time to provide double inking. This provides a brighter color in the finished job.

The press should be clean and free from any material that might contaminate the ink. Traces of dark ink on the ink rollers, for example, will reduce the brightness of the fluorescent colors. Some pressmen run an opaque white on the rollers after the first wash up in order to weed out any traces of colored ink or foreign material. After this, they wash the rollers again before putting the fluorescent ink in the fountain.

Dampener covers should be clean and free from other ink films. The dampener solution should have a pH of 4.5 to 5.0 for grained or deep-etch plates, and a pH of 3.5 to 4.0 for presensitized or direct-image plates.

It is generally recommended that all units of the press be set with a light, even pressure when these inks are being run.

Since the ink must be run three or four times heavier with fluorescent colors than with other types of inks, some pressmen set the ink fountain roller for the maximum throw and control the volume with the fountain keys. Fluorescent colors should be used just as they come from the can with as little doctoring as possible. Most conventional additives may be used in spare quantities, but it is necessary to tap out the additive in the ink to test the two for compatibility.

These inks are fast setting. They usually set tack-free in 20 minutes in the stack and are usually hard dried in 4 to 6 hours. The drying rate can be increased by the addition of a varnish made with chinawood oil, either the overprint or mixing type. Since the ink is so heavy, anti-offset spray is extremely helpful.

These inks trap satisfactorily not only with each other but with most conventional inks, so that it is possible to overprint them with regular inks.

MAGNETIC INKS

Magnetic inks are available in green, red, brown, black, and toned black for both letterpress and offset presses. They are simply inks with iron oxide pigments which lay down printed films capable of being magnetized. They have no magnetic properties until they are printed on paper and run through a processing machine which magnetizes the printed film a fraction of a second before it is read electronically. A special type font (E 13B) must be used when printing with these inks in order for the machine to read them.

The signal strength of characters printed with magnetic ink is proportional to the ink film thickness. Therefore, since the offset press lays down a thinner ink film than that produced by letterpress, the magnetic strength of offset inks must be considerably greater. This is accomplished by proper ink formulation during manufacture.

Magnetic inks are designed to print right out of the can and generally require no doctoring, although slight additions (3 percent or less) of drier, solvent, or oil may be made in emergencies. Since the pigment is present in just the right percentage, any excessive alteration of the ink will result in an improper signal amplitude of the printed ink film.

Too much drier affects press stability and causes nonuniformity of the ink film. Do not add toners to increase jetness of blacks or strength of color as this will upset the ink balance.

Since all magnetic inks are short and/or heavy bodied and must contain a special iron oxide which is a poor "pigment" as far as wetting is concerned, automatic ink fountain agitators are recommended. Even with this precaution, constant checks of the ink fountain and rollers are required for good results with magnetic inks.

Exact shelf life for the inks is unknown. However, tests indicate that a closed container of magnetic ink should have a life of at least one year. The iron oxide pigments themselves are not affected by age.

PAPER

A sheet of paper may look perfectly white when you see it lying alone on the table, but if you compare it with a sheet from another batch of white stock, you may find that the first sheet is slightly offshade. Offshade whites have a slight effect on the appearance of the finished job in color printing, particularly when the job is run in transparent inks. This is because white light from the paper reflects through the ink. And the results will not be the same on two different stocks, if one is whiter than the other. You will also find that when ink is printed on two different kinds of stock, it may dry a darker shade on one than on the other. These subtleties may be disregarded for the average run or work, of course. But, if a close color match is required, pressmen generally select a pure white sheet and mix the stocks as little as possible.

In extreme cases, stocks may vary from sheet to sheet in the same package. Since the stock comes from several different rolls at the mill, every fifth or sixth sheet may vary slightly from the others in ink receptivity.

You will find that your eyes will become tired after you have been running the same color for a long stretch of time and the chances are if you close your eyes, you will see the opposite or complementary color in your mind. Because of this, pressmen sometimes have difficulty in matching colors when they switch to another job after a prolonged run of one color. The eyes become tired from the first color and tend to be oversensitive to the color which is complementary to it.

PLATES

Although deep-etch plates were formerly used extensively for process work and long color runs, today it is possible to get good results from a variety of plates. Bimetal plates are used in many instances and presensitized or wipe-on plates may also be used. Paper and plastic direct-image plates are being used for short and medium length runs, but rarely, if ever, for process work.

Presensitized plates are thinner and fit more readily to the contour of the press cylinder, but because they are so thin, they may tear if you apply too much pressure in drawing them taut on the cylinder or they may kink if they are handled carelessly.

Conventional zinc plates are developed with black developing ink. If a plate is to be run in color, this ink is usually washed out and the image areas are covered with asphaltum. The image areas on other types of plates may also be covered with asphaltum before the plate is sent to the press. If the plate is allowed to stand overnight or for any length of time while the run is in progress, you should wash the ink from the image and cover the image areas with asphaltum. Many pressmen dilute the gum arabic solution slightly when gumming a plate on the press to facilitate removing it later.

MISREGISTER

Always check the paper to see that it has been cut square along the side guide and gripper edges before you begin the run. If the paper is "out of square," you will have trouble in maintaining register.

EXCESS PRINTING PRESSURE

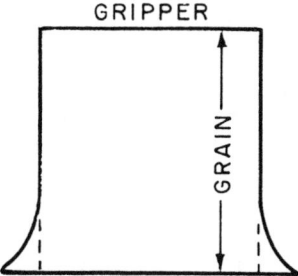

You may have trouble in registering succeeding colors if you use too much printing pressure. Excess pressure stretches the sheet and also causes it to fan out at the tail edge as it runs through the press, as shown in the illustration. Most sheets return to their original size after the impression, but some sheets may not; and this will cause a register problem when the next color is printed, because the amount of stretch will vary from sheet to sheet.

UNSEASONED PAPER

Improperly seasoned paper is another source of misregister, of course. If the moisture content of the paper is out of balance with the humidity of the pressroom, the stock may curl before it is run, even though it is perfectly flat when it is removed from the package. This is likely to cause wrinkles and may also affect the register because the paper will take on additional moisture as it runs through the press and the impression will stretch with the paper making the image on the next plate appear short.

If the stock has swollen or wavy edges, the tail edge of the sheet may fan out, as shown in the illustration, on the first trip through the press. There will be less fan out on the second trip through, so the first down color will print wider than the second. If the paper is swollen in the center and has tight edges, the sheet will fan out slightly as it passes through the first printing unit and will then return to its original shape, causing the first image to be narrower than the second.

For best results, you should always allow the paper to season awhile before you attempt to run a close-register job. It will also help to cover the stack between runs, because the sheets may develop wavy or tight edges if they are left standing open.

If the run is long, you should number the skids or dollies so that you can keep them in numerical order. Then when you begin the second run, you can start with the sheets on the first skid. You will find this system useful in maintaining register, particularly if the plate has stretched during the run, or if the blanket was lifted or other adjustments were made after the first run was started.

There may be times when paper stretch from the first run will make it difficult for you to effect register, if you run the second color too soon after the first run is completed. In such cases, it may help to allow the paper to stand for a few hours to give it a chance to shrink back to its original size.

Misregister may also be due to static in the paper—particularly if the stock is coated.

Coated stocks sometimes cause mottling and picking in color work. You may not encounter trouble of this type when you make the first run, but when you put the sheets through the press for the next color, you may find that moisture from the previous run has softened the surface of the stock. This may cause the sheets to pick or stick to the blanket, or powdery particles of the paper coating may build up on the blanket, causing mottling and scum. Alum in some coated paper will also cause a scum or tint in the nonprinting areas of the plate on long runs.

When it is necessary to run such paper, pressmen sometimes waterproof it by putting a blank plate on the press, lifting the dampeners and running a solid coating of laketine or varnish over the paper before they begin the run.

EMBOSSED BLANKETS

Embossed areas on the blanket often increase the printing pressure just enough to cause the blanket to give and throw off the register. You may even find that the register will vary slightly for a few impressions each time you wash the blanket during the run. You can eliminate this to some extent by going over the blanket with water just before you apply the blanket wash. If the blanket is badly embossed by oils from the previous run, you should change it, of course. A new blanket should be mounted carefully. It may print unevenly if it is not square or if it is drawn too tight. Excess tension shortens the image and may cause the blanket to pull out at the blanket bars.

VARIATIONS IN PLATE THICKNESS

The platemaker and pressman should work hand-in-hand when a close-register job is involved. The platemaker should mike each plate before selecting it for the job, because thickness varies from one plate to another, and conventional plates sometimes show as much as 0.002 to 0.004 of an inch difference in thickness from side to side.

When uniform plates are not available, it is generally better to put the image for the first down color on the thickest plate. If this plate is run first, it will increase the circumference of the plate cylinder and shorten the image. This will help to effect register because

354

the image generally prints short when the subsequent colors are run.

If the plates are thinner on one side than the other, the thick side will print shorter than the thin one. But the platemaker can assist the pressman in obtaining register if he positions the image so the thick side of the plates will always be on the same side of the press when the job is run.

If plates vary too greatly in thickness from one side to the other, it may be necessary to build up under the blanket to provide the proper contact on the low side. This distorts the image slightly during the impression, of course, and the extra pressure may batter the blanket unless you back off the impression cylinder on the side affected.

CYLINDER GRIPPERS

Misregister may occur if the cylinder grippers are not properly set, particularly if the blanket is tacky and prevents the sheet from transferring properly from one printing unit to the next.

You can check for varying register during the first run by putting some of the printed sheets through the press a second time. If the second image registers with the first, the run is proceeding properly. But if the second image does not match the first, you can look for trouble when you run your next color, if close register is involved.

You should study 10 or more consecutively printed sheets when you are checking for misregister because it may take several sheets to give you the true picture of the situation. Some pressmen check register by positioning 3 or 4 sheets one over the other and examining them over a light table.

CHAPTER 27

EQUIPMENT RECOMMENDATIONS

(Specialized equipment is covered under many other chapters)

In an effort to analyze various quick printing operations and as an excuse to travel, I interviewed, over a period of four years, several hundred quick printers. Magazine articles paid part of my travel expense and provided a playback from responding readers. I discovered there are many ways to be successful in quick printing and a lot more ways to fail.

A description of equipment being used would fill a book this size. There are no "best" types of equipment for every shop. Quick printing has moved into an age of specialization. The equipment must fit the specialty. The equipment recommended here is basic equipment used successfully in thousands of shops, including our own.

EXPERIMENTAL SHOP

We wanted to try various types of equipment and methods that seemed to be working for other quick printers. To accomplish this, we have for the past year operated an experimental shop. In this shop, we are using equipment and methods considered too risky for a strictly money-making shop. This is providing me with "hands-on" opportunities that would not be practical in our other shops. Some completed experiments are reported in this book. Others will be reported in our pricing advisory bulletins. All of the equipment we test is purchased, not loaned or donated. This gives me complete freedom in reporting results.

PRICES

The prices of equipment are not included in this book. Many of the prices would be obsolete by publication time. We will, however, be reporting equipment prices in our pricing advisory bulletins. These bulletins are part of our counter price book and computer pricing programs. Within these services we have set up a system to provide us with current prices — selling prices of printing and actual cost prices of paper and major equipment. There are many deals on equipment. Much of the equipment is sold below advertised prices. The actual selling prices are what we are interested in and will be reporting.

"STANDARD SHOP" NOT ANYMORE

There are quick printing shops with web offset

equipment, Heidelbergs, Systems platemaker/ presses, and two-color presses. Some use only Electrostatic equipment. One, at least, specializes in short-run process color work for advertising agencies. Many shops have elaborate typesetting, layup, and camera departments. As new skills and equipment are acquired, quick printers are finding customers for them — at least most of the time.

BASIC EQUIPMENT

The equipment selected for this chapter is basic, proven equipment. The word "proven" is important. You can gamble on unproven equipment up to a point, but the price of a mistake can be high. I estimate that I have bought over $50,000 of unusable equipment over the years, most of it in the early days when we had to take chances. In just one year's time, we have accumulated quite a bit of "junk" in our experimental shop.

You don't have to gamble as I did as there are plenty of places to test new equipment now. You are not going to be left behind just because you are not first. If you have a small shop, let the big shops test and prove equipment before you buy. Don't go too far the other way either and sit with outdated equipment that is costing more in manpower than new equipment would cost. It is difficult to know where the middle path is, but it is the only reasonably safe path to profit.

IDENTICAL PRESSES

Sooner or later most quick printers expand into two

or more presses. An important consideration is the advantage of having identical presses. Parts, plates, and operators can be interchanged. This can be a gigantic advantage in a small shop. There is one thing you can be sure of — you will have down time on any press. Parts should be available, but often are not for a week or two. You cannot afford to be down for a day, let alone a week. With identical presses, you will rarely be completely out of operation for even a few hours.

OFFSET PRINTING PRESSES

The A.B. Dick 360CD (chain delivery) is still the most popular press in quick printing. Other manufacturers are producing excellent presses, but A.B. Dick has the momentum. A.B. Dick has not done as well with their platemaker/processors or their photocopiers.

Quick printing, as we know it today, started with the combination of the A.B. Dick press, the Itek camera/platemaker, and Eastman photo-direct paper plate material. In the mid 1960s, this combination clicked. The buying public accepted the level of quality this combination was capable of producing. Inroads into this original combination are being made, however. The Japanese have developed what many consider a superior plate material to Eastman. 3M is making gains on the Itek camera/processor, and more and more Japanese presses are showing up in quick printing shops.

A. B. Dick is currently pushing their "Pro" models. However, our most recent acquisition is the standard model because we felt the Pro models had not been sufficiently "proven." We may try a Pro in our experimental shop later this year.

WHY A.B. DICK

The question is often asked why A.B. Dick grabbed the lion's share of the quick printing market over such old-time favorites as Multilith and Davidson. When I bought my first Model 1250 Multilith in the late 1940s, A.B. Dick was a mimeograph and spirit duplicator manufacturer. They later bought the Lithomat Company, where I was involved in promoting the first commercial direct-image paper plate and platemaker. This was A.B. Dick's entry into offset printing and my temporary exit from the business.

Integrated Ink and Water System

A. B. Dick's big edge in quick printing was their dampening system — a system that carries water on top of the ink instead of using the conventional molleton system. The so-called "integrated" system used by A.B. Dick has proven superior to the molleton system for most of the work done by quick printers. The principal advantage of the integrated ink system is the rapidity that can be achieved in balancing ink and water as compared to the molleton system.

In quick printing, it is necessary at times to shift rapidly from slick card stock to absorbent rag and back again to many different papers requiring different water settings. You may print a few hundred copies of an 8½ x 11 with heavy solids on vellum stock and follow two minutes later with two words on a 110 lb. index 3 x 5 card. A molleton can absorb an excessive amount of water, and it takes time to dry it out. The integrated system stores very little water, so it can be adjusted rapidly

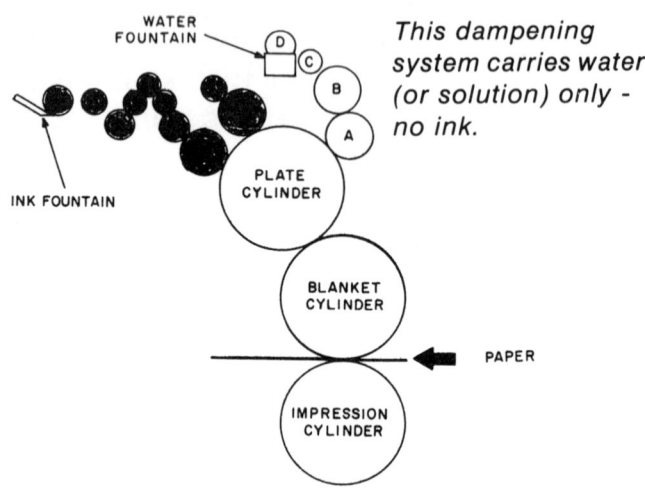

This dampening system carries water (or solution) only - no ink.

Figure A

Conventional dampening and inking system. Illustration is a standard AM 1250 offset press inking and dampening system. A knurled fountain roller (D) revolves in the water fountain, picking up a thin film of water which it yields to the molleton-covered ductor roller (C). The ductor roller (C) swings back and forth, alternately touching the fountain roller (D) and the rider roller (B). The rider roller (B) receives the water (or solution) from the ductor roller (C) and distributes it to the form roller (A). The form roller contacts the plate, keeping it moist.

Integrated System

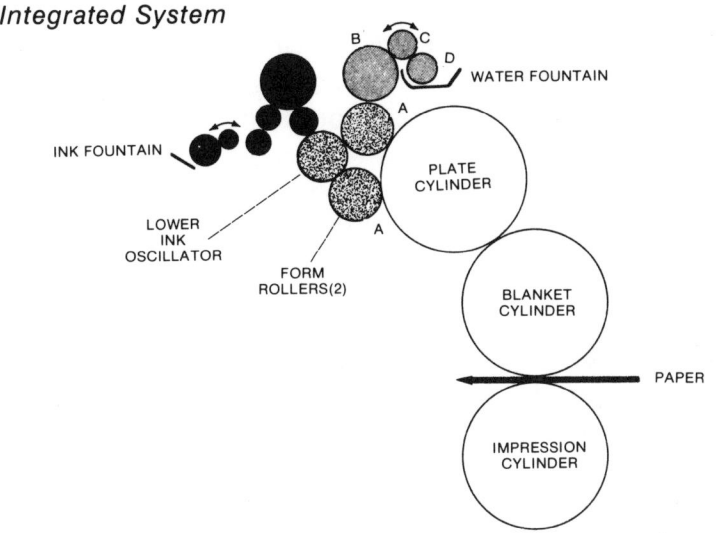

INK FOUNTAIN

WATER FOUNTAIN

PLATE
CYLINDER

LOWER
INK
OSCILLATOR

FORM
ROLLERS(2)

BLANKET
CYLINDER

PAPER

IMPRESSION
CYLINDER

Figure B

Dampening and inking system of a standard A.B. Dick 360 offset press. Unlike a conventional dampening system, ink is distributed to all rollers, including those in the dampening system (the "360 Pro" model differs in this regard). None of these rollers require molleton or paper covers like those used on the rollers in a conventional dampening system. The water (or solution) is carried on top of the ink. A copper-plated fountain roller (D) revolves in the water fountain, picking up a thin film of water which it yields to the water idler roller (C). The idler roller (C) swings into a controlled contact with the oscillating water roller (B). Water is distributed over both ink form rollers (A) and the lower ink oscillator roller. The two form rollers (A) contact the plate, each distributing both water and ink to the plate.

The illustrations and descriptions in Figures A and B explain the two basic systems of dampening. Many manufacturers now offer presses with integrated ink systems. Whichever press you select, I recommend the integrated system over the molleton system for general quick printing work.

DRY OFFSET

Several years ago the 3M Company introduced a plate designed to run on a standard offset press without water. Before using the plate, the dampeners are disengaged. The process is not widely used, if at all, by quick printers. Apparently, the driography plate is still in the process of development to a quality level acceptable by quick printing customers.

The driography plate is exposed and processed much the same as a regular plate. The nonimage area has a coating that will repel the special driography ink that is used. Scratches in the nonimage area will pick up ink. The 3M genius for developing new processes may eventually propel this plate into standard usage in quick printing. (Tory Industries also manufactures a dry offset plate.)

CAMERA/PLATEMAKERS

The 3M camera platemaker is used by many quick printers, however, the leader is still Itek. Itek has several new models, but the two models used in most shops are the 175 for electrostatic and the 1218 for photo direct. Like A.B. Dick with supporting equipment, Itek has not been a leader with other quick printing equipment. Their press and phototypesetter trail far behind the leaders in sales.

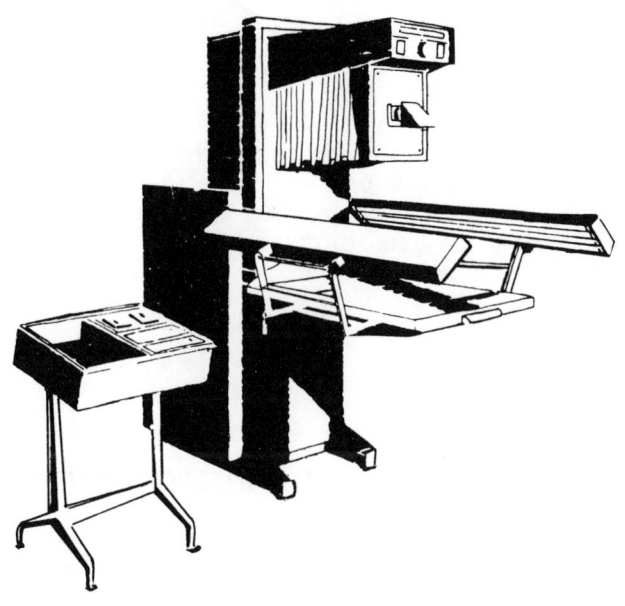

The Itek 12-18 Photo Direct platemaker (shown above) and the Itek 175 Electrostatic platemaker (not shown) are similar in appearance. The 175 is shorter as it has only one tank for toner, whereas the 12-18 has two tanks - one for developer and one for stabilizer.

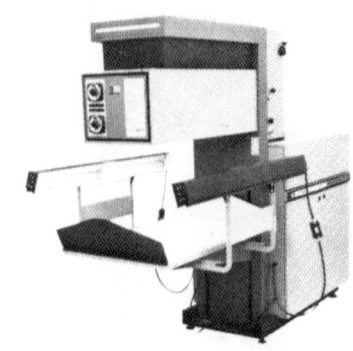

The 3M-412 (shown above) is the most popular model with quick printers. Like the Itek, it will reduce to 45% and enlarge to 150%. Unlike the Itek,* the 3M can be used to make paper stats, film line negatives, and transparencies. *12-18 model.

ELECTROSTATIC OR PHOTO-DIRECT

The big controversy today is which process to use — Electrostatic or Photo-Direct. When the price of silver temporarily skyrocketed, many quick printers panicked and dumped their photo-direct Itek 1218s because of the high cost of silver-coated plates. They switched to the Itek 175 or similar electrostatic platemakers which use nonsilver coated plates. Electrostatic plates come in several grades, but the best costs only about one fourth as much as the best silver-coated plates. Even though the price of silver has crashed, this price difference exists. In fact, the price ratio existed from the first introduction of electrostatic plates in the mid 1970s.

Many quick printers are sorry they switched. Some jobs, involving fine lines and halftones cannot be produced at a satisfactory quality level with electrostatic plates. Also, the relative thinness of the electrostatic plate causes straightening and wrinkling problems. The time lost in straightening and frequent remakes often negates the savings.

In a large shop, I recommend both types of camera/platemakers — electrostatic and photo-direct. Fountain solutions, however, are not compatible and plate thickness is different, so it is desirable to assign separate presses to each type of process. There are many jobs that do not require photo-direct plate quality or hairline straightness. If large quantities of this type of work are processed, the saving in electrostatic plates can be considerable.

SYSTEMS PLATEMAKER/PRESSES

A "system" platemaker/press automatically processes and installs an electrostatic plate, cleans the blanket, counts the copies, and automatically recycles. In-line collators are often attached. System presses use only electrostatic plates. In many urban areas, system presses have grabbed the lion's share of the multiple original, short-run duplicating business where quality is not of prime importance.

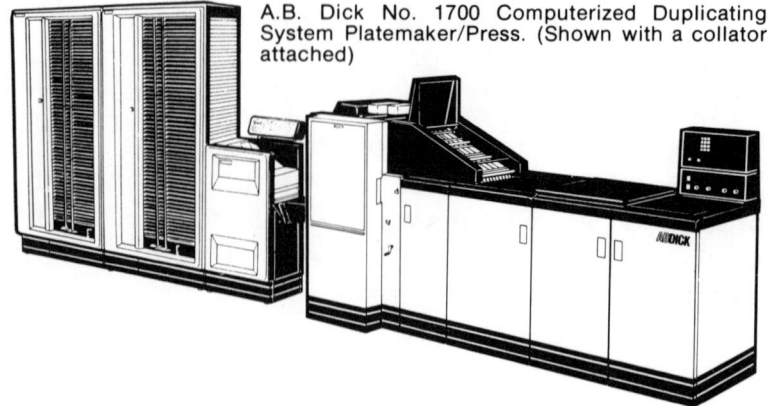

A.B. Dick No. 1700 Computerized Duplicating System Platemaker/Press. (Shown with a collator attached)

The problem many quick printers are having is finding enough low-quality, short-run business to justify the enormous cost of the system presses — several times the cost of a small press. The low selling price of systems copies dictates a regular, high volume of multiple copy business to break even.

A.B. Dick and A.M. lead the field in system presses. Both have several models, and opinion is about equally divided as to which manufacturer produces the best equipment. The availability and quality of service takes on greater importance with system presses than with standard small presses.

ADDITIONS TO A BASIC PRESS

There are several worthwhile attachments that will improve most small presses for certain jobs. There is rapid development by outside sources of these attachments. Many are inexpensive, but add a lot. Unfortunately, some of the most expensive attachments add very little to profit.

TWO-COLOR ATTACHMENT

The Thompson T51 color head attachment is used by many quick printers. Models are available for A.B.Dick and most popular brands of small presses. They work!

Two-color work produced by quick printers has increased over the past few years, but is still a small percentage of the total. I recommend you first try to build a large two-color business and, only if successful, install a T51 color head. The volume of two-color business you are able to land may not be worth the extra cost and bother of this extra equipment.

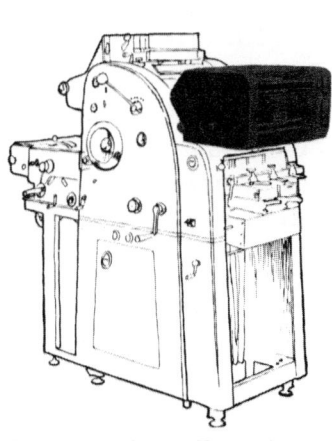

Outline of a T-51 head mounted on an A.B. Dick No. 360CD press.

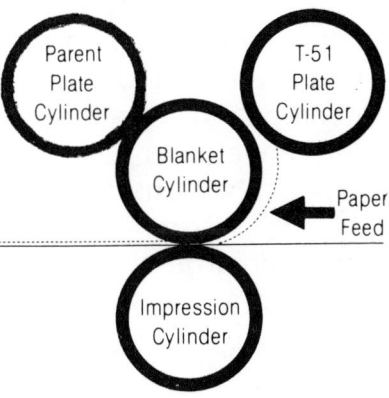

The above illustration shows how a T-51 works. It allows you to print both colors simultaneously by applying a second color to the blanket of the parent press. The common blanket prints both the T-51 and parent press images in perfect register.

ENVELOPE FEEDER ATTACHMENT

Envelope feeders have been a disappointment for many quick printers who have installed them. The problem is the same as with most other specialty equipment — insufficient volume to warrant the expense and bother.

If you have only a few thousand envelopes to run at a time, you will waste more time attaching, adjusting, and disassembling a feeder than you will save in production time.

However, shops with a large, steady volume of envelope orders find an envelope feeder attachment indispensable. Don't make the mistake of thinking you can build a repeat business of large envelope orders with a small press. Customers using a large volume of standard envelopes can buy printed envelopes for less than you are probably paying for plain envelopes. Like business cards, the envelope business is a highly automated, mass production business. Competing with a high speed envelope press on large orders is like taking on a Greyhound bus with a Volkswagen.

Press Specialties and Sandmar make roll-up envelope feeding units in the $2,000 range. Interestingly, many of the trade business card and stationery companies, such as Regency, use envelope feeders attached to A.B. Dicks for raised ink envelope production.

WASH-UP ATTACHMENT

No small press should be without a wash-up

attachment. It saves work and wash-up mat cost. All small press manufacturers offer models to fit their presses. Baldwin has a good unit. Most sell in the $150 range. Of course, all rollers should be hand cleaned regularly whether you use wash-up attachments or mats.

POWDER ATTACHMENT

This attachment has big advantages and equally big disadvantages. There are some jobs you will need to turn down unless you have a powder spray attachment. Some jobs can be speeded up by using powder. The problems are: white dust in your shop which should be kept neat as the press is usually in full view of your customers (most operators use much too much powder); when powder is mixed into the ink system, it increases the problems involved in running direct-image plates.

The powder can become a "crutch" to replace good ink control habits. It is often better practice, when offsetting or drying problems are encountered, to find the problem. The problem is probably too much ink, low Ph, static electricity, incorrect fountain solution, too many sheets in a lift, or the wrong ink.

I recommend a small powder spray attachment with the warning that it should be used with discretion. There are many good units on the market, however, there are two important considerations in selecting powder spray equipment. (1). The unit should have its own air pump, otherwise it will rob your press of air needed for proper sheet feeding. (2). It should have a trigger that cuts on the powder only when a sheet of paper is under the spray heads. This helps protect your shop from a coating of white dust.

SPECIAL ROLLERS

For special purposes such as heavy solid coverage, some of these rollers have an advantage to offer. However, we have found the disadvantages often outweigh the advantages. Unless you have a special reason to change to special rollers, you are probably better off with standard rollers.

TELESCOPING FEEDER FEET

These attachments sell for about $45.00 per set and are supposed to improve the ability to pick up envelopes and difficult stock. The advertisements seen in most trade publications appeal to printers having problems feeding envelopes — which includes just about every printer.

We tried them five years ago and they didn't work for us, so we junked them. Recently we bought a set of the new "improved" version. We tried them and they didn't work for us, so we put them in the junk box with the first set.

BACK CYLINDER CLEANER
FOR A.B. DICK

The back cylinder of an A.B. Dick is hard to get at and needs frequent cleaning. Several tools have been introduced by independent manufacturers that will do this job faster than fingers and cotton pad. The best one we have found is the one sold by Printers Shopper.

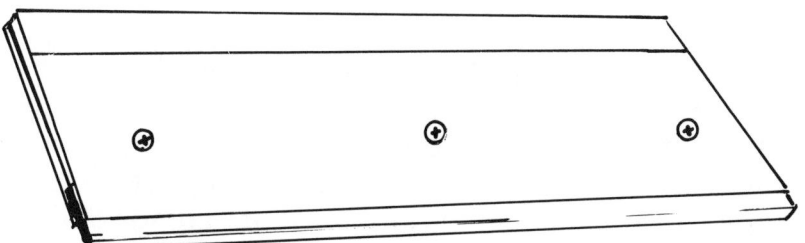

Impression Cylinder Cleaner for A.B. Dick 350/360 A replaceable felt pad clamps between two aluminum plates. The tool fits into the narrow access gap at the feed end of the press. The felt pads can be cleaned with blanket wash or replaced. Sold by Printer's Shopper for about $30.00.

CUTTER

A paper cutter is the third most important piece of equipment in a quick print shop. All too often too little importance is given to selecting this item of equipment.

A lot of cutting is done in the average quick printing shop, and it needs to be reasonably accurate. Of course, a sharp blade helps, and an extra blade should be standard equipment with any cutter. Cheap cutters will not cut straight with the sharpest of blades.

One of the saddest mistakes is to try to get by with a manual cutter. You can operate with a cheap power cutter in the $3,000 range such as a Triumph, but I recommend you spend double this amount on a 21" to 30" cutter. One of the best lines of small cutters is Challenge.

FOLDER

All folders, even the most expensive, present difficult feeding problems requiring operating skill and patience. Table model folders test the patience of otherwise calm and collected quick printers. Most quick printers do not have sufficient folding volume to warrant an investment above the table model level. The jump from table model to floor model is about $800 to $8,000 and up.

We recently bought the highly advertised table model, Pro-Fold, which sells for about $1600, thinking there might be a middle ground improvement over the cheap models. The Pro-Fold weighs more and may last longer than the $800 varieties, but it doesn't work any better. In fact, the model we bought has serious problems with single folds of heavy stock such as 67 Vellum Bristol, and we use our $800 model for all right-angle folds. G.B.C. says the problems are corrected on their new models.

We've had reasonably good luck with the Martin Yale table model folder. I recommend you stay at the $800 level unless you feel you can move all the way up to a Baumfolder floor model.

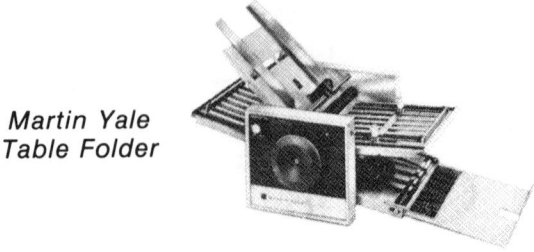

Martin Yale
Table Folder

DRILL

Challenge makes a good single spindle drill. This will do the job for you unless you intend to specialize in some area where sophisticated drilling is required. Don't buy one of the cheapies that will drill only a hundred or so sheets at a time. Be sure and get a sharpening tool, a supply of wax, and a good supply of wood blocks as these are important accessories needed for good drilling.

*Challenge
Model JO
Drill*

COLLATOR

You can start out with hand collating, but sooner or later you will find it profitable to obtain a good table or floor model 10-bin collator. There are several good ones on the market and new developments are coming along rapidly. It is not unusual to see large collators in shops specializing in multiple copies of short runs.

STAPLERS

A good power stapler that handles standard staples for shallow work will cost about $200.00, but it is a worthwhile investment as it is a big labor saver and will help speed up the rush jobs that so often need to be stapled. Several standard hand staplers are handy to have around.

A saddle stapler is a must. I recommend a small saddle stapler that will handle 11 x 17, and as your business grows, you will probably need a heavy duty saddle stapler that will handle standard and larger staples. A good power saddle stapler will cost at least several hundred dollars. Unless you develop an unusual volume in saddle stapled booklets, you don't need a power unit.

This covers the basic units of equipment needed to operate the average quick printing shop — press, camera-platemaker, cutter, drill, collator, and staplers. **Keep in mind that space is expensive in a quick printing shop. On the average, the space cost is four to five times as great as it is in a conventional printing plant.** The reason is obvious because of the location needed for quick printing. Big clumsy equipment can cost more than it is worth in space costs.

The following equipment falls into a special category, but it is the type of equipment that most quick printers grow into:

PROCESS CAMERA

There are several small cameras on the market that can be a real asset for most quick printing shops. A dark room is necessary, but you can get by without running water. A small darkroom can be built around an upright camera without taking up a lot of space. You can buy a small camera with a good lens for as little as $1,500 that will produce acceptable quality for most of the work done by quick printers.

One of the biggest advantages of having a process camera and darkroom is the stat-making ability it gives you. Sharp black and white stats can be obtained by using the Agfa-Gevaert or Eastman (PMT) process along with an inexpensive, one-chemical processor.

Many of the jobs that come your way cannot be handled by the Itek camera-platemaker because of multicolored original, weak copy, partial copy reductions, or reproductions needed for a multiple run. Much time can be lost trying to shoot difficult copy on your Itek. The quality of reproductions that go through the press for pasteup is much lower than can be produced by a stat and is often most needed when your press is tied up on a long run.

A small camera will produce acceptable negatives for conventional platemaking, however, for difficult halftones, it is best to use the services of a trade shop with the skill and equipment to produce top grade halftone work. 85 line negs and stats can be made of a good quality, simply by using a greyline contact screen. If you have the facilities for a small darkroom, I recommend a small process camera as one of the most profitable pieces of equipment. (See photographic chapters for more information.)

NUMBERING MACHINES

In recent years, numbering has taken on increased

importance to quick printers because of the volume of NCR forms being done by most shops. It is difficult to job out NCR numbering. You can get by with a small hand numbering machine, but it is time consuming and difficult to obtain straightness and multiple copies.

We used an old Chandler & Price letterpress for a couple of years, but ran into a space problem on top of difficulty and slowness in feeding sets of NCR.

For medium volume, I recommend an electric table model numbering machine. A brochure can be obtained from Printers Shopper, P. O. Box 1056, Chula Vista, CA 92012. They sell two units in the $400 to $600 range. Many other suppliers sell comparable units. These units work like an electric stapler, requiring hand feeding and hand positioning. Several units are now being advertised that attach to the feeding end of the press. These units range in price from $1000 to $1800, and are next to useless for carbonless sets. If the press pulls a double or misses a sheet, the sequence is out of order.

BOOKBINDING EQUIPMENT

Plastic spiral binding equipment is used profitably by many shops. G.B.C. is the leader in equipment. Good quality plastic combs are sold by several manufacturers.

Other types of binding equipment, such as perfect, heat seal, and plastic clamps are marginal in acceptance. Unless you have developed a special

*GENERAL
BINDING
CORPORATION (GBC)
SPIRAL PLASTIC
PUNCH/BINDER.*

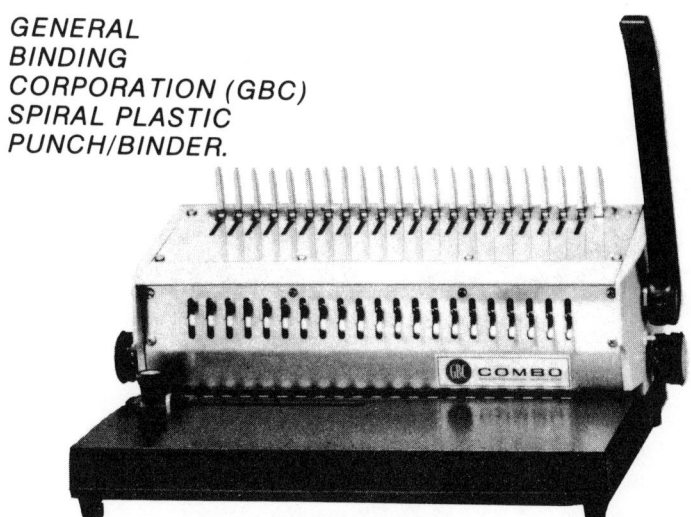

clientele, I recommend you limit your equipment to plastic spiral and job out the rest.

Of course, hard cover binding is restricted to large binderies with very specialized and super expensive equipment.

TYPESETTING EQUIPMENT

Typesetting and other specialized equipment is covered in detail under chapters dealing with the various equipment.

CHAPTER 28

PHOTOGRAPHIC
EQUIPMENT - MATERIALS
AND
PROBLEMS

Not many years ago, the only photographic equipment used by an average quick printer was a camera/platemaker. In today's quick printing shops, it is not uncommon to see process cameras, phototypesetters, contact printers, stabilization processors and, of course, photocopiers. These and other photo-related equipment and materials have added considerable complexity to shop management.

Photographic-related problems can rarely be handled "by the numbers." There are too many variables. It is important, however, that you know the "numbers" — a starting point! If corrections are made in part of a process without returning other parts to a starting point, you can end up with a mind-boggling, unworkable solution to the original problem.

CAMERA/PLATEMAKERS

Two basic types of camera/platemakers are used by quick printers — photo-direct (using silver-coated plates) and electrostatic. Both have one thing in common — camera-ready copy is placed on a copyboard, a button is pressed, and a press-ready plate is produced automatically.

Photo Direct

The photo-direct camera/platemaker came into wide commercial use in the mid 1960s, sparking the quick printing business as we know it today. It is still the most popular system in use. (See chapter, "Equipment Recommendations," for more details.) The system uses a paper or plastic printing plate coated with a silver-based photographic solution.

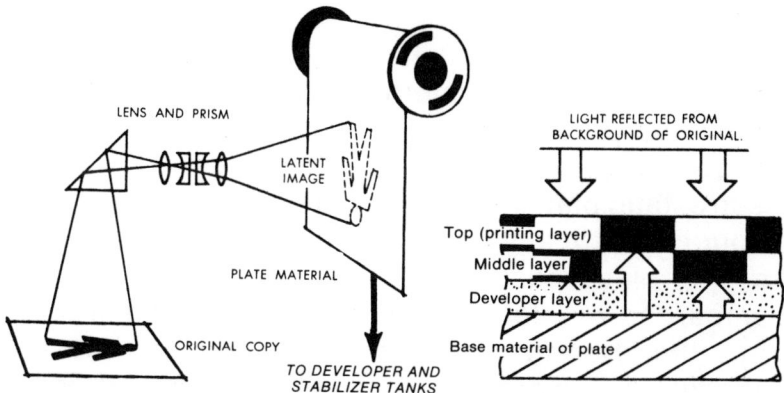

Figure A - HOW A TYPICAL PHOTO-DIRECT CAMERA/PLATE-MAKER WORKS. The plate is coated with a three layer emulsion. During processing, the middle layer is hardened wherever it is struck by light during exposure. A developer from the bottom layer travels through the unhardened areas of the middle layer to make the top layer ink-receptive in the image areas. The hardened areas in the middle layer prevent the developer from passing through and prevent the top layer from becoming ink-receptive in nonprinting areas.

(Figure A) After exposure, the plate is automatically developed and stabilized in two large tanks filled with an activator or a stop bath. The plate material comes on a roll. It is automatically cut to size and carried through the processing solutions by a series of rollers and belts.

Electrostatic

Electrostatic camera/platemakers have been used by quick printers since the mid 1970s but, as some manufacturers claim, they are not a likely replacement for the conventional silver-base systems. (See chapter, "Equipment Recommendations," for more detail.)

The process described here is a wet method as opposed to a dry method. The dry process dominates photocopying, but the wet method of processing prevails in platemaking. The electrostatic plate material is fed from a roll, passing through electrically charged wires in a corona unit. As the plate passes through the corona, it is bombarded by electrons. When the plate emerges from the corona, its zinc oxide coating has a negative charge of static electricity. (Other methods that do not include zinc oxide coating are used by some systems.)

After being automatically cut to the desired length, the plate is exposed to light through a lens much the same as a silver-coated plate is exposed. The zinc oxide coating loses its electrical charge whenever it is struck by light reflected from the white (nonimage area) of the copy, but remains charged in the image areas. Unlike a photo-direct plate, an electrostatic plate cannot be held in the exposure unit for multiple exposures. The electrostatic charge is temporary and exposure must be completed immediately.

As soon as the exposure is made, the plate passes through a tank filled with a liquid composed of two elements; a black fluid called "toner" and a clear kerosene-like fluid called a "dispersant" which acts as a carrier for the toner.

The toner consists of carbon particles which have been given a chemical positive charge. The carbon particles do not actually mix with the dispersant, but are held in suspension by it. As the plate travels through the tank, the toner is attracted to the unexposed (charged) areas, but does not stick to the nonprinting areas which have lost their electrical charge.

After the plate emerges from the toner, it passes through a squeegee and drying unit. The plate is treated with a conversion solvent before being placed on the press.

The plate is used on an offset press much the same as other types of paper plates. However, most electrostatic plates require a special fountain solution. The thinness of the plate material makes them more susceptible to wrinkling than photo-direct plates which have a heavier paper or plastic backing.

Quality and run length are less than are normally obtained with photo-direct plates. However, the much lower plate material cost and the shorter processing time have earned electrostatic plates a permanent place in quick printing.

All so-called "system" platemaker/presses use the electrostatic process. To my knowledge, no manufacturer is offering a completely automated platemaker/press using photo-direct, silver-base plates.

PHOTOCOPIERS

Shortly after World War II, office photocopiers using a silver-base photo process were introduced. At that time, I handled a line of crude copiers which sold for $52.00 and the paper for 5¢ a sheet. After exposure, the treated paper was dipped in trays containing developer and fix. Bright lights had to be turned off during the process. The paper was dried using clothespins and a line. The demand was great even for this crude process. I sold over a thousand dollars worth of paper per month.

In the early 1950s, Remington and others introduced automated exposure units. But the real photocopier boom was started in the late 1950s by Xerox with their electrostatic automated copiers.

Today, hundreds of manufacturers in all parts of the world are vying for a piece of this gigantic and growing market. Japanese firms have gained a strong position in photocopy sales.

All of today's photocopiers use a version of the electrostatic process. Most use a dry process where powdered toner adheres to a drum and is, in effect, printed onto untreated paper. Xerox is still the leader in equipment. Savin and Canon copiers are used by many quick printers. Kodak copiers are becoming popular as are many other brands. (See chapter, "Photocopies," for more details.)

PROCESS CAMERAS

Process camera work can open profitable doors for quick printers. A darkroom is required and can be as simple as two six-foot partition walls enclosing a corner with a black cloth-covered opening. Plumbing is a convenience, but not a necessity.

Figure C shows the two basic types of process cameras. Vertical cameras are more popular with quick printers because they require less floor space.

FIGURE C

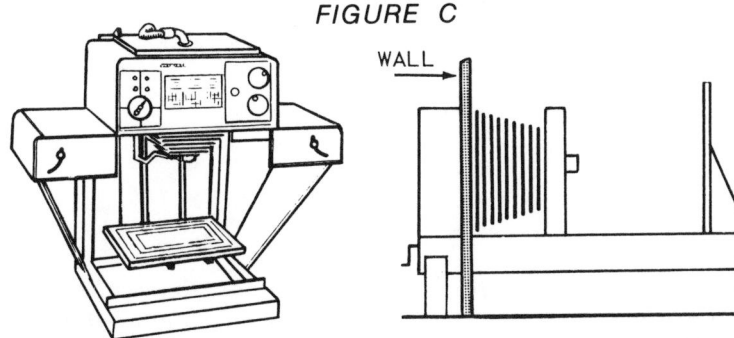

FREE STANDING VERTICAL CAMERA. This is the most popular type with quick printers because it does not have to be built into the darkroom wall and requires less floor space.

HORIZONTAL CAMERA. There are free-standing horizontal cameras, but most, like the above diagram, are built into the darkroom wall. Only the back of the camera protrudes into the darkroom.

POSITIONING THE CAMERA LAMPS

As a rule, the lamps are attached to the copyboard and travel along with it. However, they may be adjusted within certain limitations to provide for even illumination. Figure D shows how the lamps may be positioned in relation to the copyboard to prevent glare. To check for even illumination, turn on the lamps and hold an object centrally in front of the copyboard. The light is balanced when the shadows on both sides of the object have the same tone. It may be necessary to adjust one of the lamps in order to achieve this balance.

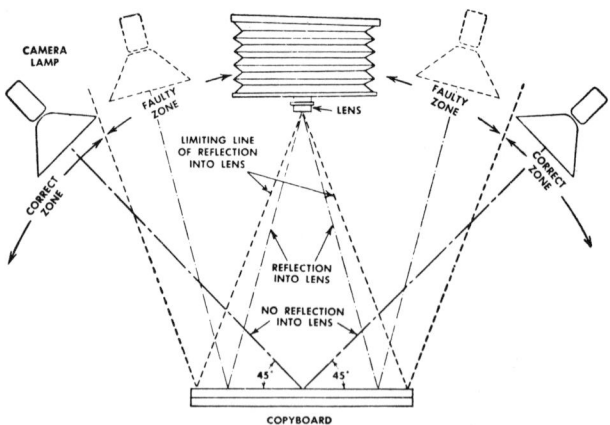

Figure D — *Positioning camera lamps. Remember that each change in the distance or angle of the lamps affects the amount of light reflected from the copyboard into the camera. Exposures vary directly as the square of the distance from the copy to the lamp.*

THE LENS

The lens is an extremely delicate piece of equipment and must be handled with great care. Never touch it with your fingers, as fingerprints will cause loss of definition on the negative.

You may brush dust particles from the lens surface with a camel's hair brush, and clean it occasionally with soft tissue (called lens tissue) moistened with a small amount of commercial lens cleaner. Do not use alcohol, polish, or other solvents on the lens.

Never take the lens apart for cleaning; that is a job for the manufacturer.

Lenses should not be stored in places where they are apt to be exposed to extreme temperature changes, nor should they be left exposed to light or air. Always close the filter slot and place a cap over the lens barrel when the camera is not in use.

FILTERS

Although filters are not a part of the camera proper, their use is so closely connected with the lens that they will be discussed at this point. Filters are not widely used by quick printers at the present time, but with the rapid growth of sophistication in quick printing, it is anticipated that filter usage will increase.

Filters are used to alter the color and intensity of the light for color correction and (in process color work) to separate the primary colors of the copy.

If you look at a colored picture through a **blue filter**,

you will notice that the filter practically neutralizes the blues in the picture, while making the yellows look darker so that it will be easy to photograph them. Similarly a **red filter** will cancel out the reds in the picture, but will make the greens look black.

Yellow filters are frequently used for photographing colored copy. Yellow absorbs blues and some of the violets and gives the negative a more balanced appearance. Yellow filters are also used in copying old papers or photographs that are yellow with age, because the yellow filter causes the yellow background to photograph as white.

Colored filters always absorb a part of the light reflected from the copy. Therefore, a longer exposure is necessary when they are used. The number of times by which the exposure must be increased when a filter is used is known as the filter factor. The exposure time varies not only with the color of filter being used but with the type of film and the nature of the light as well. Normally, the film manufacturer supplies this information on the film container or on an information sheet which is enclosed in the box.

Filters may throw the image out of focus, so final critical focusing for exact size and sharpness should be made on the ground glass after the filter is in position.

CAMERA LAMPS

The sources of illumination of the copyboard on a process camera are termed camera lamps. The lamps may be attached to the copyboard and travel with it or they may be free standing units. The free standing type are positioned according to the position of the copyboard. You will see this type of lamp in use in large commercial shops.

The principal requirement of the light source is that it must produce an extremely bright white light which is suitable for both color and black-and-white reproduction. This type of light is said to have a high actinic value, that is, it readily affects the silver salts in the film emulsion.

The most useful light sources for graphics art reproduction are the carbon arc, the quartz iodine lamp, the pulsed xenon lamp, and the mercury vapor lamp.

The use of carbon arc lamps is gradually being phased out in the trade. The other types of illumination eliminate many of the shortcomings of the carbon arcs. The arcs require a burning-in, have minor fluctuations of light, and produce gas fumes and an ash residue.

Camera lamps are placed into one of two categories: the incandescent type or the electric discharge (arc) type.

The pulsed xenon lamp, for example, is of the arc variety. It consists of a tube of quartz glass which is filled with xenon gas and has an electrode at each end. The lamp is said to be "pulsed" because it flashes 120 times a second, although the light output seems constant to the eye. The tubes may be fashioned as coils, semicircles, or angles to fit particular requirements. For example, many of the new lamp holders designed for exposing photo-offset plates are fitted with coiled pulsed xenon tubes.

The iodine quartz lamp is of the incandescent variety, but it bears little resemblance to the conventional light bulb. It consists of a short tube of quartz glass housing a coiled filament which runs the length of the tube. In ordinary incandescent lamps, tungsten evaporates from the filament and settles on the glass to gradually darken the bulb. In the case of the iodine quartz lamp, however, iodine vapor combines chemically with the tungsten and causes it to redeposit on the filament. This prevents the tube from becoming tarnished with age. Although the iodine quartz tube is very small (about the size of a fountain pen), it puts out such an intense light that it is particularly suited for use with photolithographic equipment designed to conserve space, such as vertical cameras.

The short-arc lamp, which differs from the pulsed xenon lamp in that there is a shorter gap between the electrodes in the tube and the tube has a bulge in the center which corresponds to the location of this cap. Although **mercury lamps** produce a very intense light and are often used for black-and-white work, they cannot be used for color work because they do not contain all the colors of the spectrum. They have no red radiation, for example, and this causes all reds in the copy to photograph as black. Xenon lamps produce a light which more closely resembles that of natural daylight.

DARKROOM SINKS

The sink is where film is normally processed. Most darkroom sinks have room for three trays of processing solutions and perhaps a viewing glass where the negatives may be examined.

Another type of darkroom sink is the temperature controlled model. This type is preferable because it ensures that a constant temperature of the processing solutions is maintained. In addition, the temperature controlled sinks have a refrigerated compartment below where film can be kept.

All darkroom sinks should be thoroughly cleaned at the end of each day. Many expensive sinks have been ruined because they have been neglected. The water bath in the sink collects chemicals which will corrode if it is allowed to stand.

Always make sure the power is secured when the sinks are empty. Viewing attachments must be inspected often for leaks that would allow water to reach the wiring and cause an electrical hazard.

FILM PROCESSORS

I have had several inquiries regarding film processors. This is not quick printing equipment. It is expensive and takes up a lot of floor space. To satisfy curiosity a diagram is shown in figure N.

DENSITOMETERS

I have seen a few densitometers in quick printing

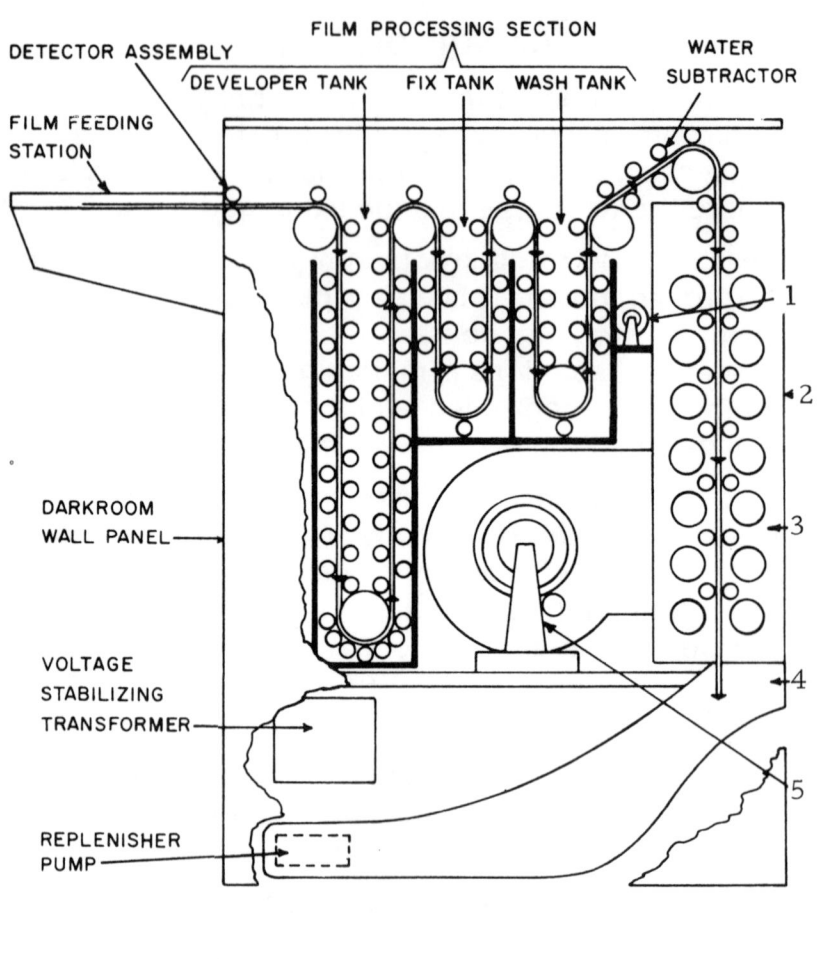

Figure N — Film processor.

shops. It is, however, a luxury piece of equipment for a quick printer. A densitometer is used to measure accurately the density (darkness) of negatives or opaque copy, such as photographs.

Some densitometers are designed to measure the transmission densities of negatives; some are designed to measure the reflection densities of opaque copy, such as photographs; and some are designed to measure both. These "combination densitometers," as they are called, are generally used in the camera department, since the cameraman deals with both negatives and opaque copy.

SAFELIGHTS

Film is sensitive to almost every kind of light if exposed to it long enough. For practical purposes, however, you can use certain colored lights in the darkroom. These lights are called safelights. The type of safelight required depends on the kind of sensitized material you are handling.

Since photographic materials cover a wide range of sensitivity to light and color, a corresponding series of safelights is needed if you plan to handle different films. Most quick printers get by with a red light for film and perhaps a yellow light for metal plates.

The red (series 1) filter can be used with certain films that are sensitive only to violet and blue colors. (These films are known as monochromatic or color-blind films.) Other films coated with orthochromatic emulsions are sensitive to all colors except red and can be handled safely under a red (series 2) or a light red (series 1 A) safelight. Panchromatic film emulsions are sensitive to all colors and should be processed in total darkness. (Panchromatic film may be inspected under a green light (series 3) after the first few minutes of processing.) Orange and yellow-green lights are usually safe for photographic paper.

If you are in doubt as to whether the safelight that you are using is safe for a given type of film, check the specifications printed on the film box. Always keep your work at least 3 feet away from the safelight. Light leaks, high-wattage bulbs, and bleached lamp filters may fog the film.

Ruby or amber light bulbs are sometimes used for general lighting (depending on the purpose of the darkroom). They should be placed high on the wall or overhead. They are not safe as safelights, but will not cause appreciable damage if you keep the work at a satisfactory distance from them.

FILM DRYERS

After developing and fixing, the negatives are washed in plain water. When the washing is completed, the film must be dried. In small shops, film is dried by hanging it with clips or pins to a line much the same as you would hang clothes from a clothesline. Many quick printers use ordinary hand held hair dryers to speed drying. There are many brands of film dryers designed for high volume film usage.

TIMERS

The timer shown in Figure O is a clocklike device that can be set to signal the camerman when a predetermined time has elapsed.

Electric timers like those found on the cameras and on photographic enlargers are generally set by moving a pointer to the figure indicating the desired time and then operating a pushbutton switch mounted below the dial. The electric timer terminates the exposure automatically at the completion of the set time. It is especially useful when repeated exposures of the same duration must be made.

MISCELLANEOUS DARKROOM EQUIPMENT

Figure O shows several miscellaneous pieces of darkroom equipment. Always handle thermometers carefully as they are very fragile. High temperatures may burst the bulb and severe jarring may separate the mercury column. You can sometimes reunite a separated mercury column by swinging the thermometer rapidly with the bulb outward or by heating it gradually in a pan of water. Graduates, funnels, pans, stirring rods, and trays must be kept spotlessly clean to prevent the chemicals from being contaminated and to prevent dried crystals from flying about in the air.

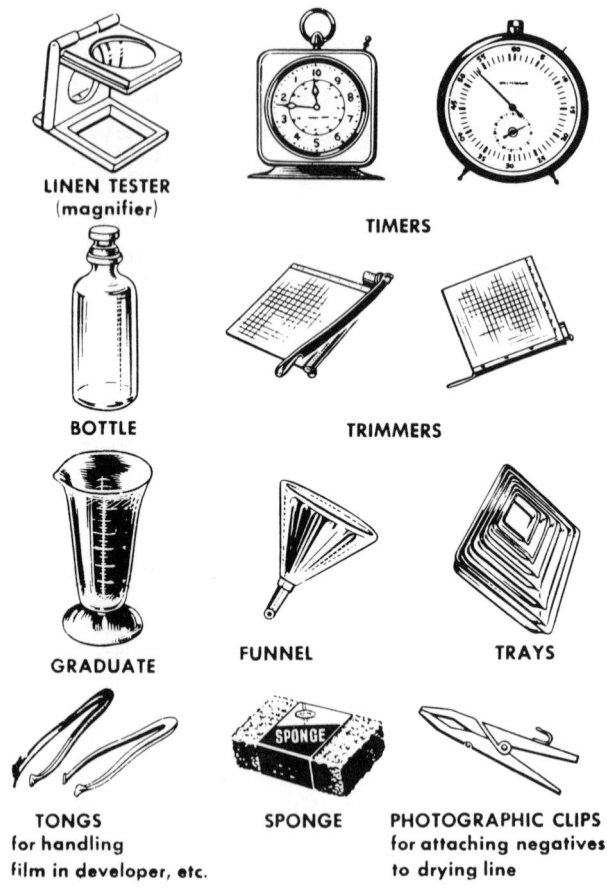

LINEN TESTER
(magnifier)

TIMERS

BOTTLE

TRIMMERS

GRADUATE

FUNNEL

TRAYS

TONGS
for handling
film in developer, etc.

SPONGE

PHOTOGRAPHIC CLIPS
for attaching negatives
to drying line

Figure O — Miscellaneous darkroom equipment.

DIFFUSION TRANSFER PROCESS

One of the biggest advantages of having a process camera and darkroom is the stat-making ability it provides — both line copy and halftones.

Stats

Diffusion transfer stats are produced by exposing a paper negative in a process camera. The exposed negative is placed on a "receiver" sheet and processed through a simple, one-chemical processor. After a thirty-second wait, the negative and receiver sheet are pulled apart, leaving a high quality black and white reproduction on the receiver sheet. To prevent yellowing, the stat requires a rinsing with plain water.

In the past, most quick printers used their camera/platemakers for reproductions needed for pasteups. This method is still preferred on bold line copy, especially when several pasteup copies are needed. However, much time can be lost trying to shoot difficult copy on your camera/platemaker. The quality of reproductions that go through the press for pasteup is much lower than can be produced by a stat and is often most needed when your press is tied up on a long run.

Eastman and Agfa-Gevaert are the leaders in stat supplies. Just about any brand of processor will do an adequate job. The same type of processor is used for treating electrostatic plates with conversion solution. However, most quick printers prefer a higher speed processor for electrostatic plates. A high speed unit is not an advantage for stat processing.

Clear plastic receiver sheets are available for

producing transparencies. Negatives that produce reverse copy use the same basic process.

Halftone Stats

Good quality halftones can be produced with diffusion transfer stats. The big advantage of a stat halftone is that it can be combined with line copy and processed on a camera/platemaker. Even if a film negative and metal plate are to be used, the stat halftone will save film stripping time, especially if captions are placed in close proximity to the halftone.

We use an 85-line grey contact halftone screen for photo-direct halftones. Timing of the exposure depends, of course, on the individual camera, but most halftones come out well with about a twenty-second shot at 100% with the lens wide open. We follow the main exposure by removing the photo, replacing it with plain yellow paper, and exposing another two to four seconds.

Difficult photos may require three exposures by adding a short exposure before placing the halftone screen over the negative. This exposure is made with the highest F-stop for about five or six seconds at 100%. Experimentation with different time combinations is necessary to develop times for individual cameras. We rarely find need for a three shot halftone stat.

Air deteriorates developing chemicals. A processor should be emptied each night or during any long period when it is not in use. If stored in a closed bottle, the developer can be reused many times. The tip-off to depleted developer is grey copy.

Diffusion Transfer Plates

An Eastman PMT paper and metal plate can be produced using the same equipment as for stats. Eastman claims up to 2,500 impressions for the paper plate and up to 25,000 for the metal plate. We have not tested this type of plate because we have yet to receive a favorable report from quick printer users.

PHOTOTYPESETTING FILM

(Also see Typesetting chapter)

A decision when purchasing a phototypesetter is the type of film and processor you plan to use. Most quick printers use stabilization paper. A few use RC paper and processor. The RC paper costs about the same, perhaps a little less. An RC processor costs five to ten times as much as a stabilization processor (about $700 for a stabilization processor — $4,000 to $8,000 for RC). Both produce sharp copy, but the stabilization paper will darken after a few months. It is only stabilized, not fixed. Air, humidity, and light will speed the darkening process. If stored in a file folder in a closed file cabinet, copy produced on stabilization paper will remain usable for up to a year — possibly more.

RC paper is "fixed." It is permanently black and white. This can be a big advantage if the typesetting is to be reused over a period of years. The high cost of the processor is the only reason few quick printers use RC paper.

CHAPTER 29

PHOTOGRAPHIC

PRINCIPLES

Knowing the theory or principle of a process helps to keep equipment operating properly. Complicated photographic equipment is now a part of quick printing. In the near future a knowledge of photography will be a requirement for profitable operation of a quick printing shop.

Photographic equipment is covered in another chapter. This chapter is intended to provide a basic understanding of how photographic equipment works.

LIGHT

The sun, light bulbs, fire, and so on are said to be luminous because they generate light. You see nonluminous objects because they reflect light from luminous sources.

A large volume of light is called a beam, a narrow cylinder of light is called a pencil, and the smallest portion of light is known as a ray.

Light travels through the air at a speed of 186,000 miles per second in the form of electromagnetic vibrations or waves. Light waves, gamma rays, X-rays, radio waves, and electric (power) waves are all a part of the electromagnetic spectrum. All these waves of magnetic energy are the same; they vary only in frequency and wave length.

WAVE
LENGTH

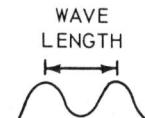

WAVE LENGTH IS THE DISTANCE FROM
A POINT ON ONE WAVE TO A CORRE-
SPONDING POINT ON ANOTHER

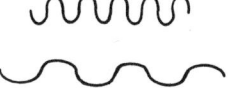

FREQUENCY IS THE NUMBER OF
WAVES GENERATED IN ONE SECOND

Figure A — If you tie a piece of string to an object and then shake the string, a wave will travel from your hand down the length of the string. You might compare this wave with that produced by a luminous light source, such as a light bulb, which acts as an oscillator, creating waves of light. The wave motion of the string, however, does not represent the true motion of light because light waves move in all possible directions. You could get a clearer picture of light travel if you had a number of parallel strings each shaken in a different direction.

Wave length and frequency go hand in hand. Wave length is the distance from a point on one wave to a corresponding point on the next wave. Waves vary in length according to the type of wave, from less than a millionth of an inch to several thousand miles. Frequency is the number of waves generated in one second. (See Fig. A.) As waves become shorter, they increase in rapidity or frequency, and as they lengthen, their frequency is reduced. In other words, short waves have a high frequency and long waves have a low frequency. The frequency of visible light waves, for example, is millions of times greater than that of radio waves.

COMPARISON OF SOUND WAVES AND LIGHT WAVES

Sound waves are not a part of the electromagnetic spectrum. They differ from light waves in that they consist of a physical compression of the air while light waves are an electromagnetic vibration. However, the two have certain properties in common, which make it possible to compare them. Figure B shows what happens when you strike a tuning fork. Notice how the air is compressed and how the sound travels in circles or waves as it moves away from the tuning fork. As the waves travel away from the source, they spread and become weaker, until finally the sound becomes inaudible.

Light waves act in much the same manner. They are always stronger near the source because the rays are closer together at this point. As the waves move away from the source, the rays fan out or spread and the waves become weaker.

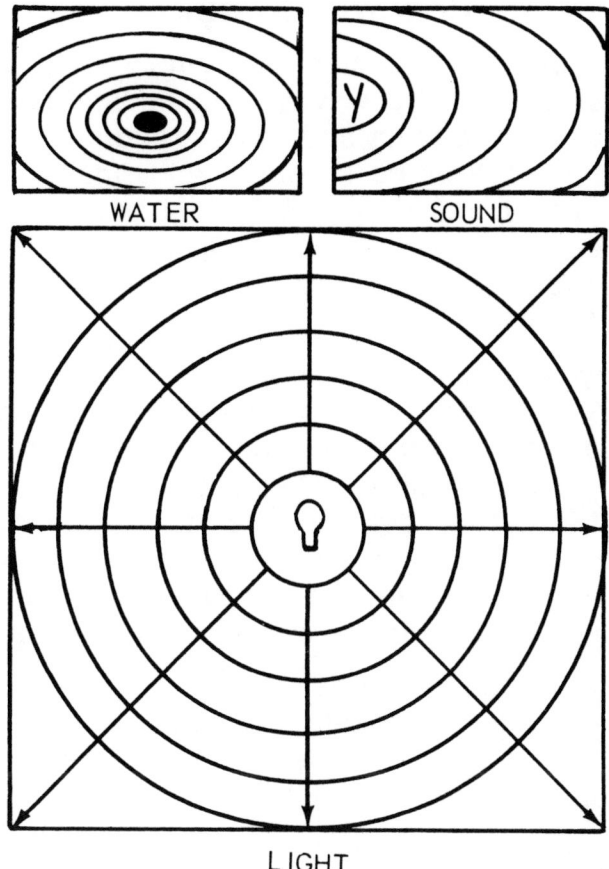

WATER   SOUND

LIGHT

Figure B — If you drop a pebble in a pool of still water, you will create a series of ever-expanding waves. Sound and light also spread from their source in circular waves, but moving in all directions. The light rays used in illustrations are radii from the light source. They show the direction of light travel. Each line represents an infinite number of rays radiating in all directions from the source, but for practical purposes, each line is referred to as a light ray.

HOW WE SEE COLOR

Your ear cannot detect extremely long sound waves, but as the waves become shorter, they increase in frequency and become audible — first as a low rumble or bass sound; and finally, as the frequency increases, as a treble sound or a screech. If the sound waves become too short, their frequency will become so high that the ear cannot detect them.

The eye records visible light waves just as your ear records tones. The longest waves (lowest frequencies) that the eye can see are those which produce the sensation of red. There are longer ones, called infrared, but they cannot be seen. The shortest waves that you can see are the violet. Ultraviolet waves are too short and their frequency is too high to be detected by the human eye.

If all the optical wave lengths are combined, your eye receives the sensation of white. But a colored light will result if one of the wave lengths predominates the others.

Light waves may be transmitted, absorbed, or reflected. If an object reflects all the wave lengths equally, it will look white; but if it absorbs some of the wave lengths, it will appear to be colored. A red object, for example, appears red because it reflects red light waves and absorbs the light waves of all the other colors. A colored object always reflects the light waves of its own color, and it appears black (colorless) if it absorbs all the colors or if the light striking it does not include the wave lengths of its particular color.

When light passes through a substance such as glass, which is denser than air, its speed is reduced. If the light rays strike the substance at a 90° angle, they will pass through without bending. But if they strike at any other angle, the change in speed will cause them to bend. This is known as refraction.

REFLECTION

Light rays which are not absorbed or transmitted by an object are thrown back or reflected. If a beam of light strikes a smooth surface, such as a mirror at a 90° angle, it will be reflected at a 90° angle; if it strikes the surface at a 45° angle, it will reflect at a 45° angle and so on. But when a beam of light strikes a rough, uneven surface, the rays may be reflected or thrown back in several different directions.

Most surfaces reflect both types of light. Since diffused light is more common, it is of the greatest value in photography.

BASIC PRINCIPLE OF PHOTOGRAPHY

Perhaps you have noticed how certain colors fade or bleach when they are exposed to sunlight. The radiant energy of the light sets up a chemical action wherever it strikes the dyes, causing them to change color. Photographers use this "actinic" action of light to produce images on film coated with light-sensitive salts.

You can capture an image by attaching a piece of film to the back of a camera. Film is simply a sheet of transparent acetate coated with a layer of gelatin in which are suspended millions of tiny particles of silver salts. When film is exposed in the camera, these silver particles are ionized or broken up wherever they are struck by the light. Shadows and dark areas reflect little light; therefore, little change occurs in the film emulsion in areas where the subject is dark. But there is a good deal of change in areas where the emulsion is struck by strong light reflections.

When the film is placed in a chemical "developing" solution, the exposed particles change to black, metallic silver. In areas where the film was struck by strong light reflections, the silver deposit will be very dense or black; in areas where the light reflections were weaker, the silver deposit will be thinner and have a gray appearance on the film. Areas of the film which correspond to the dark or shadow areas of the original subject may have received no light reflection at all; consequently, the silver salts in these areas are not exposed and will not turn dark in the developer unless development is continued too long.

However, these unexposed salts will still be affected if they are exposed to light. Therefore, the film must be "fixed" in another chemical solution called "hypo." This solution dissolves the unexposed salts and leaves clear, transparent areas on the film. The film is then washed and dried. The developed film is called a negative because the light has registered on it in reverse. That is, it is dark where the original subject was light and transparent where the original subject was dark.

THE PROCESS CAMERA

The camera used in graphic arts photography is called a process camera. Although larger than the type of camera you use to take snapshots, it is similar in principle. Since the process camera is built for copying, it is equipped with a copyboard and has other features not associated with the average camera. There are two types of process cameras: horizontal and vertical. There is a considerable saving of floor space with the vertical cameras. The back of most horizontal cameras extends into a darkroom, and the front is housed in a separate room.

As you can see in Figure C, all process cameras,vertical or horizontal, have three planes or surfaces: 1. The copy plane (copyboard to which the copy is attached). 2. The lens plane (lensboard or front of the camera into which the lens is fitted). 3. The focal plane (back of the camera which consists of a film-holding device). The image projected through the lens is focused onto this surface.

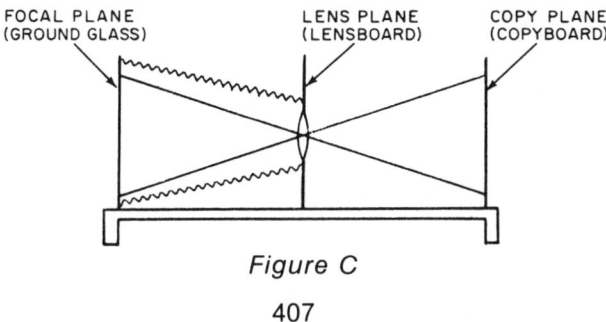

FOCAL PLANE
(GROUND GLASS)

LENS PLANE
(LENSBOARD)

COPY PLANE
(COPYBOARD)

Figure C

407

Handwheels or cranks are usually provided to enable the camerman to move two of these planes forward or backward along the tracks when he is focusing (setting the camera so that the light rays will come together to produce a sharp image of the proper size on the ground glass).

The positions of the copyboard and lensboard affect the size as well as the sharpness of the image. Most process cameras are equipped with scales that show the camerman where to set the copyboard and lensboard for the amount of enlargement or reduction required. The film holding device usually consists of a vacuum back which holds the film perfectly flat by suction.

THE LENS

The lens is the camera's eye. In order to understand how it works, study the pinhole camera shown in Figure D. This is the simplest form of camera. In fact, it is so simple that you can make one yourself by attaching a piece of film to one end of a cardboard

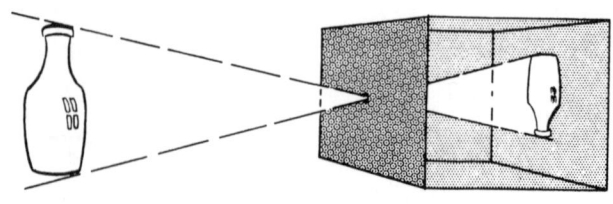

Figure D — Image formation in a pinhole camera.

408

box, punching a hole in the opposite end, and then sealing the box so that all light is excluded except that entering through the pinhole. Although an extremely long exposure is required, you can use the pinhole camera for taking pictures of objects where no motion is involved.

IMAGE FORMATION

As you can see in Figure E, each point on the copy reflects light rays in all directions, but since the pinhole is so small, only one ray from each point on the copy can pass through it to reach the film. If you think of the copy as consisting of millions of these tiny points, each reflecting a light ray to a corresponding point on the film, you can understand better how these points combine to form an image or likeness of the original copy on the film.

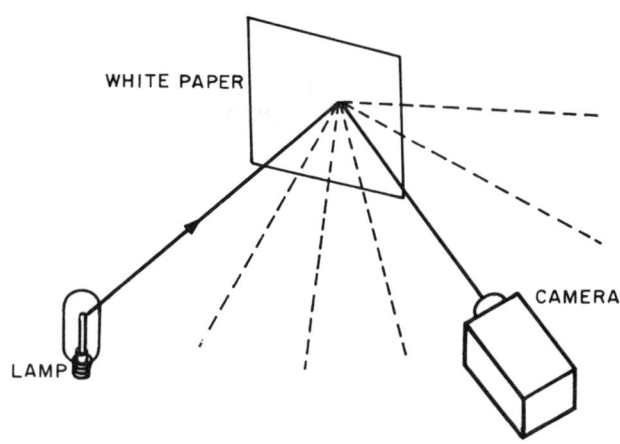

WHITE PAPER

CAMERA

LAMP

Figure E — How light rays are reflected from a point on the copy.

Unfortunately the pinhole camera has little practical value because of the extreme length of time required to expose the film. Of course, you can cut down exposure time by making a larger pinhole. The larger opening will let in more light, but it will also cause the image to be blurred, because it will allow more than one ray from each point on the copy to enter the camera, and this will cause the rays to overlap on the film.

IMAGE FORMATION WITH A LENS

When you use a larger opening, you must have some means of controlling the light rays—and that is where the lens comes in. The lens is a piece of optical glass, scientifically ground to catch the light rays reflected from each point on the copy and bend them so they will come together again at a point inside the camera.

As you can see in Figure F, the lens is capable of receiving numerous light rays from a single point and bending them so that they will all converge or

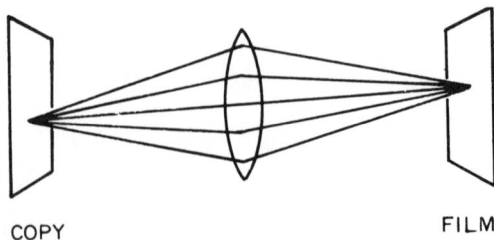

COPY   FILM

Figure F — The lens can capture any number of rays emanating from a single point on the copy and bend them so that they will come together again to form a similar point inside the camera.

come together again to form a similar point behind the lens.

A simple lens, like the one shown in the diagram cannot form a sharp image however, because the light rays passing through its edges are bent more than those passing near the center. Therefore, some of the rays coming from a particular point on the copy do not meet at the same point on the film, and this causes a slight fuzziness. Lens manufacturers correct this fault by combining lenses that spread the light with lenses that cause the light rays to converge or come to a point. (See Fig. G.) Two or more of these individual lenses (called elements) are fitted together in a metal tube known as the lens barrel. The entire assembly is then referred to as the lens.

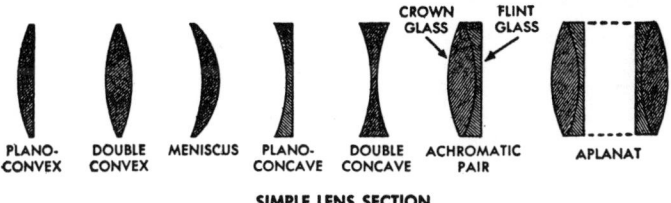

Figure G — A simple lens does not form a true image, and so types of converging lenses must be combined with types of dispersing lens for best results.

411

FOCUSING

If you will look at Figure H for a moment, you will see that if the light rays come from an object near the camera, they focus or come to a point a considerable distance behind the lens. If the object is moved farther away from the camera, the light

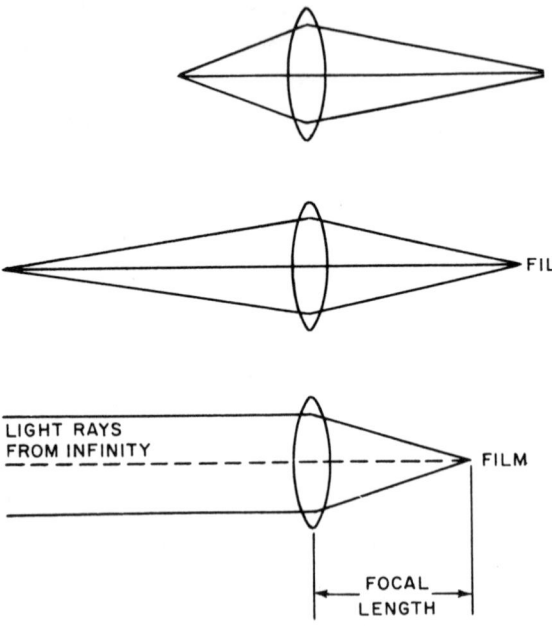

Figure H — Light rays coming from a distant object come to focus at a point closer behind the lens than those coming from a near object. When the lens is focused on an object 600 or more feet away, it is said to be focused at infinity, and the image will form at the closest possible point behind the lens. The distance from this point to the center of the lens is known as the focal length of the lens.

rays come to focus closer to the lens. If the object is moved far enough away from the camera (approximately 600 feet), the lens is said to be focused at an infinite distance or infinity, and the image will form at the closest possible point behind the lens.

When you focus a lens, only those objects that are a specific distance from it will be in absolute focus. Objects farther away or closer to the camera will be slightly fuzzy, although the distortion may be so slight that the eye will not notice it. The ability of the lens to produce (at one setting) a reasonably sharp image of several objects at varying distances from the camera is known as depth of focus. Depth of focus (also called depth of field) is not as important in process camera work as it is in other types of photography, because you are shooting flat copy, all portions of which are the same distance from the film. But it does allow you a slight tolerance when you are setting up the camera, particularly when you are focusing for reductions.

When the copyboard and the film holding device are focused at the same distance from the lens, the image formed is the same size as the original copy. If the cameraman wishes to enlarge the image, he moves the lensboard away from the film and then moves the copyboard into focus. If he wants to reduce the image, he moves the lensboard closer to the film and then adjusts the copyboard.

ILLUMINATION PRINCIPLES

When the lens is moved away from the film, the light

is spread over a greater area and the image is enlarged. But spreading the light weakens its intensity, and the more it is spread, the weaker it becomes.

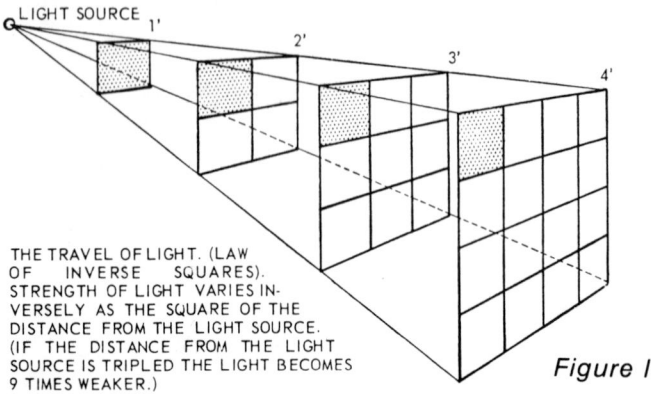

THE TRAVEL OF LIGHT. (LAW OF INVERSE SQUARES). STRENGTH OF LIGHT VARIES INVERSELY AS THE SQUARE OF THE DISTANCE FROM THE LIGHT SOURCE. (IF THE DISTANCE FROM THE LIGHT SOURCE IS TRIPLED THE LIGHT BECOMES 9 TIMES WEAKER.)

Figure I

Look at Figure I for a moment. If it takes 15 seconds to make a proper exposure when the distance between the lens and film is 1 foot, it will take 60 seconds (four times as long) to get the same exposure if the distance is increased to 2 feet. This is due to the fact that when the distance between the film and lens is doubled, the light is spread over four times its former area, and it is so weakened that it will take four times as long to get the proper exposure.

Tripling the distance will enlarge the image nine times and an exposure nine times longer than the original will be required. This loss of strength as the light travels through the air can be expressed by a mathematical rule known as the "law of inverse squares" which states that "the strength of light varies inversely as the square of the distance from the light source."

You can compensate for this loss of light strength in two ways. You can use a longer exposure, or you can use a larger lens opening to let more light enter the camera in the same amount of time.

LENS DIAPHRAGM

Each lens barrel contains a device known as the iris diaphragm. The diaphragm consists of a series of thin metal or composition blades which are so arranged as to form a circular opening in the center of the lens barrel. This opening is known as the lens aperture. By turning a collar on the outside of the lens barrel, the cameraman can adjust these blades to increase or decrease the size of the aperture and thus regulate the amount of light entering the camera. (See Fig. J.)

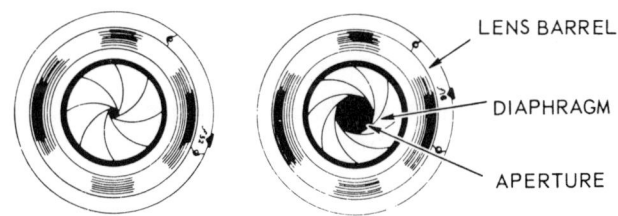

LENS BARREL

DIAPHRAGM

APERTURE

Figure J — The aperture setting is made by adjusting the lens diaphragm.

F-NUMBERS

To maintain the proper relation between the amount of light let into the camera and the distance it must travel once it gets inside, photographers have adopted a scale of values called f-numbers or f-stops which show the relation of the lens opening to its focal length.

The f-numbers are marked on the lens collar and are used in setting the aperture. Each f-number represents a fractional part of the focal length of the lens. When the cameraman sets the collar at f/8, the diaphragm will automatically form an opening in the lens barrel that is 1/8 as wide as the focal length of the lens. If the focal length of the lens is 16 inches, the diameter of the lens opening will be 2 inches. Similarly, setting the aperture at f/16 will mean 1/16 of 16 or a 1-inch opening, and so on.

LENS SPEED

The smallest f-numbers represent the largest apertures. The speed of the lens is determined by the largest f-number that can be used with it. A lens with an f/1 opening is faster than one with a maximum opening of f/8 because the f/1 opening is relatively larger and lets in more light thereby reducing exposure time.

For many years, it was believed that greater detail and sharpness was obtained from process camera lenses when they were stopped down to the smaller aperture settings. Tests have proved that the sharpest image is realized when the lens is stopped down one or two stops from the largest lens opening. For example, if the camera you are operating has a f/11 lens, the lens aperture setting should be set at f/16 or f/22 for a same-size exposure. When the aperture setting is f/45 and smaller, the tests show that there is considerable loss of detail and sharpness.

The length of an exposure depends to some extent on the lens aperture setting. Using the next larger or smaller major lens opening either halves or doubles your exposure time. For example, a 10-second exposure at f/11 will require 20 seconds at f/16 or 5 seconds at f/8.

LENS DIAPHRAGM CONTROL SYSTEM

The basic exposure time and aperture setting for same-size (1:1) work varies with the speed of the film and the particular camera set-up you are using. A series of test exposures will determine the basic exposure time and aperture setting for the camera you are operating.

The intensity of light received by the film varies as the distance between the lens and the film is changed. A change in film-lens distance occurs when the camera extension is changed for an enlargement or reduction of the original copy. The purpose of the lens diaphragm is to open or close the lens aperture, thereby regulating the amount of light the film receives. The amount of time of the exposure remains the same regardless of the camera extension.

There are several types of diaphragm control systems, but the one typical of those found on many process cameras consists of a pointer which is attached to the lens collar and a metal plate which is attached to the lens barrel. The plate has a series of scales—one for each major f-stop—and each scale is graduated to show percentages of enlargement or reduction. The cameraman determines the percentage of enlargement or reduction with a scaling wheel. He then simply moves the pointer to the proper place along the selected f-stop scale. Since the pointer is attached to the lens collar, the aperture is set automatically.

SHUTTERS

Process cameras are equipped with a shutter which opens to admit light through the lens or closes to stop the passage of light. The shutter is located behind the lens and is electrically operated. It is connected to a timer which is set for a predetermined length of time. When the starting button on the timer is pushed, the shutter and the camera lamps are simultaneously activated. When the time of the exposure has expired, the camera lamps are turned off and the shutter automatically closes.

LENS ABERRATIONS

A single lens cannot form a sharp image because it cannot bend all light rays uniformly. The light rays passing through the outer edges of the lens are bent more than those passing near the center, for example, and they will not meet at the same point.

Rays of certain colors are also bent more than others. If you look at printed matter through a magnifying glass, you may find colored outlines around the letters. These outlines are there because the lens does not focus all colors on the same plane. White light is composed of a series of colored waves, some of which are longer than others. Colors of the shorter wave lengths are bent the most as they pass through the lens and colors of the long wave lengths are bent the least. Since these rays do not come together at a single point, they tend to overlap and create a blurred or outlined image.

These lens defects are known as aberrations. There are several types of aberrations common to all lenses:

1. Chromatic aberration is the inability of the lens to focus all colors on the same plane. (See Fig. K.) You

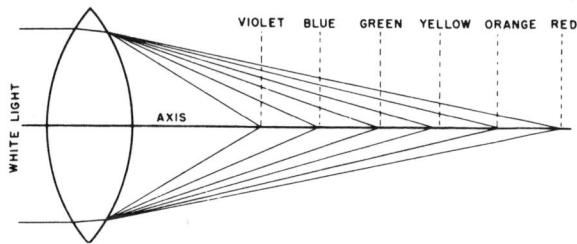

Figure K — Convergence of colored rays from white light.

can minimize it by using a smaller lens aperture, or the manufacturer can correct it by using a combination of lenses made of different types of glass. Crown and flint glass are generally used for this purpose, and the lenses are ground so that they bend the light rays in opposite directions. One spreads the light while the other brings the rays together to a point. This combination causes the longer wave lengths to be refracted more sharply and the shorter wave lengths to have less refraction so that most chromatic aberration is cancelled out before it reaches the film. Lenses corrected to bring two of the primary colors together on the same plane are known as achromatic. Lenses corrected to focus all the primary colors are called apochromatic lenses.

2. Spherical aberration occurs when the light rays passing through the outer edges of the lens focus on a different plane from those passing through the center. This causes the edge of the image to be out of focus when the center is sharp and vice versa. The manufacturer corrects this condition by combining positive and negative lenses, by calculating suitable curvatures for each lens element, and by varying the thickness and separation of the elements. Stopping down the lens with the iris diaphragm will also reduce spherical aberration.

3. Coma is characterized by fuzziness along the margins of the image due to the light rays forming ovals (pointing to the center of the image) instead of points. It is caused by the unequal refracting power of the different areas of the lens. The image of a point of light is formed by numerous light rays which are refracted through a relatively wide portion of the lens. In order for them to form a sharply defined point of light inside the camera, the rays which pass through the outer edges of the lens must come to focus at exactly the same point in the focal plane as those passing through the center of the lens. When a lens is causing coma, rays of light emanating from a point on the copy which is not in line with the center of the lens (lens axis) pass through the center of the lens to form a well-defined point, but those rays passing through the outer portions of the lens do not converge to form a single point. Instead, they form several overlapping points, and this creates an egg- or pear-shaped blur along the margin of the image.

Coma can be corrected by the use of a combination of negative and positive lenses, and it can be minimized by stopping down the lens.

4. Astigmatism is the inability of the lens to project a sharply-focused image of both horizontal and vertical lines on the same plane.

When this aberration is present, the lens seemingly has two focal lengths—one for the horizontal lines and another for the vertical lines, especially when these lines are in the margins of the image. For example, if you were photographing a crossmark (+), you would find that the vertical line would be out of focus when the horizontal line was focused and vice versa. If you adjust the focus between the horizontal and vertical focuses, the image of the crossmark will be slightly blurred, but the lens will form its best image at this distance. You can reduce the blur somewhat by stopping the aperture down and using only the center portion of the lens.

Astigmatism is corrected by the use of a combination of lenses of different kinds of optical glass. When lenses are corrected for astigmatism and chromatic aberration, other aberrations are corrected simultaneously. However, it is difficult to eliminate astigmatism and at the same time retain a flat field so there is a negligible amount of aberration in even the best lenses.

5. Curvature of field causes the center of the image to be out of focus when the margins are in focus and vice versa. It is due to the fact that a curved lens cannot form a perfect image at all points on a flat surface. The usual compromise with such lenses is to focus midway between the two extremes and reduce the size of the aperture. The manufacturer corrects this aberration by combining positive and negative lenses of varying radii of curvature. When the lens has been corrected in this manner during manufacture, it is said to have a flat field. The best modern lenses have a noticeable degree of this aberration however, when used with large apertures.

6. Distortion causes the straight lines of the image to appear curved, particularly along the outer margins. It is due to the fact that some areas of the lens magnify more than others. Since the lines are bent in one direction if the aperture is placed in front of a simple lens and are bent in the opposite direction when the aperture is placed behind the lens, it is possible to correct this form of aberration by placing the aperture in the center of the lens barrel between the lens elements.

FLARE

Flare or hot spots are nebulous patches of light

caused by internal reflections in the lens. Occasionally they originate from spots within the lens mount where the blacking has worn off. You can have these spots repainted to eliminate future trouble.

Flare may also be caused by the lens itself. When the light strikes the first element in the lens, part of it goes through and part of it is reflected. Similarly when it strikes the next element, part of it goes through and part is again reflected. This time the reflected light bounces from the second element back to the first and from there it is reflected again back to the second. Part of it may eventually get through to form a ghost or flare on the negative. (See Fig. L.)

Some flare is present in all lenses, but you can reduce it by the use of a lens hood, a dull, black lensboard, a dust-free lens, or a change in the angle of lighting. Lenses are often coated with a chemical solution to reduce optical flare.

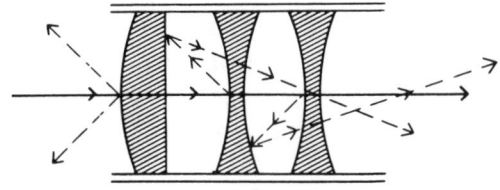

Figure L — How ghosts are formed in the lens barrel. Center arrow indicates path of light forming image. Broken line represents reflected light.

CHAPTER 30

FILM NEGATIVES

More and more quick printers are running jobs requiring film negatives and metal plates. By so doing, they increase their worth to customers and prevent inroads from being made by unskilled competitors.

A darkroom and process camera are needed to make film negatives. Some systems use "hands through holes" cameras to try to bypass a darkroom. Others use camera/platemakers. There is not, however, a good substitute for a darkroom and standard process camera for producing film negatives.

FILM

There are many kinds of film. Most quick printers, however, limit usage to one type of film for making negatives — a process film designed for single-color subjects. The film referred to in this chapter is

424

a standard orthochromatic process film in sheet form. One exception to "standard" is a film designed to reach full development and stop, thereby preventing overdevelopment. This "autostop" film is useful where unstable temperatures cause development timing problems.

PROCESS CAMERAS

There are many good, small cameras on the market. NuArc makes a 14" x 18" vertical model (VV1418) that sells for about $2500. It will enlarge and reduce 3X. If price is a factor, the Sandmar 12" x 18" upright sells for about $1400 and does a good job. It will only enlarge and reduce 2X which is the major disadvantage. We have tested the Sandmar. It is simple to operate and makes good negatives.

MINIMUM MISCELLANEOUS EQUIPMENT

In addition to a process camera, you will need at least the following small equipment:

1. **Trays** for developing film (Few, if any, quick printers use expensive film processors.)
2. Darkroom **timer**
3. Line and clothes pins, or **film dryer** (A few quick printers use film dryers. Most use hand-held hair dryers or simply hang film to dry.)
4. Small **light table** (a necessity for stripping)
5. **Exacto knife** and **scissors** for cutting film and masking sheets

MINIMUM SUPPLIES

1. **Film** - standard orthochromatic sheet film or

"autostop film." "Autostop film" reaches full development in about one minute and then stops developing. However, the timing of the exposure is more critical. With standard film, incorrect exposure can be adjusted by development time. You can reduce film inventory by stocking one size (11" x 17") and cutting all other sizes.

2. **Developer** and **fix** concentrates. If the mixtures are stored immediately after use in capped bottles, they will last for weeks or even months, depending, of course, on usage. Longer development time is the tip-off to depleted developer. Always change the fix when developer is depleted.

3. **Masking sheets** (goldenrod). I recommend masking sheets that are precut (to your press size) and preprinted with guide lines.

4. Lithographers **tape.—** a transparent red tape that permits visual inspection when blocked out areas of a negative are examined over a light table. Because of its color, it won't allow light to pass onto the light-sensitive coating of the plate. It may be used for attaching negatives to masking sheets, stripping in halftones, or masking out parts of the negative.

5. **Opaque.** I recommend two kinds: a water soluble red opaque which is applied with a brush and a transparent red opaque that comes in a pen, much like a Marks-a-lot. The pen is handy for small opaque jobs.

6. **Brushes** for opaque. A No. 1 for close work and a No. 3 for larger areas.

7. **Metal plates.** Unless you expect exceptionally long runs, I recommend presensitized aluminum plates. You can buy presensitized plates that are good for runs of 100,000 or more, but the longer run plates cost more. 25,000 run plates are usually sufficient. Foil plates are cheaper than aluminum, but they are thick, and unless press cylinder pressures are adjusted to accommodate them, they will pull loose from pinholes on gripper plate. Also, run length is shortened with too much pressure. If aluminum plates are too thin for your press setting, the solution is a simple underlining with a sheet of paper.

8. Metal plate processing **chemicals.** Plate manufacturers recommend their own chemicals, but the usual is a desensitizing solution or process gum and a red lacquer or developer. Gum arabic is used for preventing oxidation during long storage periods. Process gum will prevent oxidation for shorter periods.

9. **Sponges** or pads for applying solutions to metal plate.

MAKING LINE NEGATIVES

Many poor quality offset printing jobs can be traced to negatives that have been underexposed, overexposed, or improperly developed.

In order to obtain consistent results, it is necessary to standardize operations whenever possible. If you use the same materials in the same way each time, you can expect to get reasonably uniform results.

Another important point is to make just one change to your operations when you are having problems. For example, if the image develops slowly when you are processing a negative, the cause can probably be attributed to underexposure, cold developer, or old developer. To remedy this problem, you should make an exposure adjustment or check your developer. By making one change or check at a time, you can isolate the cause and observe the results to the change you have made.

JUDGING ORIGINAL COPY

When shooting line work, most cameramen expose for the background rather than the image. If the copy is prepared on tinted or colored paper or on paper having a very rough surface, less light is reflected into the camera and a longer exposure is necessary than is required if the copy is prepared on a smooth, white paper. There is no formula for determining how much the exposure must be increased. This is something you must learn from experience and test exposures.

FILTER FACTOR

If the copy background is colored, it may be necessary for you to use a filter. Since filters absorb part of the light, you must increase the exposure time. The term filter factor describes the number of times the basic exposure must be increased when a filter is used. The filter factor varies according to the filter itself, the type of light source used for the exposure, and the particular type of film you are using. To find the filter factor for the film and light source you are using, consult the film data sheet packaged with the film.

DETERMINING EMULSION SIDE OF FILM

The emulsion side of film should face the lens when the camera is closed for the exposure. If you are using ortho film, you can determine the emulsion side by examining the film at a reasonable distance from the safelight. The emulsion side is always the light, dull side. Another method of determining the emulsion side is to moisten your lips and press a corner of the film between them. The emulsion side will stick to your lip.

EXPOSURE TIME

Although it is impossible to designate an exact exposure time for a particular film and camera setup, you can find a recommended exposure from the manufacturer's film data sheet. Of course, if your setup varies, your exposure times will also vary. The age and speed of the film you are using as well as the nature of your copy are factors that will affect the length of your exposures.

Timing adjustments are also made for reductions and enlargements. Time is increased for enlargements and decreased for reductions. The percentage of time increase or decrease is the same as the percentage of reduction or enlargement. A substitute for timing changes is an F stop change. Each F stop point doubles or halves the time required for a shot.

FILM PROCESSING

A few quick printers have a temperature controlled sink and can obtain uniform results when developing negatives by the time-temperature method. (Auto-stop film does not require precise timing.)

If you do not have a temperature controlled sink, you should keep a thermometer in the developer and make a time-temperature chart based on your experience with different films.

Once you have determined the correct development time, set the darkroom timer for the amount of time required. Immerse the film uniformly in the developer by first drawing it emulsion side down through the developer. Then quickly flip it over and let the film rest on the bottom of the developing tray. During the development, you should agitate the developer continuously with a smooth, rocking motion of the tray.

When the developing time has elapsed, remove the film from the developer and rinse it in a tray of plain water or stop bath solution, then into the fixing solution. When the milky appearance is gone from the image areas, you can turn on the regular lights.

The total time the negative must remain in the fixing solution varies according to the type of film and fixing solutions you are using — usually a minute or more. More time is better than less.

You can determine the correct amount of time by consulting the film data sheet. After fixing, the negative should be given a thorough wash in running water to remove all traces of the processing solutions. Ideally, the film should be washed for a minimum of ten minutes, but this is rarely done. A quick rinse to remove the fix will suffice if the film is not going to be reused over a long period of time.

DEVELOPMENT BY INSPECTION

Under conditions where the temperature cannot be fully controlled, you can develop film by inspection instead of a set time method. You should look at the film frequently until the image starts to form, and at 5 to 10-second intervals thereafter. Total development time should be about four times that required for the image to first appear.

Compare your negatives to the samples shown in Figure A. The good negative has sharp, clear transparent areas. The other two negatives lack the sharp detail in the image areas. When examining negative quality, have a specific point in mind to check. Some experienced cameramen use the small openings in the letters "A" and "e" as to their quality checks; others look at the tips of the letters "m" and "w." If the images are sharp and clear in these areas, the negative should be acceptable.

SENSITIVITY GUIDES

Some cameramen use a sensitivity guide similar to the one shown in Figure B when they are photographing line copy. The guide is placed in an open area of the copy. The image of the guide as it appears on the film being developed is used as a gauge to indicate when the film has been developed to the correct point.

CORRECT

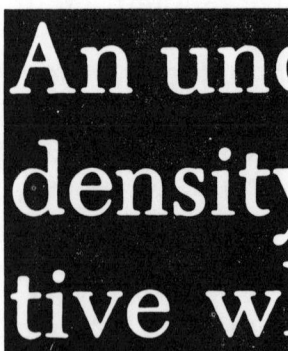

Figure A. The image of a negative should appear sharp and clear as example on right.

└─────── INCORRECT ───────┘

Figure B. The Stouffer Sensitivity guide may be used as a visual aid to determine when the correct development of line negatives has been attained. The two patterned areas at the top can be used to check the camera's focusing system.

432

NEGATIVES FOR COLOR REPRODUCTION

If the colors do not overlap, a single black-and-white drawing is all that is required. It should have a tissue overlay attached to indicate the parts of the drawing that are to go in color and the colors to be used. You then shoot as many negatives from the original as are necessary to reproduce the number of colors desired, and mask off each negative so that only the desired color areas are printed on the plate.

If the work is very simple, you may be able to use a paper mask and shift it about so that plates for all colors can be made from the same negative.

When colors overlap, it is best to have a separate black-and-white drawing for each color and to make a separate negative from each drawing.

COLORED COPY

You may be able to photograph colored copy without the use of filters. Sometimes, however, there is so little contrast between the subject and the background that filters are indispensable. When the subject is to be made dark against a light background, select the filter which will transmit the color of the background and absorb the color of the subject so that it will photograph as black.

If you write on paper with a red crayon and try to read it by the red safelight in the darkroom, the lettering is practically invisible. But if you were to look at the lettering under a mercury-vapor lamp, it would appear black because this lamp gives off no red radiation. That is the effect of the filter. Filters transmit some colors freely, making them photograph as white or light shades of gray; and they absorb the radiations of other colors, making them photograph as black or deep shades of gray.

Orthochromatic film is the workhorse of the litho shop because it is suitable for almost all types of work. However, panchromatic film must be used when red filters are required because ortho films are not sensitive to red. No image will register on the film if a red filter is used with ortho film because all light striking the film will be red.

Hints

You may find the following hints helpful:

1. To **drop** a color, use a filter of the same color, preferably darker than the color you wish to drop.

2. To **hold** a color, use a filter which is complementary to the color which you wish to hold.

3. Use a green filter to intensify **pencil** drawings.

4. To obtain a negative of a **blueprint**, use panchromatic film and a red filter.

5. If the copy you are photographing has a **signature in blue ink**, use a yellow filter.

6. **Yellow stains** and other discolorations can often be dropped from the negative by use of a yellow filter. If the stains are severe, however, it may be necessary to retouch the copy to obtain a satisfactory negative.

7. **Overexposure** will help to drop a color when no filter is used. **Underexposure** will help hold a color when no filter is used.

NEGATIVE DIFFICULTIES

Image does not develop because:
Negative has not been exposed. *Check lens, shutter, and camera lamps for failure to operate properly.*
Oxidized developer (age or contaminated). *Replace with fresh developer.*
Cold developer. *Heat to 68° F.*

Develops too slowly because:
Underexposed. *Check aperture and full coverage of lamps; check filter factor, colored background; increase exposure as necessary.*
Cold developer. *Heat to 68° F.*
Old developer (muddy color, slow action on test strip). *Drain developer, clean tray, replace with fresh developer, check water for impurities, use distilled water if necessary.*

Develops too quickly because:
Overexposed. *Check aperture and lamps, correct position, reduce exposure time.*
Warm developer. *Cool to 68° F, if possible, otherwise dilute developer or reduce developing time.*

Clears too slowly or not at all in fixing bath because:
Old or spent fixer. *Drain fixer, clean tray, replace with fresh fixer.*

Negative veiled or fogged in clear areas because:
Overexposure. *Reduce exposure so image first appears in 30-45 seconds (process film at 68° F).*
Overdevelopment. *Develop only for required time,*

reduce temperature to 68° F, check for underexposure.
Old developer (requires excess developing time). *Replace with fresh developer.*
Reflected light. *Adjust lights to prevent reflections from lamps or copyboard.*
Lights leaks. *Check camera bellows, lensboard, and darkroom seals.*
Dirty copyboard glass. *Clean both sides of glass, keep cameraroom clean and well ventilated.*
Old or fogged film. *Replace film, use film before expiration date.*

Uneven development because:
Uneven contact with developer. *Immerse film quickly and evenly into developer with emulsion side down.*
Uneven action of developer. *Agitate to mix developer and equalize temperature.*

Negative lacks overall density because:
Underexposed or underdeveloped. *Check aperture and lamps for exposure, check developer for age or adjust development time.*

Negative thin in corners because:
Uneven illumination. *Increase distance of lamps to copyboard and correct exposure, mount diffusers or reflectors to spread light to edges of copy, stop lens down and increase exposure time.*

Blurred image because:
Out of focus. *Adjust focus.*
Camera motion. *Check for vibration.*

CHAPTER 31

HALFTONES

Halftone negatives are made by placing a halftone screen over the film during exposure. A halftone screen is made up of clear glass or plastic, crosshatched with opaque lines similar to Figure A. The crosslines form a pattern that breaks up the light and causes it to register on the film as a series of small individual dots, each varying in size according to the amount of light being reflected from the copy at that particular point.

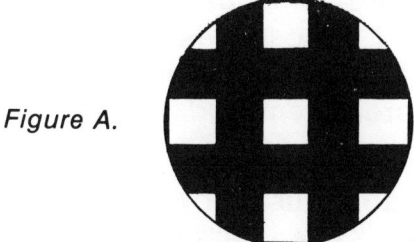

Figure A.

Because some areas of the copy are whiter and reflect more light than other areas, dots of varying sizes are produced on the film and this creates an illusion of tone ranging from light grey to black.

Glass halftone screens were used for years and are still used in some commercial shops. Today, however, most commercial printers and nearly all quick printers use thin plastic or acetate contact screens. There are several types of halftone screens. The screen most used by quick printers is known as a "grey contact screen."

Halftone screens are available in standard rulings of 50 to 400 lines per square inch. A 100-line screen, for example, has 100 lines and 100 transparent openings to the linear inch. 85-line screens are most popular with quick printers. Commercial printers favor 133 line screens.

Making Exposures with a Grey Contact Screen

Only one exposure is required for line negatives. Halftone negatives can be made with one exposure, but two will produce better results. With some copy and screens, a third exposure will improve the halftone. This third exposure is called a "bump" exposure and is a short shot with a large F stop setting with the screen removed.

The grey contact screen has a built-in bump exposure, and it can be used for either black-and-white or color work. "Magenta" contact screens are used by some quick printers. The principal disadvantage of magenta screens is the effect they have on some colored originals due to the filtering factor of their color.

The following procedure will produce good halftones from most good photographs:

1. Use an 85-line (not more than 110) grey contact screen with elliptical or square dots. (I prefer elliptical.) Why an 85-line screen? Because presses, papers, pressures, and inks used by most quick printers will cause plugging (holes filled with ink) of fine line halftones. An open 85-line halftone looks much better than a plugged 133-line halftone.

2. Place the halftone screen over the negative. Negative should be emulsion side up and screen emulsion side down. Screen should extend at least one inch beyond all sides of the negative. Turn on vacuum and smooth the screen with a clean, dry cotton pad or a soft rubber roller.

3. Open lens to the widest opening and turn on camera lights. Exposure time will vary depending on film, camera, and darkness or contrast of copy. 20 seconds is a good starting point for 100% copy. For reductions or enlargements, increase or decrease exposure time by same percentage as the percentage of reduction or enlargement. Example: if 20 seconds is the correct time for 100%, then a 70% reduction would require .70 x 20 seconds or 14 seconds. 130% enlargement would require 1.30 x 20 seconds or 26 seconds. If a 50% reduction is used, the lens can be closed one F stop instead of decreasing time, since each F stop closure cuts the light in half — the reverse for enlargements.

4. After main exposure, leave screen in place with vacuum on, but remove photo and replace it with a

blank piece of yellow paper. Most screens are protected with yellow back cardboard folders. If this yellow cover is clean, it can be used. Also, goldenrod paper can be used. Expose the yellow paper for several seconds, about one fifth the time of the main exposure. Develop the film and you should have a good halftone.

5. Make notes after each experiment, and you will eventually zero in on the best timing for your particular camera and film.

ELLIPTICAL (CHAIN DOT) GREY CONTACT SCREENS

In addition to the conventional square dot grey contact screen, there is also an elliptical (chain-dot) grey contact screen which varies slightly from the regular grey screen.

Figure B
Square dot on top - Elliptical dot on bottom.

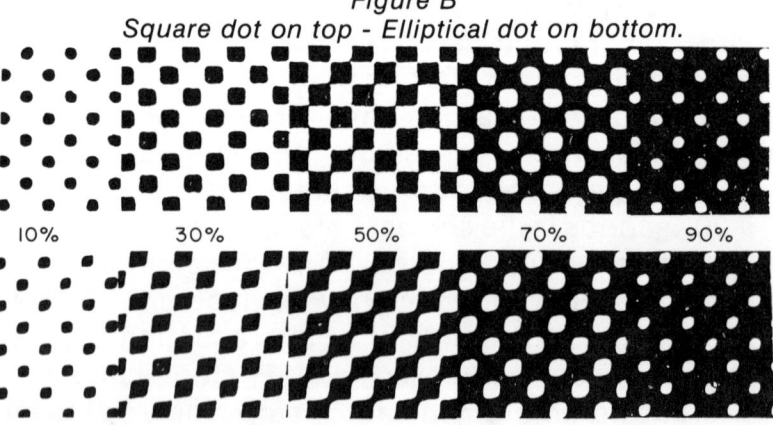

This screen is designed to produce an elliptical dot in the middletones (40 to 60 percent tone areas). Elliptical dots have an advantage over the conventional square dots. In the 50 percent middletone areas, the square dots join each other at all four corners in a checkerboard pattern. Elliptical dots join each other at only two corners. (See Figure B.) The square dot produces a rather harsh transition from the highlights to the shadows while the elliptical dot produces a more subtle transition. It is easier to print halftones made with the chain-dot screen because the image does not fill in as readily on the press. The elliptical dot screen also minimizes grain when the original copy has considerable grain showing in the print.

JUDGING DOT SIZE

The size of halftone dots is controlled primarily by exposure times. Ideally, the light grey areas of a photo should be printed with 90% of the copy white and 10% covered with black dots. Dark grey areas should be 90% black with 10% covered with white dots.

If your inks tend to plug the dots in the dark areas, you can open them with a longer flash exposure. (Yellow paper replacing the photo on the camera copyboard.) Dot size in the light grey areas can be controlled by the main exposure.

USING A GREY SCALE

A grey scale is a strip of paper printed with a scale showing different shades of grey. It can be placed alongside a photograph during exposure to serve as a guide to correct exposure times. See Figure C. It is difficult to reproduce both ends of the grey scale

Figure C. This is an illustration of a NEGATIVE. The small black dots on the negative become small white dots on the printed paper.

REDUCED EXPOSURE will move all dots up, darken middletones, and reduce contrast. A reduced exposure may require a LONGER FLASH to enlarge the small dots.

LONGER EXPOSURE will move all steps down and lighten middletones.

Longer FLASH will open the small dot and move it down to 0 on the scale.

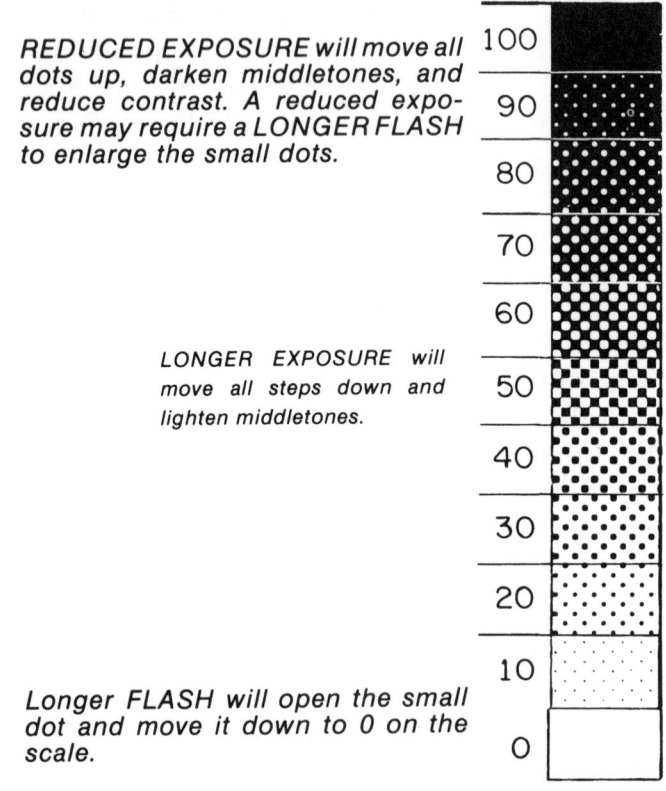

accurately. If the copy is contrasty, you can capture the detail and highlight portions with the main exposure, but you must flash the negative through the screen to provide shadow dots in areas where the copy does not reflect sufficient light.

CONTROLLING CONTRAST

You can increase contrast by placing the screen on the vacuum back with the emulsion side out rather than against the film emulsion. Contrast is also increased by faster or longer agitation of the film in the development tray.

You can also control contrast by manipulating the flash exposure to produce the desired dot sizes in the shadow areas.

COMBINATION COPY

(Halftones and line copy on same negative)

If line copy is exposed through a halftone screen, lettering and other lines will have white dots in the normally black areas. This problem may be handled in several ways.

Most quick printers and an increasing number of graphic artists make their halftones on stat paper instead of film. Making a stat halftone is similar to making a film halftone. Only the timing and developing procedures are changed. The halftone stat is trimmed and pasted onto the original with the line copy. Then a line negative is made of the entire job. The dots in the stat halftone will reproduce with very little loss in quality.

Another method is to make two negatives — one line and one halftone. The halftone portion is then spliced into the line negative. See stripping chapter for details.

A third method, seldom used, is to strip line copy

and halftone copy onto separate masking sheets and make a double burn on the plate. This method is used when the line copy is too close to the halftone for normal stripping.

OVERPRINT LETTERING

Lettering over a halftone requires that a film positive be made from the line negative. The film positive must be made as large or larger than the halftone area which it is to cover so that it will not leave a ragged line or shadow when it is printed on the plate. This positive copy is stripped over the halftone negative and printed on the plate with a single printing.

Tints and tone backgrounds can also be stripped over transparent sections of line negatives in this manner.

COLOR SEPARATION

Halftone color separation, known as full color or process work, is both difficult and expensive. If the copy is to be reproduced in full color, it is necessary to make four separate press plates for it. Most color separations are done by computerized cameras.

Since colors normally photograph as black or shades of grey, regular black and white halftone negatives are used for color-separation work. In order to separate the colors in the original copy, the cameraman photographs the original through a series of filters.

The negatives are then developed and printed on the offset plates in the usual manner. The original

444

colors are restored when the plates are run on the press in the proper colors of ink. Since impressions from the yellow, red, blue, and black plates must be made on the paper one over the other to restore the full color to the finished print, the cameraman changes the angle of the halftone screen for each shot so that some colors will overlap and some will print side by side when the plates are run on the press.

RESCREENING HALFTONES

Often you will need to copy a clipping — a halftone which has been previously printed in a magazine or newspaper. If the screen used for the halftone in the clipping is coarse and open (not finer than 100 lines per inch), you may shoot the job as a same-size line shot; if it is not, you must copy the job through a halftone screen.

When the job is rescreened, the new dot formation often overlaps the old, and a disturbing pattern called a moire is formed. If the halftone must be rescreened, you can reduce this pattern or eliminate it by reducing the image or by tilting the copy to about a 30° (off vertical) angle on the copyboard.

CARE OF THE CONTACT SCREEN

Fingerprints, waterspots, and dust will affect the dot formation of contact screens. You should handle the screen by the edges and keep it in a container when not in use.

You can clean the screen with film cleaner. If dirt is stubborn, immerse the screen in plain water at room temperature or in a solution consisting of 4 ounces of alcohol, 1 cap full of Photo-Flo, and one gallon water. (If the screen is cleaned with plain water, you should treat it with a wetting agent such as Photo-Flo before hanging it up to dry.) Go over the screen lightly with a piece of saturated cotton to wipe away the stubborn spots. Do not allow the screen to soak more than 5 minutes.

Never use a camel's hair brush on a contact screen; you can dust the screen by wiping it lightly with a piece of photo chamois or by going over it with a Staticmaster brush which is designed to remove dust particles and eliminate static. If you do not have such a brush, you should tap the edge of the screen lightly against a table top before using it. This will disperse static and eliminate stray dust particles.

Perhaps the worst problem for the camerman is the half-moon creases that occur when a wrinkle is snapped out of the screen when it is picked up. To prevent these half-moons from forming, you should handle the screen carefully and raise the sides from the diagonal corners to form a kind of roll in the middle as you pick it up.

Before handling the screen, your hands should be clean and free from all chemicals — even if they are dry. All photographic processing chemicals are harmful to screens, particularly hypo. It can ruin a contact screen in less than a day.

CHAPTER 32

STRIPPING
FILM NEGATIVES

Attaching negatives to a masking sheet is an operation referred to as "stripping." The term "stripping" is also used to describe the merging of line and halftone negatives into a single negative. This process involves cutting windows in the line negative and taping in halftone negatives.

GOLDENROD (MASKING SHEETS)

Masking sheets are referred to as "goldenrod." Normally this means a coated, 80 lb. paper, goldenrod in color. Most quick printers use a goldenrod sheet precut to their press size and preprinted with grid (guide) lines. The guide lines on this goldenrod allow you to position the negatives accurately without requiring you to rule-in lines as must be done when using plain goldenrod paper. As a further time-saving aid, preprinted goldenrod has other information you will find helpful such as press gripper margins, standard page areas, and centering reference points for various page sizes.

LIGHT TABLE

A glass-topped table, which is illuminated from below, is a necessity for film negative corrections and stripping. Some of these tables are equipped with built-in movable horizontal and vertical straightedges that move on gears or cables.

Negatives are attached to the goldenrod with either clear cellulose tape or with red or black tape, which is called lithographer's tape. Lithographer's tape is translucent and permits visual inspection when blocked out areas of a negative are examined over a light table. However, because of its color, it won't allow light to pass onto the light sensitive coating of the plate.

When you use tape to attach negatives to the goldenrod, make sure that two pieces of tape do not overlap each other. Otherwise, the double thickness of tape will cause poor contact between the negative and the plate. This condition will cause the image on the plate to spread.

Use enough tape to prevent the negatives from slipping out of position or catching on something and tearing away from the goldenrod. A small strip at each corner and one along each side will usually be sufficient, but large negatives may require more.

CUTTING TOOLS

Razor blades, cutting knives with replaceable blades and scissors are all used to cut film and goldenrod. When you cut film with a razor blade or knife, the film should be cut part way through and then bent so that the film separates along the cut line. When the film must be cut all the way through, place a piece of scrap film or other protection under it to prevent the cutting tool from marring the light table glass.

USING CUTTING TOOLS

After the negatives are positioned and taped to the goldenrod, you must cut out areas of the goldenrod to expose the image areas of the negative. These openings are referred to as "windows." The goldenrod masking sheet with the windows is called a "flat."

Window openings in the goldenrod are made either with a razor blade or cutting knife. The cut must be made through the goldenrod only, not into the negative below the sheet. Type matter (line) windows may be cut out freehand, leaving about ⅛" of space around the image area of the negative. You must remove enough of the goldenrod to ensure that all of the image is uncovered.

When you are cutting windows for halftone negatives, use a straightedge to obtain a window the exact size of the halftone image. After ruling-in an outline of the window on the goldenrod with a pen, place a straightedge along each side of the outline to make the cuts straight and square. The cuts must not run over each other at the corners or a mark may appear at the corner of the halftone image. If your cuts do overlap at the corner, apply tape over the cuts as shown in Figure A.

Figure A. A method of correcting overcuts with lithographers tape.

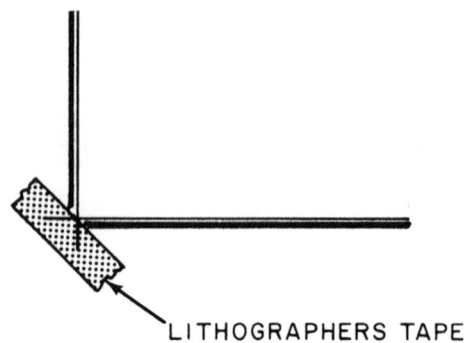

LITHOGRAPHERS TAPE

CORRECTIONS

Opaque is a light-proof paint which is used to spot out pinholes, shadow lines, and other undesirable markings on negatives. It can also be used to crop halftone negatives and to mask off parts of negatives which are used in color separation work.

Two types of opaque are in general use. Water soluble black opaque, with a pigment of carbon black, is generally used for fine detail work. Water soluble red opaque is somewhat thicker and more suitable for covering large areas. Red opaque is often used to label or to put other identification markings on negatives.

Applicator pens are becoming popular. We use one similar to a "Marks-a-lot" that is filled with red transparent opaque.

Opaque is applied to negatives with brushes or the tip of an applicator. The type of brush used depends

450

upon the kind of opaquing necessary. A No. 1 round-tipped brush is ideal for fine detail work. Smaller brushes, such as 0 or 00 may also be used, but you will seldom need them. On the other hand, you will probably have frequent use for larger brushes, such as No. 3 or No. 5. A No. 8 brush can be used to cover large areas easily.

Opaque may be applied to either side of the negative. However, if opaque must be removed, the negative is less likely to be damaged if the opaque has been applied to the harder, nonemulsion side.

Mix the opaque with water in a small container until it reaches the proper consistency to flow freely on the negative, yet dry almost immediately. Many quick printers use the opaque jar's metal cap as the mixing container.

To test the correctness of the opaque texture, they make several short strokes with the opaque brush on a scrap piece of film. When the opaque is beginning to dry by the time a one inch stroke is completed, it is mixed correctly.

You can spot out pinholes and other small areas with the tip of the brush. Larger areas, such as shadow lines, should be covered with long, flat parallel strokes of the brush.

Do not apply the opaque in heavy coatings. If it is necessary to recover an area, turn the negative over and touch up the other side. You can reduce the amount of opaquing required by covering large parts of the negative with pieces of goldenrod paper or litho tape.

CROPPING HALFTONES

You can crop halftones by ruling a straight outline on the negative with a ruling pen filled with opaque and then painting out the remaining background. The border lines should be at least 1/32″ wide because it is easier to opaque up to a line if it is reasonably thick.

You can also crop halftones by masking with goldenrod paper or with strips of red or black tape applied to the back of the negative. Be careful not to add too many thicknesses of tape or to allow the corners to overlap.

If you make an error in applying the opaque, correct it immediately so that you will not forget it. Use a clean, damp cotton swab and wipe outward from the center of the affected area.

RULING LINES

To scribe lines on a negative, square the film and tape it, emulsion side up, to the light table. If the negative requires opaquing, apply the opaque (on the emulsion side) before starting to rule it.

Mark the location of each line to be drawn with the point of dividers or engraving point. If a copy of a previously printed form is available, use it in locating the positions for your lines.

Square the printed form and tape it beside the negative. Then position the straightedge on the printed lines and scribe corresponding lines on the film. After marking the location of each line, draw a light pencil line on each side, along the margins, to

452

show the length of the lines.

It is a good idea to test the engraving tool in the margins of the negative before you begin ruling. If your lines are uneven in length, you can even them by opaquing or by applying strips of red tape to the back of the negative along the ends of the rules.

STRIPPING A FLAT

To find the center of the negative, measure the longest line of type and make a mark on the emulsion side of the film. Align the mark on the negative with the centerline on the layout. When the position is correct, tack the negative with two pieces of tape to the underside of the goldenrod.

After the negative is tacked in position, turn the flat over and fasten down the negative securely with additional tape. Do not put the tape closer than ¼" to the image areas.

Next, return the flat to its original side and cut out the opening (window) for the image area of the negative. As you gain experience, you will acquire the feel that will allow you to use just enough pressure to cut through the goldenrod without cutting into the film.

The size of the window should not be larger than necessary to uncover the image areas of the negative. Otherwise, it may be necessary to opaque pinholes or other defects in the negative which would have remained covered by the goldenrod.

Sometimes after numerous windows have been cut

in a flat, the flat will lose its rigidity. In such a case, if the negatives are not halftones, you can place strips of transparent tape on the front side of the flat in areas where it is weak. Clear tape placed over the image areas of a line negative will not ordinarily interfere with the plate exposure providing the tape is not dirty.

OTHER STRIPPING METHODS

Instead of tacking the negatives to the goldenrod sheet, some strippers position the negative under the goldenrod and cut two small holes in the layout sheet — one in the upper left corner and one in the lower right corner — and then place a strip of red tape over each hole to tack the negative to the sheet.

After the negatives have been tacked in place, the stripper turns the flat over and tapes them securely, or he may cut windows in the goldenrod sheet to expose the image areas of the negatives and then do his taping along the edges of the windows.

Some operators use this procedure when working with presensitized plates because this eliminates the necessity for having any tape on the emulsion side of the negatives and provides better contact between the plate and film when the plate is exposed.

DOUBLE BURNING

Sometimes, because of the nature of the job, it is not possible to splice the insert into the master negative. In this case, you may strip the main negative on one flat and the insert on another. Combine burning them one after the other on the plate in exact register.

At times, it may also be desirable to print black lettering or other line work over a halftone area. This is known as "surprinting." When stripping for a surprint, you must also prepare two flats. The platemaker will then burn one flat on the plate for the halftone and will burn the other flat for the line detail.

When preparing flats for double burning, you should strip your main negative on the goldenrod sheet first. You can then use this flat as a master. Fasten it to the light table and position another sheet of goldenrod over it. Strip up the insert or surprint on the second sheet in perfect registration with the main negative.

BUTTERFLY REGISTRATION MARKS

When double burning, cut crossmarks (like those shown in Figure B) through both goldenrod sheets. You should cut at least two butterflies along each side or at the top and bottom of the layout.

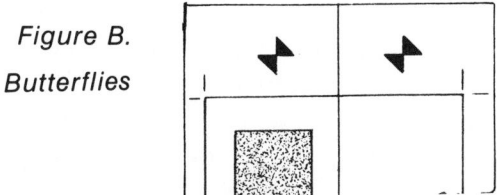

Figure B.

Butterflies

When burning the main flat, outline the butterflies in pencil on the plate. You can then match the butterflies on the second flat to the pencil marks on the plate to obtain register.

FILM REGISTER MARKS

Film register marks, like those shown in Figure C, are more accurate than the butterflies. They have two points of registration: the pin point at the center of the crossmarks and the circle.

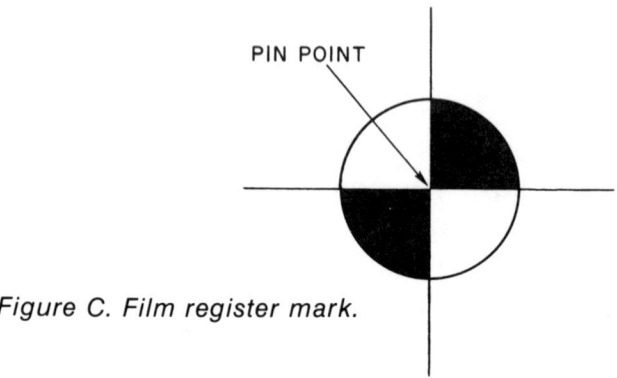

PIN POINT

Figure C. Film register mark.

Marks of this type are more difficult for the platemaker to use, however, because he must align them with a magnifying glass when he exposes the second flat. These marks are provided as film tabs. You should tape these tabs in position on at least three sides of the key flat.

After you tape your second flat over your key flat on the light table, you should cut openings in the second flat to correspond to the marks on the key flat. You can then position a register mark in each opening and align it with the register mark in the key flat. Tape the marks in position. Complete the second flat by registering the surprint negative and taping it into position.

PIN REGISTER

Still another system may be used when large flats or close registration is involved. This system involves the use of small tabs of acetate with prepunched holes and a set of plastic pins or buttons like those shown in Figure D.

TAB   **PIN**

Figure D. Pin Register Tabs

When the stripper prepares his first flat, he strips one of the hole tabs on each side of the goldenrod sheet. (He generally strips the tabs near the gripper edge of the flat so they won't interfere with the image areas.)

He then inserts the plastic pins through the holes in the tabs and positions a second sheet of goldenrod over the first flat, stripping in another set of hole tabs on this sheet in exact register with those stripped into the first. He then slips the second goldenrod sheet down over the pins to prevent it from slipping while he strips up the negatives for the second flat.

The platemaker uses a similar set of pins for positioning the work on the plate when he makes his exposures. He slips his pins through the hole tabs and allows them to lay loose on the plate until after he has positioned his first flat. Once the flat is in place, he secures the pins by taping them to the plate with masking tape.

After he makes his first exposure, he removes the flat and then positions the second flat on the plate, fitting it over the pins so that the details of the surprint will register with those of the main negative when the second exposure is made.

There are many variations of the tab and pin system. In some cases, holes are punched in the plate as well as the flats. These holes are punched on a punch table equipped with individual punches along the gripper and side edges.

REVERSE LETTERING

Effects, such as reverse lettering (white lettering against a dark background), require a film positive of the lettering. This film positive is stripped on the same flat as the main negative so that it overprints the main negative on the plate.

When stripping line negatives against halftone areas, you should arrange the work so that the halftone negative will be in direct contact with the plate when the exposure is made. This arrangement will keep the light from spreading and produce a sharper dot formation on the plate.

The film positive must always be as large or larger than the negative it is to cover so that it will not leave a shadow or edge when the plate is printed.

TINTS

Although the cameraman may provide tints by photographing a sheet of white paper through the halftone screen, many shops use commercial tints which are available in sheets in values ranging from

10 to 80 percent and in screen rulings measuring from 50 to 175 lines. Most quick printers use 110 or smaller rulings.

When a tint is required, the copy preparer may paste a piece of black paper over the desired area of the copy or he may fill in the area with india ink. The filled-in area will photograph as a transparent window on the negative.

In some cases, the person preparing the camera-ready copy may simply outline the area for the tint on the layout with india or red ink and indicate that a tint is to go in the area by marking in instructions on a tissue overlay. In such cases, it will be necessary for you to cut a window in the main negative, using the lines ruled in by the copy preparer as a guide.

The tint film should overlap the edges of the window by at least ¼". And it should be taped to the main negative in such a manner that the emulsion side of the tint will be in direct contact with the plate when the exposure is made.

Flat tints may create contact problems when the plate is exposed if they are not handled properly. Several thicknesses of tape, for example, may prevent proper contact and cause a dark rim or halo around the outer edges of the tint area when it is printed on the plate. You are more likely to have out-of-contact areas if you cut windows in the main negative than if clear openings are provided on the negative in the tint areas.

To eliminate out-of-contact troubles, some

operators treat tints as surprints instead of stripping them into or over the main negative.

STEP AND REPEAT WORK

It is sometimes desirable to run a job two or more up on the plate. This means that additional negatives must be used or that one set of negatives must be printed in two or more different positions on the plate.

If the job is very simple, it may be better to make several negatives from the original copy, but if halftones, inserts, or complicated stripping operations are required, it is usually better to make two or more exposures on the plate from the same set of negatives. This is called step-and-repeat work. There are several ways that it can be done.

Figure E shows one method of repeating the job on the plate. In this case, the stripper rules up the goldenrod in the regular manner.

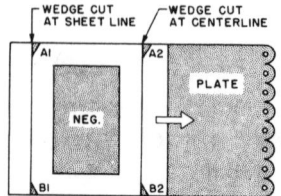

Figure E. One method of step and repeat.

It is not necessary to rule up the right side of the goldenrod because he cuts this side of the sheet off (slightly to the right of the centerline) before he burns the plate. If he did not do this, when working with large flats the goldenrod might project beyond the edge of the vacuum frame when moved for the second exposure on the plate. The uncovered portion of the plate is covered with a loose piece of goldenrod before exposure.

The stripper strips up the negatives in the regular manner on the left side of the flat. He then cuts in two sets of wedges — one set along the left edge of the press sheet outline and one along the vertical centerline, as shown in Figure E.

Before the first exposure, the platemaker takes a sharp pencil and traces the outline of the two centerline wedges on the plate. After the first exposure, he moves the flat to the right side of the plate and aligns the wedges cut along the outline of the press sheet with the pencil marks on the plate. This enables him to position the flat properly for the second exposure.

STRIPPING FOR COLOR

If you are stripping up a simple line color job where the colors do not overlap, you may use only one flat and have the platemaker mask out on the negatives those areas that are not to print as he makes the plates for each color. Flaps may even be cut in the goldenrod and folded back to expose the desired portion of the negative.

If the colors are to overlap, it will be necessary to make up a set of flats. In this case, you may use the flat for the main color as the master for the others. Line up the main (key) flat on the light table and then strip up the flats for the other colors by the same method that you use in stripping up flats for double burns. You should include reference marks (+) on all flats to be used as guides in registering the work on the press. You can cut these registration marks into the goldenrod stock or you can use register marks on tabs of film.

PROOFS

You can make proofs from your flats on blueprint or Vandyke (silverprint) paper. You can make these blueprint or silverprint proofs by exposing the paper through a negative layout in a vacuum frame for about 4 or 5 minutes — until the paper turns blue or brown as the case may be. These prints should be kept out of strong light unless they are fixed. Silverprints are fixed in hypo and blueprints are fixed in a solution of potassium ferricyanide.

The 3M Company produces thin, light-sensitive, color-coated acetate sheets which may be used in proofing color jobs. The colored coatings on these sheets match standard printers' inks. The sheets are exposed to light through the proper separation negatives and are then developed with a chemical which dissolves the unexposed areas of the coating, leaving a colored image on the acetate. Since the colors are transparent, when sheets with a magenta, cyan, yellow, and black image are registered one over another, a full-color proof results. These sheets may also be used for proofing individual black-and-white halftones.

CHAPTER 33

METAL PLATE MAKING

Quick printing was built with paper plates. The early paper plates, however, had serious shortcomings with colored inks — nor would they do a good job on fine lines or halftones. Metal plates had to be used on all but the simplest of jobs if quality printing was required.

Today's colored inks, developed especially for direct image work, run well with most paper plates. Paper plates such as the Itek Megalith do an excellent job on all but the finest of halftones. Metal plate usage, however, has increased in quick printing in spite of dramatic improvements in paper plate performance.

Quick printing skills and talents are developing beyond the scope of paper plates for a significant percentage of jobs. Double burns, screen tints, close register, difficult colors, long runs, etc. are presenting profitable challenges that can best be met with film negatives and metal plates.

TYPES OF METAL PLATES

The workhorse for quick printers is the short or medium run presensitized aluminum plate. Few, if any, quick printers coat their own metal plates. Presensitized plates have little or no grain. They are coated by the manufacturer and come ready for use. After the job is completed, they cannot be regrained and used again. However, they are often coated on both sides so that each side of the plate can be used for printing.

These plates are coated with a diazo compound which is an aromatic nitrogen by-product of coal tar that is sensitive to light. The plate is exposed and then developed with a solution which dissolves the coating in the nonprinting areas. After this, the image areas are covered with a special lacquer emulsion, and the plate is gummed.

PHOTOPOLYMER COATED PLATES

There is another type of presensitized plate that is sometimes used by quick printers when long runs are involved. Instead of the diazo coating, it utilizes a light-sensitive photopolymer coating made of plastics or lacquer. Plates made with this type of coating are good for 100,000 impressions or more. These plates use different chemistry and a different processing procedure than the diazo coated plates.

DEEP-ETCH PLATES

Deep-etch plates are more durable than surface plates, often producing sharp impressions up to 500,000 per run. Quick printing type presses are not cost efficient on such long runs, so deep-etch plates are rarely used.

Deep-etch plates are made of grained aluminum or stainless steel. The plate is coated with a solution of gum arabic and ammonium bichromate which must dry completely before the plate is exposed to light. The plates are exposed through a film positive. Because a positive is used instead of a negative, the light hardens the coating in the nonimage areas of the plate rather than the image areas. After exposure, the plate is developed with a chemical solution which removes the unhardened coating that leaves the plate bare in the image areas.

The plate is then etched with an acid solution that eats slightly below the surface of the metal in the image areas, but does not affect the metal areas hardened by the light during exposure. Next, a lacquer is rubbed into the etched out areas to form a base for the image. After the lacquer is applied, a special developer ink is spread on the plate to form the image. After this step, the entire plate is soaked in water to dissolve the coating in the nonimage areas. As soon as this coating is removed, the plate is etched and gummed to prevent oxidation.

Although the image of these plates is etched slightly below the surface of the metal, the etched area is so shallow that the plate carries ink above as well as below the plate surface. This enables deep-etch plates to produce a deeper, brighter image than conventional surface plates.

MULTIMETAL PLATES

Multimetal offset plates are only of academic interest to quick printers. They are good for as many as 5 million impressions. These plates consist of two or three layers of metal — generally copper for a top layer and aluminum or chromium for a second layer. If a third layer is used, it is simply a base for the other two metals and may be either chromium, zinc, aluminum, or steel.

The top layer is etched with a solution that eats away the thin copper top coating in the nonimage areas and leaves the second layer of metal exposed. The copper is friendly to ink, but not to water. The second layer is water receptive, but does not take ink.

PROCESSING PRESENSITIZED PLATES

Presensitized plates are coated by the manufacturer and come ready for use. In contrast to conventional zinc or aluminum plates, which range in thickness from 0.012 to 0.030 of an inch, depending on their size, these plates are relatively thin, ranging from 0.005 to 0.012 of an inch in thickness. For this reason, you must handle them carefully to prevent buckles. Also be careful of the edges. The edges are knife sharp and can inflict serious cuts.

Since the coating on these plates is also more sensitive to light than that used on conventional plates, you should keep them away from strong light. When possible, they should be handled under yellow light.

When you open a package of plates, be sure that they are carefully rewrapped to prevent accidental exposure on the shelf. Properly stored in a cool place, these plates will keep from 6 to 12 months. The expiration date is generally marked on the package and you should use the plates on a "first in, first out" basis so that the oldest plates will be used first.

BURNING THE PLATE

When you are ready to expose or burn the plate, you should place it face up in a vacuum frame of a metal plate maker. Position the goldenrod flat over it with the emulsion side of the negatives in direct contact with the coating on the plate. Locate the work on the plate by accurately aligning the gripper edge of the flat to the plate and by using other reference marks provided on the flat by the stripper for positioning purposes. If any areas of the plate are not covered by the goldenrod paper, cover them with strips of goldenrod.

In case of doubt, it is better to overexpose slightly than to underexpose the plate. If you do not give it enough exposure, no image will be formed or the image will be so weak that it will not stand up on the press. If you give it too much exposure, fine lines or halftone areas may fill in.

USING A GREY SCALE

In some shops, a grey scale, like that shown in Figure A is stripped into the flat along the gripper edge so that it will print on the plate but will not print on the paper when the job is run.

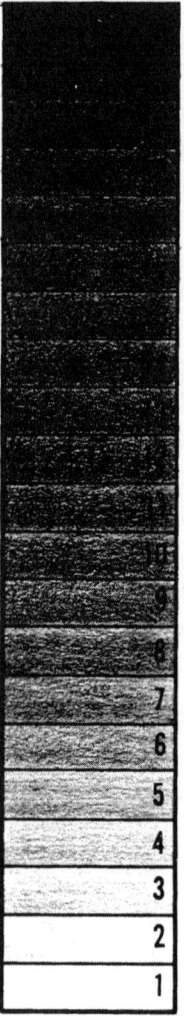

Figure A. An artist's conception of a 21 step sensitivity guide used to determine correct plate exposure. Variations of platemaking sensitivity guides are available from manufacturers of plates and platemaking supplies.

The grey scale is a strip of continuous tone film with 21 graduations or density steps. These steps are numbered, and each step is slightly more dense than the step before it. When the plate is exposed, the coating will be underexposed at one end of the scale and overexposed at the other. When developing the plate, you will generally find that the first four to six steps will be solid. The next three or four steps will show as grey areas and the remainder of the steps will wash off completely.

If step 4 is the highest completely solid step, the plate is just slightly underexposed. If step 5 is the highest step, the exposure is just about right. If more than 7 steps go solid, the chances are that the plate is overexposed.

If the press run is short, or if you are working with halftones, you may find it better to expose for a solid four, but for other kinds of work, you should expose for steps five or six. In extreme cases, you may expose for a solid seven when the image consists of line work and a long press run is required.

If the plate is underexposed, you can increase your grey scale reading by one step by increasing the exposure 50 percent; you can increase it two steps by doubling the exposure; and you can increase it three steps by tripling the original exposure. Conversely, if the plate is overexposed, you can reduce your grey scale reading by three steps by dividing your original exposure time by 3; you can reduce the reading 2 steps by dividing the exposure by 2; and you can reduce it one step by dividing the exposure by 1½.

DEVELOPING

Processing will vary from one type of plate to another. You will generally find a set of processing directions in each package of plates.

After the exposure is completed, remove the plate from the vacuum frame and place it on a table. Then go over it with the proper chemicals, following the instructions furnished by the manufacturer.

If the plate is coated on both sides, always place a piece of paper under it before you begin developing it, and change the paper before you start processing another plate. This will protect the second side from chemicals that might seep under it during processing. If you have trouble with chemicals seeping under the plate during this operation, you may find it necessary to print both sides of the plate before you process it. You can then develop one side of the plate and turn it over and develop the other in one continuous operation.

In most cases, the exposed plate is first treated (developed) with a solution that dissolves the unexposed coating and makes it water receptive. Process gum is the most commonly used developer.

Once this solution has been applied, you can put the plate on the press and run it just as it is. However, if the plate is to be held for some time, or if it is to be used for a reasonably long run, it is best to cover the image with a thin coating of lacquer. The lacquer supplies color to the image so that you can check it for defects, and it also lengthens the life of the plate by forming a tough, protective coating over the image areas. Do not use too much lacquer. A thin coating will outlast a thicker one when the plate is run on the press.

In addition to applying the lacquer, most operators also gum the plate with a solution of gum arabic to protect it from fingerprints and scratches during makeready operations.

SUBTRACTIVE PLATES

The 3M Company has developed a line of presensitized, prelacquered plates which are known as subtractive plates. The lacquer is applied over the entire face of the plate by the manufacturer. During development, the lacquer is removed (subtracted) from the nonprinting areas instead of being added to the image.

A single processing solution is used and the same solution can be used for both the long run "S" and the medium run "K"plates put out by the 3M Company. After processing, the plate is washed in plain water to remove the chemical and is then ready for gumming or for putting on the press.

STORING METAL PLATES

Before any prolonged storage, metal plates must be coated with gum arabic or asphaltum to prevent oxidation of the metal. If the coating of gum is too thick, it may crack and allow the plate to oxidize.

Once the gum is dry, the plate may be stored by hanging it or stacking it flat with paper slipsheets.

CHAPTER 34

PRESSROOM

PROBLEMS

Ink, paper, photographic, and other problems are covered in chapters dealing with special subjects. This chapter is sort of a "catch-all," covering problems not mentioned elsewhere.

A small press, like a small airplane, requires a lot of "feel" based on experience — seat of the pants flying! Airline pilots and big press operators know a lot about gauges, but put them on a small plane or press and they crash.

Advertisers trying to sell small presses to private offices portray an image of a process so simple that it can be operated by the beautiful, manicured girl shown leaning on their sparkling equipment. Press salesmen wear permanently spotted business suits — marks of their efforts to convey an impression that ink and oil never soil the person operating their "turnkey" equipment. Some of these manufacturers should leave the "n" out of turnkey to properly describe their presses.

The fact is that turning out commercially acceptable work on a small press requires years of experience and a lot of ingenuity in solving a great quantity of problems — few of which are covered in operating manuals.

COMMERCIAL VERSUS INPLANT QUALITY

Inplant operators of small presses face many of the same problems as quick printers — with one big difference. They have fewer rejections over very minor defects. Every quick printer has experienced a customer attempting to reject a job over a simple flaw — until the customer discovers the flaw is a result of his own error. Then the job is "usable."

PHOTO-DIRECT PLATE PROBLEMS

Any kind of paper or plastic plate presents more problems than a metal plate. In spite of the added difficulty, quick printers consistently turn out "metal plate quality" on paper plates. This ability has resulted in the phenomenal growth of quick printing. There is, of course, a substantial low-cost market for "quick and dirty" work. But many quick printing buyers will not return to a shop producing shoddy printing — regardless of the price!

There can be many problems affecting the performance of photo-direct plates. Here are a number of them:

pH FACTOR

Too much acid in the fountain solution is a major problem with paper plates. The pH values are measured from 0 to 14. A value of 7 is neutral. Paper plates run best with a pH from 4.5 to 5.5. If the pH reads 3.5 or lower, many problems can occur. A pH test kit is available from most printers supply dealers.

The solutions: (a) Wash plates with water after processing. Processing chemicals left on the surface of photo-direct plates carry a lot of acid to the fountain solution. (b) Use the proper type and mixture of fountain solution. This can be critical. The type and mixture depends on the type of plates and inks you are using. It pays to experiment with different solutions. (c) Use distilled water if necessary. Chemicals in some water complicate pH control. (d) Drain and replace water if pH is too low. (e) Select ink that will work with a low pH. (f) Select paper with low acid content. Some rag stocks will lower the pH from 5.5 to 3.5 in 1000 sheets. (g) Some pressmen even use Maalox (a stomach antacid) in the fountain in emergencies.

FORM ROLLER ADJUSTMENT

Plates come in a wide thickness range. Form rollers should be set for the caliper of your principal plate. Form roller pressure is especially important with an integrated ink system. Too much pressure will squeegee the water away from the ink; too little pressure will result in mottled ink. Pressure requirements differ with each type of plate. A 3/16" stripe is a good starting point for ink rollers. Watch for "180 degree off" problems. Some presses use a cam-like adjustment. If your operating manual indicates that a clockwise turn will increase pressure and you are getting a decrease, you are 180 degrees off. Make a one-half turn and start over.

PLATE TO BLANKET PRESSURE
If plate to blanket pressure is too great, plate life will be shortened. If pressure is too light, ink will pile on the plate and print quality will be off. If your cylinder is adjusted for a thick plate, you can use a paper underliner when running thinner plates.

PRESS NOT LEVEL
This is an often found problem. If a press is not exactly level, water will be unevenly spread across the plate. If one side of your plate tones more than the other, check your press level.

HAND OIL ON CAMERA GLASS
Natural oil from hands on the camera glass will diffuse the light and cause an uneven exposure of the plate. Clean both sides of glass with glass cleaner. While you're at it, use a razor blade to remove hard hickies. Be careful not to scratch glass.

FOAM PAD UNDER CAMERA BOARD SMASHED
Some camera/platemakers have foam padding under the copyboard. The foam can become compressed. You can get by for a while by padding with paper under the copy area.

DEVELOPER TEMPERATURE OFF
Photo-direct platemakers have heating elements in the developer tanks. Some plates, such as the Itek Megalith, should be developed at 81 degrees. Others require 91 degrees. Adjustment of the thermostat is simple. Use an immersible thermostat to check.

INCIDENTAL LIGHT ON COPYBOARD
Nearby strong overhead lights or even sunlight

reflected through windows can cause uneven exposure of the plate. One solution is to place an overhanging piece of plywood on top of the camera/platemaker. You can then hang red Rubylith or black cloth to block out the offending light.

CAMERA LIGHTS UNEVEN
Most camera/platemaker lights, in time, are knocked out of proper alignment. To check alignment, hold a piece of paper beyond the edge of the copyboard. Turn on the camera lights and check the edge of the shadow area for all lights. If shadow length is not the same for all lights, adjust or bend the offender back in line.

REPLENISHMENT BOTTLES EMPTY
Most camera/platemakers have replenishment bottles of chemicals that keep the processing solutions at the proper level. This level is critical to proper plate emersion timing.

WORN OUT CHEMICALS
Camera/platemaker chemicals are worn out by a combination of time and usage. With infrequent usage, they may last five or six weeks. Heavy usage can deplete them in a day. A record of time and plate usage since last change is helpful in determining if worn out chemicals is your problem when toning occurs.

COPY NOT ALIGNED ON PLATE
Misaligned copy causes much lost presstime and remakes of plates. A sheet of white paper, waxed or rubber cemented in place on the copyboard, helps

align originals. It's easier to see than yellow lines. If plate is twisting on the vacuum plate holder, you might try taping over some of the unused holes to produce a stronger vacuum under the plate. Plate twisting is not a big problem with photo-direct, but a major problem with electrostatic. (See "electrostatic" section of this chapter for solutions.)

DIRTY LENS OR MIRROR
Clean regularly. Use only lens tissue and lens cleaner. Never a rag! A scratch can be expensive. A static free lens brush may also be used.

SCRATCHES ON GLASS
Glass copyboard scratches can produce black lines on the plate. Your local glass dealer can cut a glass to size for a fraction of the camera manufacturer's replacement price.

LIGHT LEAKS
Light leaks can be hard to find. If the same portion of the plate is consistently overexposed, first check glass for hand oil, then light angles, then look for holes in bellows or perhaps a loose plug or bolt somewhere in the film exposure or storage area of the camera.

HUMIDITY
Low humidity (below 45 percent) makes plate dampening difficult to control. An inexpensive humidifier will solve this problem. Sears sells one for a little over a hundred dollars that will humidify your entire shop.

High humidity (above 55 percent) also causes problems and is more difficult to control. At times we've even alternated heat and air-conditioning to dry the shop out. Of course, if you are fortunate to be in a humidity controlled building, you have no problem.

EDGES OF PLATE TONES

This is a major problem with 11" wide paper plates on an 11" press. The problem is usually a combination of problems — ink and water balance, form roller pressures, fountain solution type and mix, type of ink, swelling of edges of blanket, etc. If all else fails, you can get by with dampened cotton pads, held in place by clothes pins, rubbing against the outer edges of the plate.

SHORT PLATE FLOPS

Some photo-direct plates are so stiff that the end of short plates cannot be held down by dampening the backside with fountain solution. We use a spray adhesive (the art department kind) to hold down stiff plates.

SPOTS ON PLATE

Spots on heavy plates such as the Itek Megalith can be removed with a soft rubber eraser. An eraser trimmed to a point or knife edge helps get in small places. Glass wax works well on some plates. There are several types of image eradicators sold by Printers Shopper and others that will remove spots.

Some other problems can be defective chemicals or plate material, improper ink, excessive heat, offset powder mixing with ink, nicks in platemaker causing scratches, improper exposure, lights not adjusted properly for reductions or enlargements, etc.

ELECTROSTATIC PLATE PROBLEMS

Many electrostatic plate problems are the same as photo-direct plate problems. Following are some problems peculiar to electrostatic:

VERTICAL LINES ON PLATE

Unwanted vertical lines are a major problem with electrostatic plates. A little detective work can usually trace the line through the processing units and find the problem.

First plates out in the morning are usually streaked by dried toner. You can save several plates by cleaning the worst areas with a rag dampened with dispersant.

Rollers coated with toner will cause streaking.

Nicks or protruding screws in the processing unit can scratch the surface of plate.

Corona guide strings can come out of grooves or break and scratch plate. Most guide strings can be replaced with 24 lb. monofilament fishing line. **(Always pull power plug before working with corona unit.)**

Corona wires get dirty. They can be *gently* cleaned with a Q-tip dampened with alcohol.

OLD TONER

Many quick printers stretch toner life too long. Keep a record of plates processed as guide.

CONVERSION SOLUTION

Conversion solution will crystallize and deteriorate if left in processor overnight. It should be emptied out of the processor into a sealed container at night.

THINNESS OF PLATE

Electrostatic plates are much thinner than photo-direct plates. This thinness increases the risk of wrinkling. Plates should be placed on the plate cylinder exactly straight. The wrinkling problem is minimized by pulling down on the tail end of the plate after each repositioning.

Form roller adjustment should be set for the caliper of your principal plate. It is not practical to alternate electrostatic and photo-direct plates on the same press because of different plate thickness and different fountain solutions.

SPOTS ON PLATE

Unless spots are detected on electrostatic plates before the conversion solution is applied, the spots are difficult, if not impossible, to remove. Before conversion, spots can be *carefully* removed with a soft rubber eraser.

CROOKED IMAGE ON PLATE

This problem is more serious with electrostatic because processors cut the plate material before the end of the plate passes through the corona unit. This leaves the plate free to twist before exposure. Taping off some of the unused vacuum holes may solve the problem.

Some quick printers use a hand trimmer with a clear plastic grid taped in alignment with the cutting edge. By lining up the copy with the grid, the top edge of the plate can be cut square with the copy.

FINE LINES AND HALFTONES

Electrostatic is not as exact as photo-direct. It is also

not as consistent. One plate may print a perfect fine line that will be broken on the next plate. You need to be backed up with either photo-direct or negatives and metal plates.

BLANKET PROBLEMS

The quality of a job is greatly affected by blanket condition. This is an area of quality control often overlooked by quick printers.

LOW SPOTS

Quick printers run a great variety of paper sizes and calibers on a single press — perhaps in one day ranging from 3" x 5" card to 11" x 17" carbonless. This variety of paper sizes and thicknesses can result in an uneven blanket surface. A low spot in a blanket will transfer a weak image to the paper. In severe cases, it will transfer no image at all. Low spots can be temporarily repaired with "blanket fix," a solution that swells the rubber surface of the blanket. Some prevention measures and cures are:

RESET PRESSURES between blanket and impression cylinders to accommodate thicker papers. A few small cards or envelopes can smash a blanket if pressures are too tight.

ALTERNATE BLANKETS. Reserve one blanket for 11 x 17 work, one for 8½" papers, one for small card or envelope jobs, and perhaps one for halftones. You can buy special halftone blankets that are softer than regular blankets — they also smash easier.

REST YOUR BLANKETS. Blankets need time to swell back up. It's usually the cloth fiber that is smashed rather than the rubber. Soaking in water can help, but prolonged soaking can shrink some blankets so much that they no longer will fit the cylinder. You can store blankets face down and wet the fiber side. This helps swell the fibers back to normal.

BROKEN FIBERS can result from excessive tightening of a new blanket. A new blanket should be mounted fairly loose and retightened after four or five hundred impressions. Broken fibers will cause low spots that cannot be repaired.

USE SMALL PATCH BLANKETS. When running small cards or envelopes, you can use pieces cut from an old blanket — just large enough to cover the image area. Remove your regular blanket. Spray a coating of adhesive on the cylinder where the patch blanket will be used. Also spray the back of the patch. Use the kind of spray adhesive used by art departments. Patch blankets can also solve wrinkling problems caused by air traps in poorly made envelopes. Patches will also allow you to run catalog envelopes with metal clasps. (Cylinders should be protected from damage from metal clasps by placing masking tape where clasps hit.)

BLANKET CARE

It is common practice to use nothing on blankets but the blanket wash used to clean the ink off between jobs. That isn't good enough. Regular blanket wash is usually formularized to remove the surface ink and to dry fast. It does a poor job of cleaning the pores of a blanket.

BLANKET PORES. When blanket pores are clogged with ink and paper sizing, job quality suffers. A

periodic cleaning with a strong blanket cleaner is needed to clean out pores. Never use turpentine or kerosene on the blanket as they will damage it.
BLANKET POWDER. Blanket powder can be applied between runs if paper is sticking to the blanket. When storing the blanket, or at night, a coating of blanket powder reduces excessive tackiness and absorbs ink from blanket pores. Blankets should be hung or stored on a flat surface away from bright light.

STATIC ELECTRICITY
Static electricity will cause sheets of paper to stick to the blanket. You can relieve static temporarily by washing the blanket with water.

SWOLLEN BLANKETS
Swollen blankets can increase the blanket to plate pressure, squeegee water off of the plate, and cause it to run dry. Sometimes water seeps under the edge of the blanket and swells the underpacking or fibers enough to cause toning or scum along the edges of a job. Swelling is often caused by slow drying or greasy blanket wash. A loose blanket may allow water to seep under it, causing swelling.

FOUNTAIN SOLUTIONS
In some instances, you can get by with tap water in the fountain. Some tap water, however, contains chemicals that cause problems. Most quick printers who run with plain water use distilled water. One problem with running plain water without any fountain solution added is rapid acid buildup. If excess acid is introduced to the fountain from plate

or paper coatings, plain water will not counteract it. Controlling pH is one of the principal functions of fountain solutions.

The *best* fountain solution can only be determined by experimentation. The effectiveness of a mixture depends on a combination of factors such as the type of ink you are using, type of plate, paper, etc. It is usually best to start with the plate manufacturer's recommendation. Generally, photo-direct plates require the strongest mixture, electrostatic plates next, and metal plates the weakest mixture.

INK COVERAGE

See "Ink" and "Running Color" chapters for the many problems associated with inks. One problem that bears rehashing is the often found practice of running too much ink. Proper ink control requires close observation and frequent adjustments, at least for the first several thousand copies. Too thin ink coverage is more obvious than too thick coverage. For this reason, pressmen lean toward heavy coverage — sometimes using powder to prevent the excess ink from offsetting onto the backs of other sheets.

USE YOUR THUMB TO CHECK

If a light brush with your thumb will smear a fresh image on the paper, it is generally too heavy. If a heavy brush with your thumb will not smear a fresh image, it is generally too light.

BACK CYLINDER DIRTY

The blanket is not supposed to contact the back cylinder unless a sheet of paper is passing through the press and is positioned on the back cylinder. Malfunctions often occur, causing the blanket to print an image directly on the chrome surface of the cylinder. Usually enough ink is deposited on the cylinder surface to print the backs of the next ten to twenty sheets.

Malfunctions are often caused by improper jogging or fanning of paper before placing it on the feed table. A protruding or crooked sheet will often jam after feeding far enough into the system to trip the blanket-to-cylinder release on some presses. The offending sheet of paper will usually be nicked or marked at the hangup point, providing a clue to the problem.

Some presses have easy access to the back cylinder. The A. B. Dick back cylinder is difficult to reach. See "Equipment Recommendations"chapter for a special A. B. Dick cleaning tool.

If back cylinders are regularly cleaned with chrome cleaner, less ink will stick, making them easier to clean. If ink and dirty blanket wash are allowed to dry and accumulate on the back cylinder, the blanket can become embossed. In severe cases, paper can even stick to the cylinder and pull out of the grippers.

ROLLERS

If the rollers are not cleaned thoroughly during washup operations, the ink and other solutions will fill their pores, and the rollers will become glazed. Glazed rollers have a hard shiny appearance. Glaze is less likely to develop when the rollers are washed by hand.

The ends of rollers are often neglected during cleaning. Ink buildup on the ends of a roller will cause minute cracks in the roller surface. The roller will swell at the ends. Also, dried ink flakes off the ends of the rollers during a run and produces dirty or mottled impressions.

Burnishine Putz Pomade will remove most glaze from rollers. This compound may be added to the ink before washup, allowing the rollers to slowly idle for five to fifteen minutes, depending on severity of glaze condition. You may also use it on clean rollers, or it may be used for hand cleaning. Directions come with cans or tubes.

There are many other problems involved with operating a pressroom. Most are peculiar to the specific equipment being operated. Quick printers, however, seem to develop into "jury rigging" fixers and somehow keep the equipment turning out quality work.

GLOSSARY OF TERMS

Activator: *Name given to various developers.*
Agate line: *A measurement for depth of columns of advertising space. Fourteen agate lines make one column inch.*
Airbrush: *A small pressure gun shaped like a pencil that sprays watercolors by means of compressed air.*
Aniline printing: *Printing done with rubber plates and aniline dyes — also called "flexography."*
Antique finish paper: *Natural, rough surface on book and cover papers; may be wove (simulating cloth) or laid (ladder-like) in appearance.*
Aperture: *Opening through which light enters the camera.*
Artwork: *A catch-all phrase — it can mean a pasteup, mechanical, illustration, design, form, etc.*
Autoscreen: *Trade name for an orthochromatic film which is designed to produce a screened image from continuous-tone copy without the use of a halftone screen.*
Back cylinder: *Impression cylinder.*
Back gauge: *On paper cutters, a fingered metal bar against which the paper is squared.*
Back light: *In process camera work, to illuminate the copy from behind.*
Back up: *To print the reverse side of a sheet having printing on the front.*
Backbone: *Bound edge of a book, also called the spine.*
Basis weight: *The weight of a ream (500 sheets) of paper cut to a given standard size for that grade: 25 x 38 for book papers, 20 x 26 for cover papers, 22½ x 28½ or 22½ x 35 for bristols, 25½ x 30½ for index.*
Bastard size: *Not of standard dimensions.*
Benday: *Term applied to tint effects, such as lines, dots, or patterns applied to art, negatives, or plates.*
Bimetal plate: *Offset press plate consisting of two layers of metal. During processing, the top layer is etched away in the image areas to expose the bottom layer which is especially sensitive to grease.*

Bulk (of paper): *Expression indicating the number of paper sheets per inch of a given paper weight.*
Bullets: *Dots used as ornaments in composition.*
Blanket (offset): *Sheet of vulcanized rubber on a fabric base, treated to prevent stretch when wrapped around the press cylinder.*
Blanket dust: *Mixture of French chalk and powdered sulfur used to relieve tackiness in the blanket.*
Bleed: *Printing to the very edge of the paper. Actually, this is achieved by printing close to the edge and trimming away the unprinted part.*
Blinding: *Image areas on an offset plate that will not accept ink.*
Blueline or Blueprint proofing: *A method of proofing film negative flats by exposing them on a contact printer to blueprint paper.*
Body copy: *Text copy — does not include headlines, illustrations, etc.*
Bond paper: *A grade of writing or printing paper for letterheads, business forms, etc.*
Book paper: *Paper suitable for printing books, catalogs, magazines, etc; may be coated or uncoated, in a variety of finishes, and may or may not be sized for offset printing.*
Boxed: *Drawing a line around a certain paragraph for emphasis.*
Bristols: *Lightweight cardboards, as index bristols, mill bristols, and wedding bristols.*
Broadside: *Large advertising circular.*
Brochure: *Pamphlet or booklet.*
Brownprint: *A photographic print or silverprint which produces a brown image; not to include a sepia print or a contact print that has been toned.*
Burn: *Common term used for plate exposure.*
Burn out: *To overexpose a film or plate to eliminate unwanted dirty areas or to "thin out" thick lines.*
Business papers: *Papers used for administrative uses, such as bonds, punch cards, safety papers, and mimeograph, and duplicator papers.*
Caliper (of paper): *Term denoting the thickness of paper, expressed in thousandths of an inch. Each thousandth is called a point or, less commonly though preferably, a mil.*

Calligraphy: *A form of hand lettering frequently used on book jackets, title pages, cards, and letterheads. The calligraphic letter is based on the handwritten cursive alphabets of the 16th century.*

Camera-processor: *Automated process camera and platemaker combined into one machine.*

Camera-ready: *Copy that is complete and ready to be photographed.*

Candle power: *Unit of measure of a light source.*

Caps: *Capital letters or upper case (u.c.).*

Caption: *Identification of an illustration.*

Carbon ribbon: *A typewriter ribbon made of thin carbon paper or thin plastic — used one time only.*

Cat's whiskers: *Short pieces of wire or thin strips of metal used on feeders of some presses as separator fingers.*

Chalking: *A term which refers to improper drying of ink. Pigment dusts off because the vehicle has been absorbed too rapidly into the paper.*

Chipboard: *Rough surfaced cardboard used as backing for pads and tablets.*

Circular: *Same as flyer.*

Coated paper: *Any paper to which surface coating has been applied.*

Cobalt drier: *Liquid drier resembling dark varnish — primarily a surface-type drier for use with dark offset inks.*

Cold type: *Includes phototype, rub-on, strike-on, etc. Does not include the use of molten lead or "hot metal."*

Collating: *Gathering single sheets or leaves in sequence.*

Color key (3M): *Thin, light-sensitive color-coated acetate sheets for use in proofing multicolor jobs; colored coatings on these sheets match standard process colors. The sheets are exposed through separation negatives and developed with a chemical which dissolves the unexposed coating, leaving a colored image.*

Color separation: *The process of photographing each primary color of a full-color original on a separate sheet of film. Also the preparation of artwork for a multicolor job whereby an overlay is made for each color.*

Combination art: *Artwork containing both line and tone work.*

Combination plate: *An offset plate imaged with both halftone and line work. Also a plate on which there are two or more unrelated forms for simultaneous printing.*

Complementary colors: *Red and green, blue and orange, yellow and purple. When any two of the 3 primary pigment colors are mixed to form a secondary color, the remaining primary is complementary to the mixture. Any 2 colors of light that produce a neutral gray or white when combined are said to be complementary.*
Comprehensive: *A detailed layout with illustrations carefully drawn and type positioned. Often called a "comp."*
Contact negative: *Same-size duplicate made by exposing a sheet of film to a film positive.*
Contact positive: *Same-size duplicate made by exposing a sheet of film to a film negative.*
Contact screen: *Halftone screen made on safety base film — used in absolute contact with the film emulsion.*
Continuous tone: *Image consisting of blacks and intermediate shades of gray — not produced by a pattern of varying-size dots.*
Contrast: *Tonal range of photographs, negatives, artwork, etc. The degree of difference between the darkest shadows and the brightest highlights.*
Copy: *Can mean pasteup, entire original, typesetting, etc.*
Copy fitting: *Calculating the proper type size and line width to accommodate copy within a given space.*
Cover papers: *Paper which serves for covering printed material, made in a wide variety to provide a desirable choice.*
Creep: *Stretch, slippage, or any movement of the blanket that causes misregister during press operation.*
Crop marks: *Marks on an illustration to show which portion is to be reproduced.*
Cut: *An engraving used in letterpress printing. Also commonly used to refer to small illustrations used in offset printing.*
Cylinder gap: *The gap or space in the cylinders of a press where the mechanism for plate (or blanket), clamps, and grippers is housed.*
Deckle edge: *The untrimmed feathery edges of paper formed where the pulp flows against the deckle.*
Deep-etch plate: *A metal offset plate used for long runs where the inked areas are slightly recessed below the surface.*
Densitometer: *A sensitive photoelectric instrument which measures the density of photographic images. Use as a guide in timing halftone exposures.*

490

Descender: *That part of a letter which extends below the line.*
Developer: *The chemical used to render photographic images visible after exposure to light.*
Diffusion transfer: *A system consisting of a photographic emulsion on which a negative is produced, and a receiver sheet on which a positive of the image is transferred during processing. It is the principle of Polaroid film.*
Dingbats: *Stars or ornaments used in type composition.*
Direct-image plates: *Plates which are imaged by typing, drawing, lettering, or imprinting directly on the plate.*
Display type: *Type larger than body type used to draw attention.*
Distributor rollers: *Inking rollers which break down the ink by sidewise as well as rotary movement.*
Dot etching: *Reducing the size of halftone dots by etching with silver solvents.*
Dowel: *A short register pin of plastic or metal attached to a film support or plate. Used to position a film or flat for double printing or for step-and-repeat exposure.*
Driography: *Plates which print without water on the press. They consist of ink on metal for the image areas and silicone rubber for the nonimage areas.*
Dry offset: *Offset process using relief plate and no water.*
Ductor: *Roller in the inking or dampening system which alternately contacts the fountain and distributor rollers.*
Dummy: *A rough layout of a print job — also blank pages folded and marked to guide layup of a booklet.*
Duotone: *A halftone that has its shadow detail printed in a dark color and its highlight detail in a lighter color.*
Duplex paper: *Paper with a different color or finish on each side.*
Electrophotography: *Image transfer systems used in copiers and platemakers to produce images using electrostatic forces. Some use a zinc oxide coating; Xerography a selenium surface.*
Electrostatic plate: *A type of offset plate made by a process similar to the xerox or photocopy process.*
Elliptical dot halftone screen: *Contact screen which produces an elliptical dot instead of the conventional square dot.*
Em: *A printer's measure, the square of the body of the type; e.g. 8 points by 8 points.*
Embossed finish: *Paper with a raised or depressed surface.*

Emulsification: *Mixing of water in inking system or ink in dampening system; may cause gray image (water in ink) or plate scum (ink in water).*

Emulsion side: *The side of the film coated with the silver halide emulsion which should face the lens during exposure.*

En: *Half the width of an em, also called "nut." Properly called a space as it is smaller than an em.*

Enamel stock: *Paper to which has been applied a smoothed coating. May be dull finished or high gloss.*

English finish: *Uncoated book stock with relatively high bulk and smooth surface.*

Engraving: *A metal engraved plate. Not used in offset printing.*

Etch: *Chemical treatment of plate to make nonworking areas grease resistant. Also the solutions used to accomplish this.*

F-numbers: *Fixed values at which the aperture of the lens can be set. The values are determined by the ratio of the aperture to the focal length of the lens.*

Facsimile transmission: *Process of scanning graphic images to convert them into electric signals which are transmitted to produce a recorded likeness of the original. Also called "fax."*

Far side: *Nonoperating side of press.*

Feed rolls: *Forwarding device on small presses used to move stock from front guides into impression cylinder grippers.*

Felt side (of paper): *Smooth or top side — preferred side for printing.*

Filling in (or filling up): *Filling of areas between halftone dots or small letters caused by excessive ink or thin ink.*

Film processor: *Machine which automatically develops, washes, and fixes film in one continuous operation.*

Film speed: *Relative sensitivity to light.*

Filter: *Piece of colored glass, film, or gelatin used to separate colors, reduce glare or vary contrast.*

Filter factor: *The number of times an exposure must be increased when using a filter.*

Fixer: *Photographic solution which stops the action of the developer, dissolves unexposed silver salts in the emulsion, and hardens the colloids. Commonly called hypo or stop bath.*

Flash: *A supplementary halftone exposure of short duration made to introduce a fine, pin-point dot into the shadow areas.*

Flat: *Sheet of acetate or paper on which negatives or positives have been mounted in proper position for printing.*

Flat negative: *Negative with little contrast.*
Flush: *Even with the margin or even with the widest line in the column or page.*
Flyer: *Same as circular.*
Folio: *Page number.*
Font: *Complete assortment of type of one size and style.*
Form rollers: *Ink and dampener rollers which contact the plate.*
Forwarding rollers: *Rollers which receive the sheet from sucker feet.*
Fountain: *Reservoir for water or ink.*
Fountain roller: *Roller which revolves in ink or water fountain.*
Fountain solution: *Chemical solution in water fountain of the offset press. Commonly called the "water."*
Friction feeder: *A type of feeder which uses a revolving friction wheel to forward sheets into the machine.*
Front matter: *In publications work, that matter which precedes the actual text, such as the title page, preface, foreword, and table of contents.*
Ganging: *Combination of unrelated jobs on a single press plate to save press time.*
Gather: *Assemble printed sheets in proper order.*
Gear streaks: *Parallel streaks appearing across the printed sheet at same interval as gear teeth on the cylinder.*
Ghost: *Reappearance on the same sheet of an image laid down near the gripper edge and repeated due to improper ink or dampener roller settings.*
Glaze: *On ink rollers, hard shiny appearance caused by improper cleaning.*
Glossy: *Glossy photograph which must be halftoned in order to print.*
Goldenrod: *Paper or plastic support for negatives used by the stripper in making flats.*
Gothic: *Class of type, usually a business-like letter without serifs.*
Grain: *The direction in which most fibers lie which corresponds with the direction the paper is made on paper machine.*
Gravure: *Process for producing an intaglio printing plate.*
Gray contact screen: *Halftone screen used for both black-and-white and color-separation work.*
Gray scale: *A strip of paper containing tones ranging from pure white to black with intermediate shades of gray. Used as a tool in contrast control.*

Gripper margin: *The margin that is needed to grip and pull a sheet of paper through the press — usually about ¼ inch.*

Grippers: *Metal fingers that clamp on paper and control its flow through the press.*

Gum arabic: *Dried sap from acacia trees. Soluble in water. Used to form a protective coating over the plate.*

Gutter: *The blank space or inner margin, from printing area to binding.*

Halftone: *A photograph that has been rephotographed through a dotted screen. This process produces a combination of small and large dots that are seen by the eye as varying shades.*

Headline type: *Large type for heads or emphasis — usually refers to type larger than 14 point.*

Hickey: *Any imperfection on the press sheet caused by dirt on the press; dried ink on the plate or blanket; picking; paper dust, etc.*

Highlight: *Lightest areas on the copy; darkest on the negative.*

Highlight exposure: *One of the multiple halftone exposures made when copy has considerable tonal range.*

Hot type: *Typesetting made from hot metal cast in relief. Used mostly in letterpress printing. May also be used to make black-and-white "proofs" which are pasted up for offset.*

Hypo: *An abbreviation for sodium thiosulfate, or sodium hyposulfite, a chemical used to fix the image on a photographic film after it has been developed. Commonly called stop bath or fixer.*

Image: *All areas of a printing job that are transferred by ink to the paper.*

Imposition: *A plan for placing of type forms or negatives in proper order so that pages will be in desired sequence after printing and folding.*

Imposition chart: *A piece of blank paper the size of the sheet to be printed, numbered and folded as it will be in the bindery after printing. Used in makeup to show where each page should go in relation to the other pages.*

Impression: *Inked image printed on paper as it runs through the press. Also the squeeze between the impression cylinder and the blanket.*

Impression cylinder: *Cylinder against which the paper picks up the impression from the inked blanket in offset printing.*

India ink: *Black ink preferred for drawings used for offset reproduction.*

Intaglio printing: *Type of printing done from plates which have the image etched below the printing surface as in engraving and gravure.*

Italics: *Type with a right-hand slant.*

Joggers: *Metal plates that move back and forth on the delivery table of the press to keep the stack of printed sheets even.*

Jogging: *Jarring paper to align and stack sheets in an even pile.*

Justify: *To adjust the space between words (or letters) to make all lines come out to the same length.*

Kerning: *Adjusting the spacing between two letters so that part of their letter shapes overhang.*

Keyline: *Same as pasteup, original, mechanical, or camera-ready art.*

Knife folder: *Folding machine which employs a knife-like bar to start the crease in the sheets.*

Lacquer: *A clear coating applied to a printed sheet for protection or appearance.*

Laid paper: *Paper with a pattern of parallel lines at equal distances, giving a ribbed effect.*

Lamination: *A plastic film bonded by heat and pressure to a printed sheet for protection or appearance.*

Laser: *The laser is an intense light beam with very narrow band width that can produce images by electronic impulses.*

Layout: *A sketch or outline of a proposed printing job.*

Lead (pronounced led): *A thin (2-point) strip of metal used for spacing between lines of type. Leads are available in 1, 3, and 4-point thicknesses also.*

Leader: *A row of dots or dashes(........).*

Leading: *Amount of space between lines. Originated from hand-set letterpress where thin strips of lead were used to increase space between lines of type.*

Ledger: *Smooth, strong paper which readily accepts printing and writing inks. Used for bookkeeping records requiring permanence and frequent use.*

Letterpress: *A printing process where ink is placed on hard type faces and the type faces are pressed against the paper to be printed.*

Letterset (dry offset): *The printing process which uses a blanket (like conventional offset) for transferring the image from plate to paper. Unlike lithography, it uses a relief plate and requires no dampening system.*

Lift: *Refers to the number of sheets or the height of a stack of paper.*
Line copy: *Printing that does not include halftones.*
Linen tester: *A fixed-focus magnifier.*
Lithography: *Same as offset. Based on the separation of water and ink on a flat, chemically treated plate which is imaged photographically. To prevent the roughness in paper from destroying the plate surface, the inked image is transferred (offset) from the plate to a smooth blanket and from the blanket to paper, hence the nickname "offset printing."*
Lower case: *Small letters as distinguished from the capitals or upper case.*
M: *Designation for 1,000 sheets or impressions.*
Magenta contact screen: *A magenta colored contact screen used for making halftone negatives.*
Magnetic ink: *Ink having a metallic base which allows for electronic sorting in data processing work. Used on bank checks.*
Makeready: *Preparation of the press to obtain proper printing impression.*
Mark up: *To write up instructions, as on a dummy.*
Mask: *Opaque material used to protect selected areas of a printing plate during exposure.*
Masking: *Protecting or blocking out parts of the copy or negative.*
Master: *A plate for a duplicating machine.*
Matte finish: *Dull paper finish without gloss or luster.*
Mechanical: *Same as pasteup, keyline, original, or camera-ready art.*
Mercury vapor lamp: *An enclosed light source containing mercury, sometimes used to expose plates or as an illuminant for cameras.*
Middletone: *Any of the various tones in photographic copy ranging between black and white. Also a halftone exposure.*
Mimeograph paper: *A paper with the toothy, absorbent surface required for mimeographing.*
Moire: *A disturbing dot formation caused by rescreening a printed halftone.*
Molleton: *Cloth covering used on the dampening rollers of an offset press.*
Mottling (of ink): *Dirty or speckled appearance of print due to dirty ink, nature of ink pigment, insufficient printing pressure,*

excess tack, or excess cutting of ink.

Mourning bands: *Ink pigment adhering to molleton dampener covers in the form of a ring or band, usually on the ends of the rollers.*

NCR paper: *"No carbon required" paper manufactured by the National Cash Register Co., having a chemical coating on the back of one sheet which combines with the coating on the front of another sheet to produce a duplicate copy on the second sheet when pressure is applied to the first.*

Negative: *Usually refers to a film replica of the original. Used in offset platemaking to transfer the image onto a metal plate. Paper negatives are also used in some types of platemakers.*

Newsprint: *Paper made mostly from groundwood pulp and small amounts of chemical pulp. Used for printing newspapers.*

Offset paper: *Book paper made for offset printing.*

Offset printing: *Nickname for lithography.*

Offsetting: *Wet ink that transfers to the back of a sheet stacked on top of the wet sheet.*

Opaque: *To paint out areas on a negative not wanted on the plate. In paper, the property which makes it less transparent.*

Outline halftone: *A halftone from which the background has been cut away or eliminated.*

Overlay: *A sheet of acetate or tracing paper fastened over the original copy to indicate position and color of various elements.*

Packing: *Paper used to underlay the plate or blanket to get proper squeeze or pressure for printing.*

Panchromatic film: *Film having an emulsion sensitive to all colors, but least sensitive to green.*

Pasteup: *Same as mechanical, keyline, original, or camera-ready art.*

Pepper: *Specks of excess ink floating in water on the surface of an offset plate and "peppering" the normally clean area of paper.*

Perfect binding: *Binding where pages are fastened by adhesive, as in the case of a telephone directory.*

Perfecting press: *Press capable of printing on both sides of the sheet in a single run.*

Perforating: *Piercing the paper with a series of tiny dots or slits.*

pH: *A number used for expressing the acidity or alkalinity of solutions. A value of 7 is neutral in a scale ranging from 0 to 14. Solutions of a lower value are considered acid while those higher are alkaline.*

Photoengraving: *Etching metal plates to cause the image area to stand in relief. Also a term applied to a cut made by this process.*

Phototypesetting: *A photographic method of setting type that is rapidly replacing most mechanical methods of typesetting.*

Pica: *A measurement used for line length. Approximately 6 picas = 1 inch. Also used to describe a size of typewriter typeface.*

Picking: *Lifting of particles of the paper by the blanket due to excessive tackiness of the ink.*

Piling (ink): *Ink building up on blanket instead of transferring to the paper.*

Pinholes: *Small transparent holes in the opaque portions of a negative.*

Plate: *An offset plate is a smooth, chemically processed sheet of paper, plastic, or metal that is photographically imaged and placed on a round cylinder on the press. The surface is bathed with ink and water and the inked image is transferred to a blanket and then to paper.*

Plugging: *Filling in of halftone shadow areas in developing the negative or in printing.*

Ply: *Refers to the number of layers of fabric in the blanket's construction. Also a term used to express the thickness of card stock, bristols, or blanks.*

Points: *A measurement used for type height and for spacing (leading) between lines of type. 72 points = 1 inch.*

Positive-working plate: *Plate coated with a light-sensitive material which is intended for printing from a film-positive layout.*

Powdering: *Practice of dusting a blanket with powder after washing to offset tackiness. Also used to describe ink that dries but pigment does not hold to stock. Sometimes called chalking.*

Presensitized plate: *Precoated plate which can be printed photographically from line or halftone negatives.*

Press proofs: *Produced by a short run made on the press in advance of a production run for the purpose of proofing actual colors.*

Pressure-sensitive paper: *Material with an adhesive coating, protected by a backing sheet until used, which will stick without moistening.*

Primary colors: *The primary colors for additive combinations consist of blue-violet, yellow-green, and red-orange light, and the secondary colors consist of blue-green (cyan), yellow and magenta. Color scientists consider these secondary light colors to be the true primary pigment colors instead of the traditional red, yellow, and blue, and these colors are used by printers as the basis for mixing colored inks and for process color work.*

Process camera: *Copying camera used in reproduction work.*

Process color: *A loose term for full color printing.*

Process colors: *The subtractive primaries: yellow, magenta and cyan, plus black in 4-color process printing.*

Process printing: *The printing from a series of two or more halftone plates to produce intermediate colors and shades. In four-color process: yellow, magenta, cyan, and black.*

Proof: *Usually a photographic copy of the pasteup or original. Used before printing to make sure everything is right.*

Proportional spacing: *A principal difference between ordinary typewriting and typesetting. Each letter is spaced in proportion to its width.*

Rag paper: *High grade paper made from rags.*

Raised ink printing: *Same as thermography.*

Ream: *Technically 20 quires or 480 sheets, commonly 500 sheets. A printer's perfect ream is 516 sheets.*

Reducers: *Varnishes, solvents, oily or greasy compounds used to reduce the consistency of printing ink.*

Register: *Fitting of two or more printing images on the same paper in exact alignment with each other.*

Register marks: *Marks, usually crosses, placed on original art or photographic negatives or positives to aid in positioning the images in multicolor or double printing. Also called "cross marks" or "reference marks."*

Relative humidity: *The percentage of saturation of a unit of air. A relative humidity of 40% indicates that the air contains 40% as much moisture as it could carry if it were 100% wet at that temperature.*

Relief printing: *Method of printing in which the printing surfaces are raised; e.g., letterpress.*

Reverse: *Printing where the background is inked, and the type or illustrations are not inked. Often mistaken as white ink printing on black paper.*

Roman: *Class of type with open, clean cut letters and serifs. Vertical type, as distinguished from italics.*

Rotary press: *A fast press using curved printing plates and a curved impression cylinder.*

Rotogravure: *A mass production gravure (intaglio) printing process using a rotary press.*

Rough: *A layout in preliminary, rough form.*

Rub-on type: *Sheets of type or characters that can be transferred to an original by rubbing. Also available in "lift off" sheets where a thin sheet of plastic bearing the character is lifted off and pasted onto the original.*

Run: *The number of copies to be printed on a particular job.*

Run around: *Type set to fit around an illustration in a column.*

Saddle stitch: *To bind a publication along the center fold.*

Safety papers: *Stock used for printing bank checks, money orders, etc., to prevent alteration.*

Sans serif: *Term applied to all typefaces having no serifs. Also the name of a particular face of type.*

Score: *To impress or indent a rule in the paper to make folding easier.*

Screen: *(1) glass. Two pieces of optical glass ruled in opposite directions. Used in halftone reproduction. (2) Contact. A screen printed on safety base film and used in contact with the sensitized material. (3) A term used to denote the particular ruling to be used. For coarser work, 50 to 85 line screens may be used, as with newspaper reproductions. Finer work takes rulings up to 300 lines per inch.*

Screen angle: *The angle at which the screen is turned to avoid a noticeable dot pattern. A 45° angle is generally used for black-and-white work. In color work, the angle must be changed for each color.*

Script: *Class of type that resembles handwriting or hand lettering.*

Scum: *A film of ink printing in the nonimage areas of a plate where it should not print.*

Sensitivity guide: *Strip of continuous-tone film with numbered gradations or density steps which is stripped into the flat along the gripper edge so that it will print on the plate but will not print on the paper when the job is run. When the plate is* *exposed, the coating under the scale is overexposed at one end and underexposed at the other. The platemaker can regulate his exposures by exposing so that a predetermined number of the steps on this scale will print solid on the plate.*

Sensitized: *Any material coated with an emulsion that is sensitive to light.*

Serif: *"Tails" on the ends of typographic characters. Sans serif refers to characters without tails.*

Set-off: *When the ink of a printed sheet rubs off or marks the next sheet as it is being delivered. Also called offset.*

Shading sheet: *A transparent sheet with a uniform pattern of dots or other shapes used in the preparation of artwork and camera copy.*

Sheet-fed presses: *Presses which take sheets rather than rolls of paper.*

Short ink: *An ink that is buttery and does not flow freely.*

Signature: *A sheet having a number of pages printed on both sides, usually in multiples of 4.*

Silk screen printing: *Type of printing performed by squeegeeing paint through a piece of silk stretched tautly over a wooden frame. The nonprinting areas are blocked out by a stencil prepared manually or photographically.*

Slip Sheet: *To place a blank piece of paper on top of each printed sheet as it comes off the press to prevent ink from offsetting.*

Slitting: *Cutting printed sheets or webs into two or more sections by means of cutting wheels on a press or folder.*

Small Caps: *Letters having the form of capitals and the height of the body of lowercase letters. Used in text to show emphasis.*

Solids: *Large areas of solid ink coverage. Uniform coverage of large solids is difficult to obtain on a small press, especially at high speeds.*

Spiral binding: *A book bound with wires in spiral form inserted through holes punched along the binding side.*

Stapling: *See stitching.*

Stat: *A camera produced, high quality reproduction of original black-and-white art.*

Step-and-repeat work: *Two or more exposures made on the same plate from a single negative by moving it about. Also done with a photocomposing machine.*

Stitching: *Fastening the pages of a book together with wire stitches. Staplers use individual staples while the stitcher is fed from a continuous roll of wire.*

Stop bath: *Same as "fixer" — a chemical that stops the developing action of negatives or direct image plates.*

Strike-on type: *Typesetting that transfers an image by striking like a typewriter.*

Stripping: *The process of fitting a film negative onto a masking sheet for platemaking. Also the cutting and fitting of halftone negatives into a line copy negative.*

Stripping (of press rollers): *Refusing to take ink.*

Substance: *Standard by which business papers (bond, ledger, manifold, duplicator, and mimeo) are weighed.*

Tack: *The pulling power or separation force of ink. A tacky ink has high separation forces and can cause surface picking or splitting of weak papers.*

Text: *Main body of a story or publication. Also a class of type, such as Old English.*

Thermography: *Same as "raised ink" — a process in which powdered plastic is added to the ink after the ink is printed on paper. A heating process expands the plastic and produces a raised image.*

Toner: *Imaging material used in electrophotography.*

Toning: *Defined as a film of ink coating the normally clean portion of the paper. There are over twenty problems that can cause toning in direct image offset printing.*

Transparency: *A positive copy on film, in color or in black-and-white.*

Trim marks: *Marks placed on the copy to indicate the edge of the page.*

Two-up: *Two identical printing images on a press plate. Usually made by preparing the flat so it can be exposed successively in the two required locations.*

Typography: *The art of printing with type, involving the style, arrangement, and appearance of the printed page.*

Uppercase: *The capital letters of a typeface.*

Vacuum frame: *A vacuum device for holding copy and reproduction material in contact during exposure.*

Vellum: *In printing, vellum refers to a sheet of paper with a rough, blotter-like finish.*

Vertical camera: *Process camera used in reproduction work. So-called because the bellows extends vertically instead of horizontally.*

Vignette: *Type of halftone which has softened "feathered" outlines that blend into the surrounding white space.*

Walk off: *Image fades out on press during the run.*

Wash up: *Removing ink from rollers at end of day, or between different colors of ink.*

Watermark: *A design impressed into some types of paper by a "dandy roller" during manufacture. Lettering of a watermark should read from left to right when the job is printed.*

Web press: *A large rotary press that prints from a continuous roll of paper called a web.*

Winding stock: *Jogging stock to introduce a blanket of air between the sheets.*

Wire side: *The rough side of paper stock which was against the wire mesh in the paper making machine. See felt side.*

Work and flop or work and tumble: *Printing the second side of the sheet (using the same press form) by turning the sheets over from gripper to back, using the same side guide for the second run.*

Work and turn: *Printing the second side of the sheet, using the same press form, by turning the sheets from left to right, using the same gripper edge.*

Wove paper: *Paper having a uniform unlined surface and a soft smooth finish.*

Zip-A-Tone: *A waxed sheet of cellophane on which benday or other shading patterns have been printed. Used as a shading medium for line drawings.*

RESOURCES

The few names and addresses listed here will get you off of ground zero if you haven't started your own directory. A complete list of resources of interest to quick printers would more than fill a book this size.

ASSOCIATIONS

National Association of
  Quick Printers
One Illinois Center/Suite 600
111 East Wacker Drive
Chicago, IL 60601
(See page 27 for details)

American Quick Printing
  Association
1324 West Clay
Houston, Texas 77019
(See page 28 for details)

NATIONAL TRADE PUBLICATIONS
OF INTEREST TO QUICK PRINTERS

Quick Printing Magazine
3255 South U.S. 1
Fort Pierce, FL 33450

Graphic Arts Monthly
P.O. Box 1067
Skokie, IL 60076

American Printer and Lithographer
300 W. Adams Street
Chicago, IL 60606

In-Plant Printer
P.O. Box 368
Northbrook, IL 60662

QPM
Quick Printing Management Newsletter
666 Fifth Avenue
New York, NY 10103

Instant Printer
425 Huehl Rd., Bldg. 11B
Northbrook, IL 60067

Printing Impressions
401 North Broad Street
Philadelphia, PA 19108

There are many excellent regional publications that carry articles and ads of interest to quick printers. Most of these publications will have booths at regional printing shows. They are worth looking into.

INDEX

505

INDEX

INDEX

INDEX